LIFE WITHOUT MONEY

Building Fair and Sustainable Economies

Edited by Anitra Nelson and Frans Timmerman

PlutoPress
www.plutobooks.com

First published 2011 by Pluto Press
345 Archway Road, London N6 5AA

www.plutobooks.com

Distributed in the United States of America exclusively by
Palgrave Macmillan, a division of St. Martin's Press LLC,
175 Fifth Avenue, New York, NY 10010

British Library Cataloguing in Publication Data
A catalogue record for this book is available from the British Library

ISBN   978 0 7453 3316 8   Hardback
ISBN   978 0 7453 3165 2   Paperback

Library of Congress Cataloging in Publication Data applied for

This book is printed on paper suitable for recycling and made from fully managed
and sustained forest sources. Logging, pulping and manufacturing processes are
expected to conform to the environmental standards of the country of origin.

10   9   8   7   6   5   4   3   2   1

Designed and produced for Pluto Press by Chase Publishing Services Ltd
Typeset from disk by Stanford DTP Services, Northampton, England
Simultaneously printed digitally by CPI Antony Rowe, Chippenham, UK and
Edwards Bros in the United States of America

Contents

List of Boxes

Preface

The aim of this work is to show the potential of non-market socialism in addressing contemporary economic, political and environmental challenges. On the one hand, the effects of the global financial crisis that appeared forcefully in 2007 have continued to reverberate around the world while, on the other hand, delays in implementing significant international measures to combat rising carbon emissions signal deep systemic failings to protect natural environments. Such challenges highlight that capitalism – seemingly at its zenith since the fall of the Berlin Wall – can neither satisfy people's basic material and political needs nor respect natural ecosystem requirements.

The contributors to this book are activist scholars who are international experts in diverse fields. They were selected for their capacity to develop two cases: one against a system that elevates monetary values above human and natural ones, and another for alternatives that will better provide for humans' collective sufficiency and the future of the Earth. We decided to produce a readable book that activists and scholars would find intriguing and enlightening. We made sure that the book explored how non-monetary systems might work in practice, while referring to historical, revolutionary and utopian debates.

As the world heads towards environmental and social catastrophes driven by the unrestrained growth of market economies – in the tradition of Thomas More's *Utopia* – our book aims to provoke urgently needed debate about the need to dispense with money in order to achieve a sustainable and humane world. As such, we hope that *Life Without Money* helps you discover that non-market socialist models offer a future for humanity and the Earth.

Anitra Nelson and Frans Timmerman,
January 2011

Acknowledgements

Many people contributed to the development of this publishing project. We thank all those academics and activist friends who offered suggestions and support, especially: Mike Berry, John King, Joan Martinez-Alier, Bill Metcalf, Alan Roberts, David Spratt and Janna Thompson. We are most indebted to all those contributors who freely engaged in a two-way process with us to develop their chapters before we had engaged a publisher, and we thank Pluto Press's commissioning editor David Castle for all his support.

Some parts of this book have appeared before in print or are revised versions of previously published material.

Chapter 2 by Anitra Nelson ('Money versus Socialism') is a revised and updated version of 'The Poverty of Money' in *Ecological Economics*, Vol. 36, No. 3, 2001, pp. 499–511.

Chapter 3 by Harry Cleaver includes revised and updated versions of some passages from previously published work: 'Close the IMF, abolish debt and end development: a class analysis of the international debt crisis', *Capital & Class*, No. 39, Winter 1989, pp. 17–50; 'Kropotkin, self-valorisation and the crisis of Marxism', *Anarchist Studies*, Vol. 2, No. 2, 1994, pp. 119–35; and 'Socialism' in *The Development Dictionary: Knowledge as Power*, (ed. W. Sach), London: Zed Books, 1992, pp. 233–49.

Chapter 4 by John O'Neill developed out of a revised version of 'Socialist calculation and environmental valuation: Money, markets and ecology', *Science and Society*, Vol. 66, No. 1, 2002, pp. 137–51, complemented by edited extracts from his 'Socialism, associations and the market', *Economy and Society*, Vol. 32, No. 2, 2003, pp. 184–206 (reprinted by permission of the publisher, Taylor & Francis Ltd, http://www.informaworld.com) and from 'Ecological economics and the politics of knowledge: the debate between Hayek and Neurath', *Cambridge Journal of Economics*, Vol. 28, No. 3, 2004, pp. 431–47 (courtesy Cambridge Political Economy Society and Oxford University Press).

Chapter 7 by Adam Buick draws on some passages, which have been revised, from 'Where LETS schemes fail', *Socialist Standard*, December 1994; 'Marx: money must go', *Socialist Standard*, September 1985; and 'Bordigism' in Maximilien Rubel and

John Crump (eds), *Non-Market Socialism in the Nineteenth and Twentieth Centuries*, Houndmills: Macmillan, 1987 (reproduced with permission of Palgrave Macmillan). The chapter also includes an extract from John Crump and Adam Buick, *State Capitalism: The Wages System Under New Management*, London: Macmillan, 1986 (reproduced with permission of Palgrave Macmillan), and extracts from Karl Marx and Frederick Engels, *Collected Works, Volume 3*, London: Lawrence and Wishart, 1975 (reproduced with permission of Lawrence and Wishart).

Chapter 8, by Mihailo Marković, first appeared as Chapter 12 in his *The Contemporary Marx: Essays on Humanist Communism*, which was published by Spokesman Books (Nottingham), European Socialist Thought Series No. 3, 1974, pp. 208–17. The book is out of print. Copyright had reverted to Mihailo Marković, who gave initial agreement to its reprinting. However, he died before the book manuscript was finalised so we thank his son, Zoran Marković, for formalising the contributor's agreement.

Chapter 9 'Labour Credit – Twin Oaks Community' is compiled from extracts from two books by Kat Kinkade: *Is It Utopia Yet? An Insider's View of Twin Oaks Community in its Twenty-Sixth Year*, Louisa: Twin Oaks Publishing, 1994, and *'Kathleen' Kinkade, A Waldon Two Experiment; the First Five Years of Twin Oaks Community*, Louisa: Twin Oaks Publishing, 1972, complemented with material from Twin Oaks Community's February 2009 'Labor Policy'. We are very grateful that Twin Oaks Community, copyright owner of Kinkade's books, gave permission to publish all the material in this chapter.

As editors, we selected extracts by other authors to complement each chapter and to enhance the work as a whole, as a contemporary primer on non-market socialism. Therefore, we gratefully acknowledge permission to reproduce the following extracts:

Thomas More, *Utopia*, (translated by Paul Turner), London: Penguin Classics, 1965 [1516], pp. 76–7, 80, 84–5, 86, 87, 89, 128, 130 (Box 1.1, courtesy Paul Turner and Penguin).

Vandana Shiva, *Monocultures of the Mind; Perspectives on Biodiversity and Biotechnology*, London: Zed Books & Third World Network, 1993, pp. 19–21, 21, 24, 24–5 (Box 5.3).

William Morris, *News From Nowhere*, London: Routledge & Kegan Paul, 1970 [1890], pp. 79–80 (Box 7.3).

1
Use Value and Non-Market Socialism

Anitra Nelson and Frans Timmerman

In capitalist societies 'the market' is an elaborate set of social structures for exchanging commodities, which are created within a social system based on production for trade. In capitalism 'money', the medium and measure of exchange value, determines decisions on production, the success of which is measured in money, as profits and growth. In other words, money dominates the content and form of exchange in capitalism. Not only that, while many talk of money as a mere tool, the measure of a capitalist society is unending growth measured specifically in monetary terms. Most significantly, money is power.

The mystical power of money and the significance of growth in monetary terms are most obvious if you do not have any or enough to live adequately, and when economic growth falters or there are international financial crises. Although capitalism is often said to correspond to freedom and democracy, the ideals of parliamentary representation and 'one vote, one value' are limited by the monetary power of industrial and commercial interests, 'the market', and particular wealthy people and companies. Therefore, reformers and revolutionaries have developed strong critiques of capitalism throughout the centuries of its growth to international dominance today.

CAPITALIST MONEY AND NON-MARKET SOCIALISM

This book explores a relatively neglected point of view held by some critics of capitalism: the views of a heterogeneous group generally referred to as 'non-market socialists', though they go by other names. We think that the vision of non-market socialism is most significant now, as capitalism continues environmentally unsustainable practices, blocking strategies to limit unnecessary levels of consumption, carbon emissions and energy use (particularly in the so-called advanced economies), and the worldwide destruction

1

of natural habitats is resulting in significant extinctions of species. We argue that we need to dispense with monetary values and market structures in order to establish humane relationships and environmentally sound use of energy and resources.

The contributors to this collection not only develop detailed critiques of capitalism and market-based models of communism but also propose constructive ways of establishing non-monetary socialism in the future. They argue that a moneyless, marketless, wageless, classless and stateless planetary society is necessary and possible. They expand on the limited arguments and positions discussed in an earlier work edited by Rubel and Crump,[1] updating their analysis of non-market socialism and incorporating strategies and visions required for addressing current environmental crises.

We argue that dispensing with the market is a key and necessary strategy to *achieve* socialism, not simply a state that we will reach once the appropriate political or economic structures are in place or people's consciousness has become sufficiently socialist. This is an important point. Many activists, politicians and economists who established communism in the twentieth century agreed that the goal of communism was a moneyless society, but most were reluctant to implement this strategy immediately. In fact they argued that market structures could be used as a *tool* to achieve developments needed for communism. Chapter 2 includes a discussion of these kinds of debates as they occurred in the Russian and Cuban revolutions. Chapter 6 refers to similar debates amongst anarchists, socialists and communists involved in the Spanish Civil War.

In contrast to those who have focused on working out how to make market mechanisms work best to achieve at least the first stages of communism, the point that all contributors to this collection uphold is that the market system, and its quasi-god money, is a strong barrier to the political and cultural reforms needed to establish socialism. Chapters 3, 4, 7 and 8 centre on the politics of substantive democracy, arguing that we must be freed from the limitations of market-based relationships in order to share decision-making and collectively implement our decisions, and that non-market socialism offers greater efficiency in both economic and political terms.

The rather loose use of the terms 'communism' and 'socialism' here reflects a more general problem that they are used often almost interchangeably, though socialism has a longer and broader lineage. Marx and Lenin saw socialism as a transitional or halfway stage to communism. Socialists are often seen as 'soft' and less doctrinaire, violent and fundamentalist than communists. However, in Chile during the late 1960s and early 1970s, and in pre-revolutionary Cuba, communists seemed a lighter shade of red than socialists. The degree of authoritarianism, hierarchy and belief in the importance of state power are other characteristics that have been used to distinguish communists from socialists. Indeed, the vagueness around these terms arises partly because some self-proclaimed communists and socialists, and especially their parties and governments, did not conform to others' points of view. Today, it all depends on what you decide the key principles and practices are for achieving a world in which people care about one another and the planet, and share skills, knowledge and resources in sustainable ways.

'Non-market socialism' is a catch-all phrase that has been handed down to us. Rubel and Crump identify the following contributory currents: impossibilists, anarcho-communists, council communists, Bordigists and Situationists.[2] Our collection includes people who belong (or have belonged) to socialist and communist parties, and who identify as autonomist Marxists, ecosocialists, anarchists and ecofeminists. Yet many other ecofeminists, ecosocialists and anarchists are not non-market socialists. Clearly, it is necessary to check or confirm what people mean when they refer to an '-ist' or '-ism'. Here, we simply reiterate that for us non-market socialism means a money-less, market-less, wage-less, class-less and state-less society that also aims to satisfy everyone's basic needs while power and resources are shared in just and 'equal' ways.

THEORY AND PRACTICE

This book takes its structure from the contradictory unity of theory and practice. It is divided into contributions that centre more on theory, namely critiques of both existing capitalism and examples of market communism (Part I), and those that focus on practical activities and experiments involving non-market socialism (Part II). However, all of the theoretical discussions are quite practical. Scholars who are also activists have written them. Similarly the chapters that focus more on activism and practice also consider theoretical implications so that we may learn from experience and make improvements. In this way the book's structure expresses the character of the non-market socialist approach and agenda, which are interdisciplinary and about learning by doing.

Part I starts with Chapter 2, which examines the essential role of money in the economic structures of capitalism and market socialism. Chapter 3 focuses on the political implications of monetary structures and the creative power of people's refusal to deal with monetary forms. Chapter 4 delves into historical debates on the environment, non-monetary models, associational form of socialism and the potential and limitations of techniques of deliberative democracy. Chapter 5 reveals how capitalist economic and political structures determine and define the lives of women and the marginalised masses in the South. Chapter 6 serves as a bridge to Part II in that its sociological critique includes a broad utopian vision of a gift economy that might evolve from already existing transitional 'hybrid strategies', which anticipate the values and relationships of such an economy.

The chapters constituting Part II present living examples and analyse existing practical strategies and schemes for implementing non-monetary futures. In Chapter 7, a British member of an international party that advocates a non-market socialist line analyses various socialist strategies of contemporary movements. Chapter 8 speaks from the experience of socialism in Eastern Europe before the fall of the Berlin Wall. Chapter 9 analyses a communal labour-credit system in North America that has operated for decades. Chapter 10 deals with the values and practices of squatters in Spain. The conclusion (Chapter 11) draws together the main themes and proposes a global–local strategy for achieving a world without money, a world beyond money.

The following theoretical frameworks and terms help one to think about, discuss and enact non-market socialism when many of our ways of thinking, our practices and our experiences have been deeply embedded in capitalism.

EXCHANGE AND MONEY

Throughout history, in all kinds of societies, people have expressed their relationships with one another and nature through exchanges of goods and services involving obligatory or voluntary acts of giving and taking. Exchanges are embedded in a range of habitual and ritual activities that we develop as social and productive beings. So exchanges of things – 'gifts', 'goods' or 'commodities' – reflect wider socio-political structures. At the same time, doing something for another person or people, a 'service', also involves exchange and notions of debt and credit. Most exchange represents and expresses social structures, enforces status, buttresses positions of power and responsibility, and indicates values involving the use of a local natural (non-human) environment.

Ethnographers and social anthropologists study various aspects of a people's lifestyle and culture: how they produce and acquire basic needs and their cosmology or religion. They try to understand the processes and principles involved in exchanging goods and services. With respect to non-monetary societies, they refer to 'spheres of exchange', which describe the rules and protocols surrounding traditional and ritual circulation of goods, obligations and people (such as slaves and marriageable women). Such exchange is institutional and controlled by rules, protocols and attendant expectations. Most significantly, while a range of 'limited monies' or 'special-purpose monies' might prevail, they are much less important to their power structures than 'all-purpose money' is in capitalism.[3] In capitalism, exchange involves distribution and is an absolutely critical aspect of the whole process of production and reproduction. Capitalists cannot 'make money', or capital, unless they make a profit from trading in goods or services, namely commodities.

Social anthropologists point out the sharp distinctions between people who use money to exchange, as in capitalism, and those who exchange within a non-monetary 'gift economy'. In a gift economy, people base their exchanges on traditional obligations within and between families, households and broader social groups, such as tribes. Among Indigenous Australian people, traditional exchange involved totems connecting each individual with another species. These totems cemented their responsibilities towards and identity with 'country' (nature and landscape), which assisted in preventing unsustainable exploitation of the land. Barter often occurred in personal and incidental ways and trade has been a limited feature of gift economies in the past. Nevertheless, the social, political and economic bases of gift economies rely on obligatory exchange.

Historians and ethnographers have traced the disturbing influence of money within gift economies. Macfarlane writes:

> 'Money', which is a short-hand way of saying capitalistic relations, market values, trade and exchange, ushers in a world of moral confusion. This effect of money has been most obvious where a capitalistic, monetary economy has clashed with another, opposed, system. Thus it is anthropologists, who have worked in such areas of conflict, who have witnessed most dramatically the effect of the introduction of a monetized economy. They have noted how money disrupts the moral as well as the economic world.[4]

In modern capitalist societies not only do people trade a lot but also their entire process of production (and reproduction) is based on production for trade, resulting in a market economy and a market society, or capitalism. Although not all trade or monetary exchange in capitalist societies involves money acting as capital, capitalism is impossible without money. Capital has the form of money and without money it cannot operate or be defined. Investments, wages, growth and losses are all measured in monetary terms. A realm of exchange value expressed as prices denominated in currencies evolves and dominates production. Under capitalist production a mere good becomes a 'commodity' (a product created for sale in the market, to gain money). A commodity has both a use value and an exchange value (a price).

USE VALUE

Trading develops sharp distinctions between the use value of a good or service and its exchange value as a commodity sold on the market. A use value is what use and value a product or commodity is to the person using or consuming it. Food, clothes and shelter that we need to buy to live are of common, mundane use value to us but of exchange value to the producers who sell them in the market. Artistic works and public buildings also represent use values to those who use and 'consume' them. Alternatively, the exchange value of a commodity is realised in money, which is generally expressed in a specific currency, though gold (and other substances) have served as general-purpose monies.

In contrast to capitalism – where commodities are produced specifically for sale in markets to gain money and people require an income (money) to subsist – in non-monetary economies the production of use values is paramount: a household or group gains economic autonomy and cohesion to the extent that it is self-sufficient, its members securing their material needs from their own resources. In a simple economic framework where people immediately and independently satisfy wants in self-sufficient households or through having servants, tenants or slaves, only surplus production is taken to market. Long-distance traders are regarded with suspicion as outsiders. Markets are marginal to the structures of power, which are based on property exchanging hands through inheritance. However, simple, immediate and direct exchange (barter) can take place, as does delayed exchange (credits and debts), based on personal trust.

Most significantly, in non-monetary societies power and economic relations are transparent.

Today, trade and production for trade, that is, capitalism, dominates relations between people across the world, meaning that exchange value in the independent form of money is paramount. People often cannot do something because they 'don't have the money'. Success is measured by the marketability of activities. Global economic and financial crises highlight the centrality of money as a seemingly uncontrollable force. Everyone is enmeshed in a web of credits and debts that enable or limit daily activities. There are knock-on effects if even one part of the system fails. It is as if money is the blood of the economy, which has become the living body of society.

An early tract by Karl Marx, 'The Power of Money', reflects on the disturbing influence of money, as monetary flows and assets obscure who is really doing what and for whom:

> Shakespeare excellently depicts the real nature of *money*. To understand him, let us begin, first of all, by expounding the passage from Goethe.
>
> ... The extent of the power of money is the extent of my power. Money's properties are my – the possessor's – properties and essential powers. Thus what I *am* and *am capable of* is by no means determined by my individuality. I *am* ugly, but I can buy for myself the *most beautiful* of women. Therefore I am not *ugly*, for the effect of ugliness – its deterrent power – is nullified by money... Do not I, who thanks to money am capable of *all* that the human heart longs for, possess all human capacities? Does not my money, therefore, transform all my incapacities into their contrary?
>
> If *money* is the bond binding me to *human* life, binding society to me, connecting me with nature and man, is not money the bond of all *bonds*?
>
> The distorting and confounding of all human and natural qualities, the fraternisation of impossibilities – the *divine* power of money – lies in its character as men's estranged, alienating and self-disposing *species-nature*. Money is the alienated *ability of mankind*.[5]

Marx goes on to contrast the all-pervading influence of money in capitalist exchanges with direct exchange based on transparent use values:

> Assume man to be man and his relationship to the world to be a human one: then you can exchange love only for love, trust for trust, etc. If you want to enjoy art, you must be an artistically cultivated person: if you want to exercise influence over other people, you must be a person with a stimulating and encouraging effect on other people.[6]

One of the key problems for analysts of capitalism has been the increasing tendency to reduce and assess plans and developments to monetary values. Instead, the fabrication and structure of capitalism – a world ruled by trade, based on production for trade – is analysed most easily and critically by focusing on use values. That is because a use value, irrespective of any imputed exchange value, represents genuine qualities and quantities of those qualities. Use values are the most direct terms in which to assess what people need (and want) as well as the potential and limits of the ecosystems in which people live. Furthermore, analyses based on use value allow subtle, complex comparisons between capitalist and non-capitalist societies.

A good example of such a comparison is provided by Marshall Sahlins, who argues that 'the original affluent society ... one in which all the people's material wants are easily satisfied' is found in hunter and gatherer economies. According to Sahlins, 'the hunter pulls the lowest grades in thermodynamics – less energy/capita/ year than any other mode of production' even though 'in treatises on economic development he is condemned to play the role of bad example'. Sahlins continues:

> Wants may be 'easily satisfied' either by producing much or desiring little. The familiar conception, the Galbraithean way, makes assumptions peculiarly appropriate to market economies: that man's wants are great, not to say infinite, whereas his means are limited, although improvable: thus, the gap between means and ends can be narrowed by industrial productivity, at least to the point that 'urgent needs' become plentiful. But there is also a Zen road to affluence, which states that human material wants are finite and few, and technical means unchanging but on the

whole adequate. Adopting the Zen strategy, a people can enjoy an unparalleled material plenty – with a low standard of living.

What about the world today? One-third to one-half of humanity are said to go to bed hungry every night. In the Old Stone Age the fraction must have been much smaller. *This* is the era of hunger unprecedented. Now, in the time of the greatest technical power, is starvation an institution…

The world's most primitive people have few possessions, *but they are not poor*. Poverty is not a certain small amount of goods, nor is it just a relation between means and ends; above all it is a relation between people. Poverty is a social status. As such it is the invention of civilisation. It has grown with civilisation, at once as an invidious distinction between classes and more importantly as a tributary relation – that can render agrarian peasants more susceptible to natural catastrophes than any winter camp of Alaskan Eskimo.[7]

Indeed, one might ask: how many contemporary developments and proposals make little social, cultural or environmental sense but are assessed as sensible money-making ventures? The soundest critiques of capitalist developments need to be conducted in terms of use values.

Much time and effort is involved in capitalist exchanges, which entail extensive markets and advertising as well as monetary and financial transactions. Direct decision-making based on use values, people's wants and how we might satisfy them most simply and directly seems more efficient and effective. It is significant that, specifically from an economic point of view, where 'economic' means efficiency of time and effort, capitalism is found wanting.

Power of Labour

For Marx, the distinction between use value and exchange value was critical to explain the exploitation of labour within capitalism. Indeed Marx's analysis of capitalism and his dialectical method rely on the distinction between use value and exchange value and their contradictory unity in the 'commodity'. Nowhere is this social distinction more significant than in the sale of 'labour power', work for money, whereby one human purchases and controls the activity of another human for a set period of time.

Money facilitates and obscures the exchange of labour power in the market. Under the camouflage of 'equal exchange' some sell their labour power for money. The capitalist and the worker have contrasting and symbiotic roles, in the same way as a feudal lord and serf or traditional male and female role-playing create interactions that define and describe the power of the 'other'. The reproduction of workers and capitalists relies on the tendency for the production process to continually leave one depleted and the other enhanced.

Marx points out that, while capital seems to be responsible for producing exchange values, the source of exchange value and capital is labour. In crude terms, labour has the form of capital and labour is the hand in the glove of capital. Capitalism relies on the compliance of workers. Yet it is difficult for a worker to act independently because under capitalism you are either a capitalist or a worker (although self-employed are both simultaneously, and unemployed are potential workers). In these conditions social change depends on massive concerted non-compliance, which is why trade unions arose. However, unions merely support capitalism if they struggle only for decent wages and conditions.

For Marx, separating people from their 'means of production' (such as land, which is used to make necessities like food, shelter and clothing) forces workers to depend on capitalists. Marx's concept of 'primitive accumulation' refers to ways that outright force and money have been used to marginalise those who had once owned land or had use-right to it to secure independent livelihoods. This continues today, for example where transnational logging and mining companies supported by wealthy and powerful local elites with state control force Indigenous forest dwellers to give up traditional rights to basic needs. In tandem, where future 'development' involves production for trade, the ideology of capitalism runs rampant.

Economic historian Karl Polanyi has commented on such capitalist developments in his classic work, *The Great Transformation*:

To separate labor from other activities of life and to subject it to the laws of the market was to annihilate all organic forms of existence and to replace them by a different type of organization, an atomistic and individualistic one.

Such a scheme of destruction was best served by the application of the principle of freedom of contract. In practice this meant that the noncontractual organizations of kinship, neighborhood, profession, and creed were to be liquidated since they claimed the allegiance of the individual and thus restrained his freedom. To represent this principle as one of noninterference, as economic liberals were wont to do, was merely the expression of an ingrained prejudice in favor of a definite kind of interference, namely, such as would destroy noncontractual relations between individuals and prevent their spontaneous reformation.[8]

Others, such as anarcho-communist Peter Kropotkin, stress the resistance accompanying capitalist development:

The small peasants know what they have to expect the day they become factory hands in a town; and so long as they have not been dispossessed by the money-lender of their lands and houses, and so long as the village rights in the communal grazing grounds or woods have not been lost, they cling to a combination of industry with agriculture.[9]

In Marx's explanation, the process of primitive accumulation set in train workers' dependence on capitalists to provide them with jobs and wages so that they can buy back their needs and wants from capitalists through the market. This implies a systemic need for most people to remain workers and simply consume through the market. So, workers' conditions are typified by a tiresome working week that allows little space for activities other than replenishment, with just enough remuneration to enable this simple reproduction of their existence.

While workers' choices in terms of the quantity and quality of consumption goods and services might expand, this does not alter their fundamental lack of power. Workers have limited kinds of choices within capitalism and no alternatives without a means of existence beyond the capitalist system. At the same time, Marx pointed out the irony that capitalists, despite their controlling power, have little choice either. They must make profits – exploit workers, introduce money-saving and profit-producing technologies, and reinvest profits into further capitalist ventures, almost irrespective of their social and environmental costs – or they risk being marginalised, even eliminated, from the market system.

MARKETS AND SOCIALISM

As workers and entrepreneurs in advanced capitalism, we are caught in a world where credits and debts between people overwhelmingly take a monetary form. More and more daily activities are routinised in production for exchange in the market. Every day we notice that if people try to follow autonomous self-sufficient development they are considered out of date, even a threat; refusing to produce for and exchange through markets to satisfy wants is considered inefficient, primitive or quaint.

Since the 1950s, families and family obligations have altered: many more women perform paid work outside the home. The norm is either managing production for trade as a capitalist making a profit or working for a capitalist enterprise to gain a wage (or, of course, to incorporate both roles in self-employment). Today the integration of all the planet's peoples in production for trade, for money and profit, is often seen as the final unification of humankind. Major capitalist powers blatantly feel justified in achieving this by force if peaceful means fail.

The growth of capitalism has been intensive as well as expansive. Comparing contemporary life-styles with those of 50 years ago, whole areas of household responsibilities of families, particularly of females – care of children, the elderly, the ill and the disabled – have been absorbed by capitalist enterprises: eating in and taking lunches and tea from home has been replaced by eating out or buying 'fast' food; developing home gardens by sharing or exchanging seedlings, grafted plants and surplus produce has been replaced by commercial nurseries and hardware shops. The impacts have been environmental as well as social, with far-reaching ecological consequences.

People once 'made their own fun' at home, spending spare time within a radius of only a few kilometres from their homes. Now facilities and stores that provide entertainment, sport, and tourist and educational products and services have expanded, demanding energy-intensive transport and travel. Many not-for-profit enterprises have left behind their non-commercial foci, relying on business sponsors that expect them to act 'responsibly', in restrictive political and financial ways, to earn or maintain sponsorship. Similarly government organisations often incorporate 'user pays' and other capitalist principles to deliver services or combine in public–private partnerships.

During the Cold War, communism as practised in Russia, China and Cuba was commonly considered evil and best kept at a distance. However, books and discussions about communists and socialists (and anarchists) increased during the late 1960s as the evils of multinational companies, capitalist powers in the South and other impacts of commercialism caused damage and conflicts, especially for Indigenous peoples and natural environments. At the same time people were suspicious of existing communist practices because of the dominating power of political elites and party bureaucracies as well as the damage to the environment that their production techniques caused.

During this period, Che Guevara became an international figure partly because he represented a movement to realise communism in a less elitist, more pure and grassroots way. For Che, consciousness directed social change. He was particularly suspicious of using market structures within socialism and upheld voluntary labour to work directly to improve everyone's standard of living collectively. His biographer Jorge Castañeda wrote:

> The problem for Cuba, as Che saw it, was that Soviet influence no longer served to radicalize or advance socialism, but rather to undermine it ...
>
> In Guevara's view, the Soviet Union had fallen under the sway of the law of value, or the laws of the market.
>
> His real goal was to abolish all market and monetary relations based on value, both among state-owned companies and within the population as a whole.
>
> By this time [December 1964], Che had an uninhibited and definitive opinion of the Socialist countries. They were losing the race with the West not because they had followed the axioms of Marxism-Leninism, but because they had betrayed them.[10]

Indeed Castañeda cites Guevara saying in a meeting: 'It is now evident to me that wherever we use the law of value we are actually, through indirect methods, letting capitalism in through the back door.'[11]

Che tried to get other people in Cuba to see his point of view, which centred on moral rather than material incentives. Fidel Castro remained independent from this struggle waged by Che. When Che failed in Cuba he became disillusioned and joined revolutionary guerrillas in Bolivia but was killed there within a couple of years. On the one hand, Che seemed like a real-life embodiment of the utopian feeling so well expressed in the iconic song 'Imagine' by singer-songwriter John Lennon. On the other hand, his sentiment followed themes from a long line of utopian thinking (see Box 1.1).

The last decades of the twentieth century witnessed the rise of neoliberalism within capitalist countries, the fall of the Berlin Wall, and moves by China, Cuba and Eastern European countries to more intensively integrate market structures and values. It seems clear from these contemporary examples that market mechanisms do not lead to communism proper, rather the reverse. This fact encourages us to explore the exciting alternatives that non-market socialism offers, not only to advance our social needs to produce in the most efficient ways and share decision-making and work, but also to address the most urgent questions facing us in the twenty-first century, which relate to unsustainable practices that are destroying the natural wealth of our planet and ultimately threatening our existence.

Indeed, by the 1990s the lack of environmental sustainability had become the key problem for our species. To live in harmony with the earth we need to adjust our behaviour, even if that means radical change. We need to perceive and respond to non-human nature on its own terms, with even-handed respect for all species, landscapes and ecological processes. (We say 'non-human nature' because we are natural beings.) The failure of the Copenhagen climate negotiations late in 2009 demonstrates the incapacity of current political structures, which support capitalist economic institutions, to address globally unsustainable levels of carbon emissions, water use and other resource depletion.

Techniques and technologies necessary to manage our lives and natural resources sustainably are known. However, simple ways of living contradict the growth of commodities and services, which drives capitalism. Vast numbers of people would need to reduce their consumption and production, and freely share their skills and resources, for all of us to live simply. We think that our unwillingness to break with the market system and money in order to manage ourselves in an environmentally sustainable way has been the major contributor to current crises. However, experience, reading and discussion suggest key strategies for creating a sustainable future: substituting extensive production for trade with intensive local production for use while establishing 'compacts' for contracts. These ideas are discussed throughout this book but most particularly in Chapters 6 and 11.

CRITIQUES OF CAPITALISM AND COMMUNISM

Chapter 2 offers a non-market socialist reading of Karl Marx's work. Arguing that monetary structures imply growth, Anitra Nelson critiques both capitalist growth and calls to introduce a steady-state capitalist economy. Marx's analysis offers significant insights into the social character of monetary values (prices) and the market. She argues that debates amongst Russian and Cuban revolutionaries on dispensing with money are relevant to critiques of current schemes to put prices on components of ecological systems (such as forests) and to use the market (for example, through carbon-trading schemes) to achieve ecological sustainability. At particular points in the Russian and Cuban revolutions, the potential and limitations of monetary pricing and market exchange were debated fiercely. These arguments apply to the environmental challenges to capitalism today.

Chapter 3 points out both the political weaknesses of mainstream Marxist movements and the need to do without money. Harry Cleaver presents an autonomist Marxist position centring on work refusal. He argues that people must act autonomously to create a desirable and diverse new society beyond capitalism's exploitation, alienation and money form. His position challenges orthodox variants of Marxism that have led to market-based forms of 'communism', which have continued to exploit and alienate people by using money as a primary measure of value. A main strategy of autonomist Marxists is to organise around the refusal to subordinate our lives to work for capital by seizing time to live in more fulfilling ways. We should, they say, work to live, rather than live to work, as capitalists would have it.

Making decisions without reduction to a common unit such as money upholds Otto Neurath's arguments for non-market associational models of socialism, John O'Neill writes in Chapter 4. He discusses similarities between Austro–German debates on socialist calculation in the early twentieth century and debates in ecological economics as a field of study today. He traces the continuities in arguments and logic of key opponents as they undercut and defend money and markets as economic (and political) institutions. As a viable alternative, O'Neill points to 'economies in kind' and decision-making based on use values offered by processes of deliberative democracy.

Chapter 5 presents a critique of the monetary values at the heart of capitalism. Ariel Salleh's arguments are drawn from environmental ethics and ecopolitics frameworks. She argues that the global North does not give credit to the capacities of peoples on the margins of capitalism – the nations of the South, and women in particular. Most significantly this process of marginalisation is facilitated by monetary flows and functions. Salleh makes the case for restructuring society around the ecofeminist values of a 'synergistic economy'.

Chapter 6 analyses aspects of the environmental crises caused by capitalist agricultural practices to outline the benefits of permaculture approaches and provides a utopian vision of a 'gift economy' based on collective sufficiency and sharing surpluses. Drawing on his anarchist analysis of conflicts within the Left that arose in the Spanish Civil War, and the potential of contemporary social and cultural movements, Terry Leahy suggests mundane strategies to achieve the massive transformation that a gift economy would entail. This discussion of theory and practice acts as a bridge to Part II of this book.

ACTIVISM AND EXPERIMENTS

Decades ago Adam Buick joined the Socialist Party of Great Britain, a party that advocates non-market socialism. In Chapter 7 he discusses contemporary debates involving the role of money in the transition to socialism. For instance, he refutes contemporary 'alternative' economic strategies and schemes, such as labour exchange trading systems (LETS) and labour vouchers, to argue for simple and straightforward non-monetary production and exchange. He also discusses how Situationists and Amadeo Bordiga (an Italian socialist who argued against money) adversely influenced French activists in the 1970s because Bordiga's notion of moneyless communism was both undemocratic and technocratic.

Chapter 8 identifies political challenges for efficient grassroots decision-making to overcome bureaucratic management within a functioning socialist society (former Yugoslavia). Mihailo Marković argues that self-management, which rests on the principle of self-determination of individuals and communities, is not incompatible with efficiency. In fact, he argues that efficiency under capitalism is wasteful, irrational, degrading and inhuman. In contrast, self-determination and efficiency are compatible with human liberation and self-realisation provided that self-management is practised at all levels of society. This means that all elected delegates are rotated and replaceable, mass media of communication are free and are used to increase the education of all individuals, and technocratic management does not decide but merely advises organs of self-management and participatory democracy.

Chapter 9 explains the evolution and current functioning of a labour-credit system within a well-established community in the USA. Kat Kinkade describes the development of the Twin Oaks community (Virginia), which has a communal economy based on labour credit and a set of rules and practices both detaching from and accommodating the wider market reality of monetary exchange. Kinkade explains the philosophy behind their labour-credit system, some unsuccessful past experiments and some remaining failings. Her material has been updated and expanded by current members of Twin Oaks.

Chapter 10 explores the contemporary non-monetary values and practices of squatters in urban and rural areas of Spain. Claudio Cattaneo describes the ecological economics of urban squatters in Barcelona and neorural settlements in the mountains of Alta Garrotxa. These squatters avoid paid work and the use of money, that is, the market, in favour of autonomous self-organisation and collective sufficiency. He assesses the extent to which a community can organise itself and achieve material sustenance directly, independent of the capitalist market.

Finally, Chapter 11 draws on key ideas and themes emerging through this book to advocate for a global 'contract and converge' strategy of non-market socialism both to equalise and reduce consumption and to overcome environmental crises. In this concluding chapter to the book, Anitra Nelson and Frans Timmerman argue that the 'contract and converge' strategy, which was initially developed for tackling climate change by reducing carbon emissions in a socially just way, could be applied successfully to address the broader global social injustices and environmental crises.

The fact that environmental sustainability is most easily achieved by local production and exchange immediately simplifies issues of governance and control. Thus scaling-up takes the form of multiplying semi-autonomous cells – households, neighbourhoods and bioregional communities – with strong and organic multilateral networks connected through 'compacts' and global principles. Nelson and Timmerman sketch a non-monetary way forward through bioregional collective sufficiency: community-oriented production determined by self-managed democratic decision-making and activities based on use values and ecologically sound and humane values.

Box 1.1   Thomas More on Utopia, 1516

Since they only work a six-hour day [in Utopia], you may think there must be a shortage of essential goods. On the contrary, those six hours are enough to produce plenty of everything that's needed for a comfortable life ... [in contrast] where money is the only standard of value, there are bound to be dozens of unnecessary trades carried on, which merely supply luxury goods or entertainment.

When the head of the household needs anything for himself or his family, he just goes to one of these shops and asks for it. And whatever he asks for, he's allowed to take away without any sort of payment, either in money or in kind. After all, why shouldn't he? There's more than enough of everything to go round ...

... they collect details of the year's production, and as soon as it's clear which products are plentiful in each area, and which are in short supply, they arrange for a series of transfers to equalize distribution. These transfers are one-way transactions, requiring nothing in return – but in practice the free gifts that Town A makes to Town B are balanced by the free gifts that it receives from Town C. So the whole island is like one big household.

... they don't use money themselves, but merely keep it for use in an emergency ...
   In the meantime silver and gold, the raw materials of money, get no more respect from anyone than their intrinsic value deserves – which is obviously far less than that of iron.

In fact they do everything they can to bring these metals into contempt. This means that if they suddenly had to part with all the gold and silver they possess – a fate which in any other country would be thought equivalent to having one's guts torn out – nobody in Utopia would care two hoots.

Nor can they understand why a totally useless substance like gold should now, all over the world, be considered far more important than human beings, who gave it such value as it has, purely for their convenience ... what puzzles and disgusts Utopians even more

▶

is the idiotic way some people have of practically worshipping a rich man, not because they owe him money or are otherwise in his power, but simply because he's rich – although they know perfectly well that he's far too mean to let a single penny come their way, so long as he's alive to stop it.

In Utopia, where there's no private property, people take their duty to the public seriously ... where everything's under public ownership, no one has any fear of going short, as long as the public storehouses are full.

In fact, when I consider any social system that prevails in the modern world, I can't, so help me God, see it as anything but a conspiracy of the rich to advance their own interests under the pretext of organizing society ... Thus an unscrupulous minority is led by its insatiable greed to monopolize what would have been enough to supply the needs of the whole population. And yet how much happier even these people would be in Utopia! There, with the simultaneous abolition of money and the passion for money, how many other social problems would be eradicated! ... fraud, theft, burglary ... And the moment money goes, you can also say good-bye to fear, tension, anxiety, overwork, and sleepless nights. Why, even poverty itself, the one problem that has always seemed to need money for its solution, would promptly disappear if money ceased to exist.

Source: Thomas More, *Utopia*, (Paul Turner, translator), London: Penguin Classics, 1961, 2003 [1516], pp. 76–7, 80, 84–5, 86, 87, 89, 128, 130.

NOTES

All italics in quotes are preserved from the originals.

1. Maximilien Rubel and John Crump, *Non-market Socialism in the Nineteenth and Twentieth Centuries*, New York: Palgrave Macmillan, 1987.
2. Ibid.
3. Karl Polanyi, *The Livelihood of Man*, New York: Academic Press, 1977, p. 121.
4. Alan Macfarlane, 'The root of all evil', in David Parkin (ed.), *The Anthropology of Evil*, Oxford: Basil Blackwell, 1985, pp. 57–75, esp. p. 72.

5. Karl Marx, 'The Power of Money', in his *Economic and Philosophic Manuscripts of 1844*, Moscow: Progress Publishers, 1977 [1932], pp. 129–32, esp. 129–30, 130–1.
6. Ibid., p. 132.
7. Marshall Sahlins, *Stone Age Economics*, Chicago and New York: Aldine Atherton, 1972, pp. 1–2, 36, 37–8.
8. Karl Polanyi, *The Great Transformation: the Political and Economic Origins of Our Time*, Boston: Beacon Press, 2001 [1944], p. 171.
9. Peter Kropotkin, *Fields, Factories and Workshops Tomorrow*, (Colin Ward, ed.), London: George Allen & Unwin, 1974 [1899], p. 140.
10. Jorge G. Castañeda, *Compañero: The Life and Death of Che Guevara*, London: Bloomsbury, 1997, pp. 256, 257, 270.
11. Ibid., pp. 261, 434fn.

Part I

Critiques of Capitalism and Communism

2
Money versus Socialism

Anitra Nelson

In the early years of his career as a scholar and communist revolutionary, Karl Marx wrote *The Poverty of Philosophy*, an attack on Proudhon's work, *The Philosophy of Poverty*, which was first published in French in 1846.[1] He criticised Proudhon for proposing simplistic reforms to achieve social justice, proposals that Marx suggested were based on a shallow critique of capitalism. In a derogatory way, Marx called Proudhon a 'utopian socialist', though Marx too is considered 'utopian' (see Box 2.1). More significantly, his arguments against Proudhon were strong and damaging.

Today, various proponents of 'alternative economics' raise issues similar to those preoccupying utopian socialists and Marx in the nineteenth century. They suggest 'fair trade' and other schemes to manipulate prices to achieve social justice, just as some ecological economists devise market mechanisms, such as carbon-trading schemes, to embody ecologically rational policies. This chapter offers cautionary Marxist tales for such schemers. It details the contemporary relevance of Marx's philosophy of the human being in nature, and Marx's views on the potential and limitations of monetary evaluation and the market, as well as debates and experiments by practical socialists (Bolsheviks and Cubans) who focused on social transformation through monetary reforms, prices and non-monetary exchange.

ECOLOGICAL ECONOMICS

Ecological economists address issues of sustainable production and consumption, social fairness and economic efficiency. They are distinguished from environmental economists in breaking with a mainstream capitalist framework that perceives nature in simplistic monetary terms, such as marketable natural resources and externalities. However, while ecological economists have a wider purview, for instance, appreciating the complex ecological services that contribute to production for the market, many still treat prices and imputed quasi-prices as mechanisms for addressing social goals without adequately explaining the need and legitimacy of assigning artificial prices to non-marketed goods and services. Nevertheless the fundamental question would seem to remain: to what extent are market mentalities and behaviour responsible for our environmental problems?

The common vision of ecological economists is indisputable: a sustainable dynamic between human and non-human nature wherein human practices optimise the potential of non-human nature. However, they regard 'potential' variously, just as divisions arise over exactly what constitutes ecologically sustainable behaviour and the best policy prescriptions. Nevertheless, many ecological economists suggest simple reforms to both state and market, presuming that price formation and market exchanges are affected more by collective will than they seem to be in practice. The vital context for interventions in the pricing process involves mundane prices and the value of the monetary unit, which are co-created and recreated in the market. So, environmental legislation and regulation via price policies or mechanisms – such as carbon-trading schemes – would seem to be based on cavalier assumptions about the way capitalist markets function.

In parallel Marx argued that utopian socialists, such as Proudhon, exaggerated the potential of monetary and price reform to alter the social system. He was adamant that the social defects of the economic system could not be removed by tinkering with money and prices, which were surface phenomena; talk of controlling the value of money, the supply of money or redefining prices was useless and idealistic. Marxist economist Duncan Foley has neatly summarised this position:

> Money is a social relation. Like the meaning of a word, or the proper form of a ritual, it exists as part of a system of behaviour shared by a group of people. Though it is the joint creation of a whole society, money is external to any particular individual, a reality as unyielding to an individual's will as any natural phenomenon.[2]

Given that the market was not subject to social control, Marx argued that state policy involving market reforms was fraught with difficulties. He pointed out that, if prices were to be determined by other than market practices, we would not have a free market.

So, he asked his opposition: what would 'price' mean then? Marx believed faulty analysis would lead to the formation of revolutionary strategies that would be doomed to fail. He regarded it crucial to get the analysis right.

HUMANITY AND NATURE

Many environmentalists believe that Marx's work exemplifies the damaging mentality of dualism characteristic of modern western thinking. They say that Marx's emphasis on technological development highlights an exploitative mentality towards nature. Marx and Engels shared a positive view of modern technologies but Marx's analyses of capitalism included many descriptions of the destructive effects of industry and modern agriculture on nature as well as on workers. Unfortunately, policies adopted by Eastern European communist regimes, involving large environmentally destructive technologies, helped to falsify Marx's dialectical perspective to a one-sided position.

Marx's critique of capitalism did not embody the kinds of production and consumer foci that are characteristic of many contemporary trade unions. He described a communism of freely associated producers, which stressed the political importance of collective decision-making and production. In *Capital III*, Marx's respect for nature seems quite clear:

> From the standpoint of a higher socio-economic formation, the private property of particular individuals in the earth will appear just as absurd as the private property of one man in other men. Even an entire society, a nation, or all simultaneously existing societies taken together, are not the owners of the earth. They are simply its possessors, its beneficiaries, and have to bequeath it in an improved state to succeeding generations.[3]

While 'improved state' could be interpreted in a Promethean way, Benton has argued that Marx's method incorporates human reliance on nature to such an extent that it is the closest existing example of an 'ecology of the human species'; Marx's historical materialism is 'a proposal for an ecological approach to the understanding of human nature and history'.[4]

Marx explicitly acknowledged nature as the source of all materials and instruments of labour and reminded the German Workers'

Party that labour is a force of nature too.[5] John Bellamy Foster has summarised Marx's position this way:

> The human community, Marx believed, can no more free itself from the need to control its interaction with nature than it can free itself from the need to take into consideration the natural conditions of human existence. Yet rational control of the relation between nature and humanity is inherently opposed to the mechanistic domination of nature in the interest of the ever increasing expansion of production for its own sake. In a society of freely associated producers, Marx argued, the goal of social life would not be work and production, in the narrow forms in which they have been understood in possessive-individualistic society, but all-round development of human creative potential as an end in itself, for which 'the shortening of the working-day is a basic prerequisite.' This would set the stage for the realm of freedom in which human beings would be united with each other and with nature.[6]

Unlike the capitalist ideology of continuous growth in which nature is a subject and victim, historical materialism considers concrete limitations, both social and natural. In the *Economic and Philosophic Manuscripts of 1844*, Marx explicitly defined humanity as part of nature:

> Man lives on nature – means that nature is his body, with which he must remain in continuous interchange if he is not to die. That man's physical and spiritual life is linked to nature means simply that nature is linked to itself, for man is a part of nature.[7]

Marx's theory of alienation expresses his philosophy that humanity is inseparable from nature. In communism, writes Marx, humanity will attain a proper relation with nature and coalesce with it. He argues that capitalist relations of private property imply an unnatural divorce of worker from non-human and human nature. In contrast, capitalists have little regard for human or non-human nature; they turn nature into commodities and employ workers to produce profits. Marx suggests that human empathy with the rest of nature and people's identity with the products they create within nature make them unique animals, ideally suited as stewards of the earth. Marx's philosophy is unapologetically anthropocentric, and differs from a radical 'deep ecology' position, but is similar to many other environmentalists' views.

Use Value and Exchange Value

In *Capital I*, Marx's analysis of the capitalist system begins with the commodity and its 'twofold aspect': as a use value for consumption, and as an exchange value to gain money for its producer.[8] He is at pains to point out that, while wealth is based on use value and therefore ultimately nature, the social constitution of exchange value in the market is in no way associated with the natural, physical and qualitative aspects of the commodity. Therefore, it is impossible for the old economic 'paradox of value' – that diamonds are more valuable than water even while they are less useful – to arise as a serious question within Marx's analysis; distinguishing exchange value from use value dispenses with the so-called paradox.

Marx's analysis concentrates on the main object of political economy, the social relations of production and exchange value. His perspective is fairly consistent with the orthodox view that natural resources represent 'externalities'. With production for the market, monetary calculations determine what and how we produce goods and services. Financial, speculative factors tend to dominate decision-making about the use of environmental resources to the detriment of ecological concerns. Uniquely, exchange value drives capitalism.

For Marx, capitalism presents dialectical asymmetry; exchange value implies use value but not necessarily the reverse. Use values are fundamental units in discussion of economies in the general. Exchange values are secondary units, relating to markets, and fundamental only in capitalism. His framework indicates how ecological values are marginalised by the social dynamics of capitalism because monetary values dominate (see Box 2.2). Marx offers a strong contrast with the pricing-the-environment direction of many ecological economists who view the market in a naive way, like the utopian socialists he criticised. The dominance of exchange value in capitalism encourages both alienation from, and an instrumental view of, nature. Not only do capitalists disregard nature, but also production for the market means that monetary considerations have priority over ecological values in their decision-making. Therefore, to capitalists, environmental taxes and internalising externalities are seen to be costly reforms to devise, implement, monitor and revise. Finally, according to Marx, any comprehensive 'reforms' to take environmental factors into account would imply or lead to new systems of exchange and production altogether.

CAPITALIST GROWTH AND COMMODITY FETISHISM

Marx's concept of money is grounded in commodity circulation, in relations between producers expressed as relations between things, as exchange values, in prices. Money is the 'value form' of exchange value. In *Capital I*, Marx argues that the development of money inevitably leads to the concept and function of capital as a dominating power; money is, historically and logically, 'the first form of appearance of capital'.[9] Marx's theory of how money becomes capital is the first step in an argument that leads to an ecologically relevant conclusion: that capitalism collapses under sustained contraction. Further, recurrent and sharp economic cycles that characterise capital accumulation involve challenging the limits of nature, for example the 'peak oil' crisis. Delays in stopping carbon-emitting activities of capitalists are directly related to this, too.

Marx charges utopian socialists and other monetary reformers with failing to address the key question, 'Why is money necessary?'[10] He answers by arguing that workers make products that only become commodities once purchased with money (product → commodity → money, or P → C → M). The development of labour and capital is embodied in the commodity and money: 'already the simple forms of exchange value and of money latently contain the opposition between labour and capital'.[11] The existence of commodities and money allows wage labour to appear, labour becomes a commodity sold for money, and money thereby becomes capital. It is a dialectical elaboration of 'value' created by labour in production, manifested in commodity circulation as 'exchange value', necessarily becoming independent in the money form and finally preserved as capital. So, the final concept in the series is money, which procures labour, 'capital'. Thus, for Marx, the whole capitalist dynamic is monetary in form.

Production is the vehicle for exploitation in capitalism. Money is invested in workers' wages, and in the means, materials and instruments of production, to produce commodities that recoup the original money plus profits. Constant reinvestment of money and productive transformation is vital for capital accumulation; without it, recession, depression and crises occur. Capital accumulation proceeds like a spiral. Lowering social consumption is incompatible with capitalism as a social system with a peculiar dynamic and behaviour established between capitalists and between capitalists and workers. Growth and making profits are defining characteristics and intrinsic demands of the capitalist system. A capitalist economy, following the capitalist entrepreneur, must grow. The goal is unfettered growth in a reproducing cycle, which implies expansion: $M \rightarrow C \rightarrow P \rightarrow C' \rightarrow M'$ (read as money is invested in commodities, which are used in production to create a greater value of commodities realised in money). Consequently, as capitalism has expanded, capitalist activities have increasingly become the central and dominant factor structuring humanity's relations with the rest of nature. It is clear then that one of the most important requirements of ecologically sustainable development, cutting production and consumption in advanced capitalist economies, is impossible to achieve.

To the extent that policies designed to ensure biological diversity, ecological integrity and a variety of natural resources involve less consumption and production or vast changes to the ways that investment and production take place, they will disrupt the business system ($M \rightarrow C \rightarrow P \rightarrow C' \rightarrow M'$) fatally. Therefore, to the extent that we are trying to apply green policies and practices that involve environmental pricing, we are actually living in this confusion of economic disruption and crises and are doomed to lose the struggle to achieve sustainability. Subsequently, environmentalists must question whose interests price-making serves, what prices represent, and why money and monetary evaluation are considered so useful and persuasive as a sign of ultimate worth.

Commodity Fetishism

Marx provides another perspective on attempts to evaluate ecosystem services monetarily (such as pricing the water-purifying capacities of a forest), that is, as a symptom of 'commodity fetishism'. Writing 'On the Jewish question' in 1843, Marx foreshadowed his concept of commodity fetishism as a capitalist attitude and form of behaviour:

> Money is the general, self-sufficient *value* of everything. Hence it has robbed the whole world, the human world as well as nature, of its proper worth. Money is the alienated essence of man's labour and life, and this alien essence dominates him as he worships it.[12]

In these spare sentences he conveys the source and complex consequences of commodity fetishism, which is epitomised in money and monetary evaluation. Marx quotes from Shakespeare to illustrate that money is an omnipotent 'visible divinity'.[13] Within a monetary economy, demand is acknowledged only if backed by money; if not supported by money, Marx writes, real human needs are invisible, just like ecosystem externalities. In this way the market reverses 'an image into reality and reality into an image'.[14]

In *Capital I*, Marx elaborates on commodity fetishism, likening monetary values expressed in prices to religious forces:

> Value... transforms every product of labour into a social hieroglyphic. Later on, men try to decipher the hieroglyphic, to get behind the secret of their own social product: for the characteristic which objects of utility have of being values is as much men's social product as is their language.[15]

Marx's theory of commodity fetishism develops from Aristotle's question about how a variety of distinctive, and therefore incomparable, goods and services are made comparable by market exchange through monetary evaluation: 'Since exchange-value is a definite social manner of expressing the labour bestowed on a thing, it can have no more natural content than has, for example, the rate of exchange.'[16] While Marx's distinction between use value and exchange value and his theory of labour value answer Aristotle's question, in the narrow sense, of explaining how capitalism works, Aristotle's question remains pertinent.

Set prices are not market prices. However they arise, prices are abstractions created by humans and are intended to signal rational reproduction of an economic system. If you decide to evaluate natural services in monetary terms, first you must define exactly what money means and how value, in its various senses, relates to price. Given that market prices are relative and every change in one price affects other prices, is it possible to set prices involving environmental factors without influencing all prices? The pragmatic view that prices are just instruments to use to achieve desired outcomes fails to acknowledge that pricing and monetary systems are so complex that tinkering with individual prices in ignorance of systematic interactions invites unintended, undesirable and even uncontrollable consequences (such outcomes have been seen in command economies, discussed below). There is a question about whether or not prices are the most efficient way to represent ecological values and ensure we respect and maintain them. More fundamental is the question of whether or not prices and the monetary system can do the job at all.

From a Marxist perspective, artificially pricing environmental resources and services seems to be a symptom and expression of commodity fetishism. Marx studied value and price as cultural categories designed to ensure production and exchange, reproduction and expanding accumulation of a particular form of social power. In as much as monetary values and prices are assigned to human and non-human nature, they provide a one-dimensional and purely market-based point of comparison that obliterates other social and ecological qualities. That people subject to capitalist dynamics would try to artificially evaluate ecosystem services would not surprise Marx, who argued that:

> The religious reflections of the real world can... vanish only when the practical relations of everyday life between man and man, and man and nature, generally present themselves to him in a transparent and rational form. The veil is not removed from the countenance of the social life-process, i.e. the process of material production, until it becomes production by freely associated men, and stands under their conscious and planned control.[17]

Marx points here to a necessary transition to communism.

THE TRANSITION

In *The German Ideology* Marx points out that people are united to and struggle with nature via industry, attacking Bruno Bauer for drawing an 'antithesis' between nature and history 'as if... man did not always have before him an historical nature and a natural history'.[18] Marx saw advanced communism as a synthesis of naturalism and humanism, 'the *genuine* resolution of the conflict between man and nature and between man and man'.[19] While the state – like money – institutionalises and symbolises alienation, a sharing and caring society would involve social empowerment and organisation based on consensus decision-making. Communism would represent a degree of conscious social control of interactions between people, and between them as a society and nature, which is impossible under capitalism. Marx's vision of a stateless, moneyless and classless society was aimed to encourage the fullest development of human consciousness and creativity.

This reading of Marx interprets him as a non-market socialist. The ideal of non-market socialism, of a cooperative, sharing and caring society that has dispensed with money and the state, has various adherents, as testified by the contributors to this book. They all acknowledge the importance of new relationships of non-monetary exchange, while pointing out the limitations as well as possibilities of such scenarios. In the non-market socialist vision, production is not for the purpose of sale and work is not remunerated via the market. What is produced and how it is produced is decided collectively. Work is a creative right and the social product is shared freely but subject to social constraints.

Autonomist Marxist Antonio Negri characterises communism as '[e]conomy of time and free planned activity' and 'the affirmation of the most exasperated plurality – creativity.' He contrasts communism with capitalism, where 'money has only one face, that of the boss': 'Capitalist socialization exalts the sociality of money as exploitation, while communist socialization destroys money, affirming the immediate sociality of labor.'[20]

Some non-market socialists, such as John Crump, share Marx's belief that advanced capitalist technologies provide a step to create the material basis for socialism.[21] Furthermore, while admitting the need for 'temporary measures', Crump believes that we need to make a 'great leap' to socialism. He roundly rejects efforts to construct a transitional society and believes that socialism must exist worldwide. The common goal of non-market socialists is a diverse, united, global, human community.

Once the capitalist impetus to produce and exchange to make money is removed and the focus is on use values and human needs, we can more easily take environmental factors into account. Most non-market socialists argue for wholesale revolution and stress the integrity of economics and politics through an ethic of sharing. Only a few short-lived experiments have developed non-monetary alternatives, such as in the 1970s towards the end of Allende's socialism in some districts of Chile and in the 1930s in certain locales during the Spanish Civil War (see Chapter 6). Discussions of such alternatives in communist Cuba and Russia follow.

COMMUNIST SOCIETIES IN THE TWENTIETH CENTURY

In the early years of Soviet power the party elite seriously discussed instituting a moneyless economy. A debate about diminishing the role of money in Cuba occurred in the mid-1960s, too. Both discussions raised serious social issues regarding monetary evaluation and calculation. While neither discussion gave any importance to evaluating and calculating environmental resources and services in terms of ecological sustainability, both cases indicate that policies involving price-setting and non-monetary exchange must be feasible and gain popular consent to succeed.

Environmentalists have suggested a range of policy options, such as cutting and distributing work hours more evenly, reducing consumption or introducing rations and, especially, setting prices to reflect or express environmental rationalities. Minority thrusts in the Russian and Cuban socialist movements argued for non-monetary exchange but the practical focus was on alternative ways of using monetary systems to rationalise production and exchange. Rather than offering any clear way forward for those bent on pricing the environment, these case studies act as important cautionary tales.

In neither the Bolshevik nor the Cuban examples did the revolutionaries adequately theorise or plan for how socialist exchanges would differ from market evaluation and behaviour. The difficulties of finding socially just and practical forms of exchange seriously challenged the revolutionaries. They were ill-prepared for these difficulties in terms of theory and, once exchange became a practical issue, they were deeply divided over what ways socialist exchanges should be conducted, particularly over how far, or in what ways, to dispense with money. These difficulties were not simply technical or economic, but involved psychology, social behaviour and political control.

The Neglect of Money Under 'War Communism'

The Russian example opens all the main conceptual and practical issues surrounding exchanges based on socialist values, which have parallels with ecological values. Social justice and ecological sustainability both involve incomparable qualities, complex processes and diverse consequences. How do we compare and measure differences in work efforts, different work, different people doing it, and products being produced in different ways? Assessing and economising on human labour can be compared with calculating and measuring efficiencies in varieties of non-human energy expenditures. Are monetary values useful to do this? If not, is socially necessary labour time best measured in units of time or calorific energy or what? And, how are questions of 'need' addressed?

The main source for the discussion in this section is the renowned historian of Russia, E. H. Carr, along with Russian economist

L. N. Yurovsky. Unless otherwise indicated, all quotes in this section are from Carr.[22]

After the October Revolution in 1917, the Bolsheviks initially adopted what Carr refers to as 'strict financial orthodoxy' and they continued to use the printing press to meet financial needs. At the first All-Russian Congress of Councils of National Economy held in May 1918, financial matters were openly debated by the highest commissars and ministers. The Right's protagonist, Isidore Gukovsky, demanded gold support for paper money 'so long as we have money in circulation'. The Left was unconcerned about introducing what seemed to be a temporary measure because, 'when the full triumph of socialism occurs, the ruble will be worth nothing and we shall have moneyless exchange'. Grigory Sokolnikov welded these views into a practical position: gold was significant for foreign transactions but unnecessary for national ones. Furthermore, he suggested that fixing or stabilising prices would counteract the ill effects of too much money in circulation. Yet monetary taxes supported the state.

Initially the Bolsheviks aimed to control distribution but shop 'workers' were not organised and consumers' cooperatives were not well supervised. The state set prices but, because neither the disturbed market nor new state initiatives to monopolise trade and ration products were effective, speculation spread and a black market started to flourish. The civil war prompted a set of economic steps known as 'war communism'. The note-printing presses were enlisted; money steadily became valueless. This depreciation, Carr writes, 'came from 1919 onwards to dominate every aspect of Soviet financial and economic policy, and gave to the policies of war communism their final and characteristic shape'. The state increased requisitions and cooperatives became the state's main collecting and distributing structure. By 1920 the gap between official fixed and free-market prices widened alarmingly: 'the list of fixed prices grew till almost every object of consumption was covered'. Rationing was extended as barter became attractive and frequent; even factories paid suppliers and workers in products finished by them or by another factory with which it made exchanges in kind.

Carr suggests that the phasing out of money was not an original aim of the Bolsheviks but that, once money became ineffective, 'a virtue was made of necessity and the view became popular that the destruction of the currency had been a deliberate act of policy'. However, many officials, such as Trotsky and Stalin, expected a monetary economy to evaporate with the advance of communism.[23] Trotsky wrote:

> In a communist society, the state and money will disappear. Their gradual dying away ought consequently to begin under socialism. We shall be able to speak of the actual triumph of socialism only at that historical moment when the state turns into a semi-state, and money begins to lose its magic power. This will mean that socialism, having freed itself from capitalist fetishes, is beginning to create a more lucid, free and worthy relation among men.[24]

However, in reality money remained a tool of state policy. For instance, Lenin pleaded with the peasants to accept the state's tokens for their grain. Therefore, Nikolay Krestinsky pointed out that 'our ruin or salvation depends on a race between the decreasing value of money – with the consequent need for printing notes in ever greater quantities – and our growing ability to do without money altogether'. Observe the wording here. Krestinsky's logic is opposed to Carr's: the diminishing value of the currency forces the government to issue more notes (rather than the reverse). Carr suggests that only the practical circumstance of runaway inflation forced them to introduce non-monetary exchange. The role of money was now a critical issue; material circumstances determined the political and theoretical agenda.

The second All-Russian Congress of Councils of National Economy, December 1918, passed a resolution condoning 'the elimination in the last resort of all influence of money on the relations between economic factors'. However, the practical measures adopted involved settlements without cash but not without monetary accounting. Discussion about eliminating money became especially confused once the state supervised transactions in the industrial sector, so industry needed cash only to pay wages. This was understood as a step towards eliminating money. Not surprisingly banking officials thought only of monetary accounting. However, especially once unions organised wages in kind (a form of rationing), monetary accounting seemed unnecessary.

One contributor to the debate cited by Carr said, 'we shall come in the end to doing without any calculations in rubles, reckoning the energy used by number of days and hours'. He, like Larin (a select member of the Council of National Economy, who pointed out that 'the only question can be how many days must be spent to produce how many articles in a given branch of production'), anticipated the focus of future debate. Still it was Milyutin, another member of the Council of National Economy, who encapsulated the ambiguity and confusion in the debate over money and state affairs when he said, 'a system without money is not a system without payments'. Initially it seemed obvious (especially to the conservatives) that 'monetary symbols' would remain even though 'monetary tokens' were becoming less necessary. In short, money would exist as a unit of account. Given that this is money's defining function, this meant a system of monetary exchange would remain.

As the depreciating ruble was less and less a stable unit of account, the role of money as a unit of account became the theoretical and political issue of the day. According to Carr, the debate over substituting a monetary unit of account with one based on labour, in terms of time or energy expended, 'occupied an enormous place in the economic literature of 1920 and the first few months of 1921' and was influenced by Otto Neurath's work (see Chapter 4).[25] At the January 1920 Congress, it was decided that accounts could involve a unit of labour, commonly referred to as *tred* (abbreviated from *trudovaya edinitsa*). This idea was passed on to a special commission and 'occupied for many months the best economic brains of the country'. A unit of labour time was a familiar concept to readers of socialist literature and political economy. Carr's comment here that 'it also seemed to be based on sheer common sense' is worth discussing. The discussion in Russia raised the possibility that such a unit would become 'a universal unit of account of living energy – the calorie' (the *ened*). Meanwhile, this had no influence on Soviet accountants, who persisted in reckoning in rubles. They followed official directions that reiterated phasing out cash while depending on the national currency as a unit of account.

At this point any return to a 'natural economy' or advance to a moneyless communism was halted because all state industries were directed to follow *khozraschet* ('principles of precise economic accounting'): demanding monetary taxes; requiring cash for state-produced goods and services; reintroducing state budgets; and returning financial independence to local authorities. These policies renewed a reliance on money as cash, not just as a unit of account. While Lenin had acknowledged that free trade would '*inevitably* lead to... a revival of capitalist wage-slavery', he spoke of the New Economic Policy as simply '*retreating* in order to make better preparations for a new offensive *against capitalism*'.[26] Unfortunately, Lenin's tactical retreat became permanent. Carr seems correct to suggest that the fresh direction and financial imperatives of the New

Economic Policy amounted to a return to all of the fiscal, financial, banking and monetary orthodoxies of capitalism.

Carr's account suggests that no discussion of assessing the various values of environmental resources occurred in the Russian debates. This was a matter of relative neglect in Cuba as well. However, both cases indicate the social considerations environmentalists need to take into account when attempting to make prices or market-based policies reflect ecological values. Devising, implementing, monitoring and revising an artificial price system for various assets, goods and services within an otherwise free market system for environmental reasons risks being time-consuming, costly and vulnerable to avoidance tactics and corruption. In fact, this seems clear already in debates and experiences of using carbon-trading systems to abate carbon emissions.

Che Guevara and the Question of Money

During 1963–65 there was a great economic debate in Cuba, which included contributions from overseas. As mentioned in Chapter 1, the debate concentrated on whether work ought to be encouraged by moral or material incentives and whether the state ought to adhere to a centralised budgetary system or allow enterprises financial autonomy. Distinctive positions on these issues related to different interpretations of Marx's concept of value, law of value and different visions of socialist planning. Marx's concept of value is based in capitalist labour, his law of value relating to the labour that is 'socially necessary' to produce a commodity. The socialist debaters argued about whether state production still constituted production of 'commodities'. As with environmentalists wanting a sustainable planet, the issue for the socialists was not so much where we are going but how we will get there.

In this debate, Major Alberto Mora, Cuba's Minister for Foreign Trade, and Carlos Rafael Rodrıguez, Director of the National Institute of Agrarian Reform, were supported by French economist Charles Bettleheim in opposition to Che Guevara, Director of the Ministry of Industries. The main English sources for this analysis are various works by Che Guevara and the commentaries by Michael Löwy and Carlos Tablada.[27] According to Löwy, it was Che's 'revolutionary humanism' that fundamentally distinguished his perspective from that of his opponents.[28] Che used Marx to defend his position, believing that freedom meant freedom from the forces of the capitalist market, freedom from alienation, and freedom to directly control and plan human life (see Box 2.3).[29]

Indeed, a tribute to Che Guevera by André Gorz thanked him for identifying 'that socialism is the negation of money, of commercial relations and straight division of labour', which was essential to reverse the capitalist experience of work: 'not knowing for whom and or why... producing things that are only measured in terms of money or comfort; from being occupied eight to nine hours a day in exchange for a salary that, no matter how high it is, will never make up for the monotony of our work.'[30]

Marx's Law of Value

While acknowledging that investment must take account of non-economic factors, Alberto Mora suggested that Marx's law of value found its most perfect expression under socialism![31] This position was not supported by Marx's work, Mora's interpretation of value being a rather conventional 'relation between limited available resources and man's increasing wants'. Mora argued also that state enterprises should be financially autonomous, use business accounting methods of economic calculation and produce commodities for profits. Bettleheim made the point that 'if we try to apply forms of organisation and forms of circulation to the (lower) level of development attained by the productive forces, we shall achieve only a great deal of waste'.[32] In his commentary, Michael Löwy argued that without a market it was unclear what people wanted.

In opposition to Alberto Mora and his supporters, Che Guevara followed Marx, stating that 'value' related directly to abstract labour, not to wants or environmental resources. He argued that, in as much as the state sector of the economy approximated a single unit and transfers of products between state factories were all supervised within one budgetary finance system, such products did not constitute commodities. Administered prices were not market prices and Marx's law of value did not apply. This applied to transactions between the private and state sectors too.

Che argued that the plan ought not mimic market forces. Planning enabled non-economic factors to be taken into account and, as a conscious act, undermined the law of value. Che wanted 'to eliminate as vigorously as possible the old categories, including the market, money, and therefore, the lever of material interest – or, to put it better, to eliminate the conditions for their existence'.[33] He believed that 'the development of consciousness can advance ahead of the particular state of the productive forces in any given country'.[34]

Belgian economist Ernest Mandel supported Che Guevara: planning ought to minimise both the working of the law of value and the commodity character of the state workers' product. Guevara distanced himself from the Stalinist bureaucratic planning model and opposed the competitive aspects of the Yugoslavian model. He and Mandel thought that centralised budgetary planning would minimise expensive bureaucratic management.

Material or Moral Incentives

The other focus in this debate was on the relative merits of material and moral incentives. Che was the protagonist for encouraging work through moral incentives. His opponents said monetary incentives were absolutely necessary. According to Michael Löwy, Che argued that use of capitalism's 'fetishes' or 'the worn-out weapons left by capitalism' (such as profit and material incentives) would result in a 'dead end', not in communism.[35] Che said a new attitude, a sense of social duty, a collectivist consciousness and a 'new man' were necessary.

Che was pragmatic enough to recognise that such changes do not occur overnight. One policy involved phasing out material incentives and focusing social benefits on exemplary workers in social fields as well as minimising wage differentiation to accord with skill. Che stressed the importance of education in creating a new consciousness. His faith in the viability of voluntary cooperative labour was based on his political experience of popular mobilisations, which had produced results demonstrably surpassing those observed when effort was individually rewarded.

The general public was much more engaged by this debate over incentives and voluntary labour than it was over financing. Che criticised monetary rewards given to Soviet workers and likened them to North American employees.[36] For Che, voluntary labour meant breaking down the artificial separation between mental and manual labour, and creating a spirited cooperative culture.[37] Like Marx, he conceived of voluntary labour as the pinnacle of a non-alienated existence and the expression of a truly fulfilled human.

Guevara's detailed and complex budgetary finance system certainly allowed for more collective human control over production and distribution than occurs in free markets or in the economic accounting methods of his opponents in Cuba. Carlos Tablada has lauded Guevara's approach to the theory and strategic practice of realising socialism, specifically for understanding and fighting for the development of a new consciousness in the establishment of the material bases of socialism.[38] Che Guevara himself wrote that:

> [C]entralized planning is the mode of existence of socialist society, its defining characteristic, and the point at which man's consciousness finally succeeds in synthesizing and directing the economy toward its goal: the full liberation of the human being within the framework of communist society.[39]

However, Che stressed that Cuba was only in the first phase of a transition to communism and deplored the lack of Marxist theory to guide them further. Most significantly, Che's budgetary system did not do without money as a unit of account (and means of circulation or distribution).[40] Enterprises simply had no *cash* for investment because finance was organised centrally and bankers became administrators. According to Tablada, money prevailed '*as an economic indicator*'.[41] Given trade, especially in the international market, Che accepted the practical reality of money as a unit of account (a standard of price or measure of value) and called for a more rational 'world socialist pricing system'.[42] In 1987, after Che had died, Castro accurately represented his position:

> If there was one thing Che paid absolute attention to, it was accountancy and the analysis, cent for cent, of expenses and costs... Che used to dream of using information technology to gauge economic efficiency under socialism and saw this as essential.[43]

Tablada argues that Guevara was impressed by the efficient administration of the most advanced imperialist monopoly enterprises. Indeed, Che felt that their economic methods could be used 'without fear of being "infected" by bourgeois ideology' and viewed the adoption of advanced (capitalist) technology in a similar way.[44] Che Guevara's model was highly centralised and supervised by a politicised elite who still took world market prices into account when setting prices for Cuban products.

Guevara did not show how his system would lead to the state's devolving its powers over production and distribution to the people directly or to a stage where a unit of account such as money would not exist at all. Guevara did suggest that the latter eventuality relied on the progress of socialism internationally. However, he indicated how terms of exchange between socialist countries might be followed in the meantime.

Castro seemed to wholly support Guevara's idealism later in 1967 (the year Guevara died) claiming: 'We want to de-mystify money, not to rehabilitate it. We even intend to abolish it completely'.[45] But, by then, Che had suffered a resounding defeat in the great economic debate, a defeat that had given him reason to leave Cuba altogether.

Probably the most important point to make here is that the strategy of transferring power to the masses did not surface in either the Cuban or the Soviet debates. Retaining a state structure and using money went hand in hand. State planning of the economy and regulation of the distribution of goods and services seemed to need some form of money, at least as a unit of account. State-produced goods retain some characteristics of commodities and workers are likely to be remunerated in wages, or at least a package of goods and services quantifiable by way of a single unit.

Bettleheim has argued that Soviet communism equated to state capitalism precisely because it adopted monetary economic calculation.[46] Societies in transition to communism could not avoid the influences of world prices and foreign trade unless they became autarchic and self-sufficient. Alternatively, a non-market socialist movement and revolution needs to be global.

Marx's strength lies in the breadth and complexity of his social analysis. In the nineteenth century he was challenging assumptions about markets and the state that have been accepted at face value by many environmentalists. Marx's analysis reveals that when production and consumption are based on market exchange, monetary values and growth are critical and *economic* sustainability, rather than social and environmental values, is the priority. Serious and significant delays in environmental reforms, such as abating carbon emissions, occur mainly because capitalist structures are based on monetary values and power-holders. In short, it is impossible to devise a system that is sustainable both ecologically and economically if capitalism, or monetary values, prevail.

However, in practice, communist movements have found it very difficult to break from capitalist customs associated with monetary evaluation and exchange and to follow a genuinely socialist direction by substituting a state apparatus with grassroots decision-making. These strategies are at the heart of non-market socialism. Only if we move away from money, and interpret the economy as a set of social practices involving nature and aimed at physical and social reproduction of human cultures, does sustainability in ecosystem and human terms appear possible. This is the key challenge facing socialists, economists and environmentalists – indeed all of humanity – today.

Box 2.1 Norman Geras on 'Utopia'

As a goal socialism is, and it always has been, utopian, including in its most influential version to date, namely Marxism... We should be, without hesitation or embarrassment, utopians. At the end of the twentieth century it is the only acceptable political option, morally speaking... nothing but a utopian goal will now suffice. The realities of our time are morally intolerable... Minimum utopia, as here envisaged, entails so fundamental a transformation of existing structures of economic wealth and power and of the distributional norms relating to need, effort and reward that it is revolutionary in scope... I put forward the gloomy proposition that we live in a world not only replete with injustices large and small and the most appalling horrors, but, what is nearly as bad, also oversupplied with a tolerance for such things on the part of those not suffering from them... a *contract of mutual indifference*... To achieve a minimum utopia we would need to find ways of overturning, reversing, the contract of mutual indifference so that a different ethic, an ideal of multifarious care, could come to prevail...

Source: Norman Geras, 'Minimum utopia: Ten theses', *Socialist Register*, Vol. 36: Necessary and Unnecessary Utopias, 2000.

Box 2.2 Karl Polanyi on Land, Labour and Money as Commodities

It is with the help of the commodity concept that the mechanism of the market is geared to the various elements of industrial life. Commodities are here empirically defined as objects produced for sale on the market; markets, again, are empirically defined as actual contacts between buyers and sellers...

The crucial point is this: labor, land, and money are essential elements of industry; they also must be organized in markets; in

▶

fact, these markets form an absolutely vital part of the economic system. But labor, land and money are obviously not commodities; the postulate that anything that is bought and sold must have been produced for sale is emphatically untrue in regard to them... Labor is only another name for human activity which goes with life itself, which in turn is not produced for sale but for entirely different reasons, an activity that cannot be detached from the rest of life, be stored or mobilized; land is only another name for nature, which is not produced by man; actual money, finally is merely a token of purchasing power which, as a rule, is not produced at all, but comes into being through the mechanism of banking or state finance. None of them is produced for sale. The commodity description of labor, land, and money is entirely fictitious.

Source: Karl Polanyi, *The Great Transformation: The Political and Economic Origins of our Time*, Boston: Beacon Press, 2001 [1944], pp. 75–6.

Box 2.3   Che Guevara on the Transition to Socialism: Morality and Materialism

The new society in the process of formation has to compete very hard with the past. This makes itself felt not only in the individual consciousness, weighed down by the residues of an education and an upbringing systematically oriented toward the isolation of the individual, but also by the very nature of this transition period, with the persistence of commodity relations. The commodity is the economic cell of capitalist society: As long as it exists, its effects will make themselves felt in the organization of production and therefore in man's consciousness.

Marx's scheme conceived of the transition period as the result of the explosive transformation of the capitalist system torn apart by its inner contradictions...

...There still remains a long stretch to be covered in the building of the economic base, and the temptation to follow the beaten paths of material interest as the lever of speedy development is very great.

▶

There is the danger of not seeing the forest because of the trees. Pursuing the chimera of achieving socialism with the aid of the blunted weapons left to us by capitalism (the commodity as the economic cell, profitability and individual material interest as levers, etc.), it is possible to come to a blind alley. And the arrival there comes about after covering a long distance where there are many crossroads and where it is difficult to realize just when the wrong turn was taken. Meanwhile, the adapted economic base has undermined the development of consciousness. To build communism, a new man must be created simultaneously with the material base.

That is why it is so important to choose correctly the instrument of mass mobilization. That instrument must be fundamentally of a moral character, without forgetting the correct use of material incentives, especially those of a social nature.

...[I]n moments of extreme danger it is easy to activate moral incentives: To maintain their effectiveness, it is necessary to develop a consciousness in which values acquire new categories. Society as a whole must become a huge school.

Che Guevara, 'Man and socialism in Cuba', in *Venceremos! The Speeches and Writings of Che Guevara*, John Gerassi (ed.), New York: Macmillan, 1968, pp. 387–400, esp. pp. 390–1.

NOTES

All italics in quotes are preserved from the source.

1. Karl Marx, *The Poverty of Philosophy*, Moscow: Progress Publishers, 1975 [1847]; P. J. Proudhon, Système des Contradictions Economiques, ou Philosophie de la Misère [*The Philosophy of Poverty*], Paris, 1846.
2. Duncan Foley, 'Money in economic activity', in John Eatwell, Murray Milgate and Peter Newman (eds), *The New Palgrave Money*, London: Macmillan Press, 1989, pp. 248–62, esp. p. 248.
3. Karl Marx, *Capital: A Critique of Political Economy* Vol. III, Harmondsworth: Penguin, 1981 [1894], p. 911.
4. Ted Benton, Marxism and natural limits: an ecological critique and reconstruction, *New Left Review*, 178, 1989, pp. 51–86, esp. pp. 54–5.
5. Karl Marx, *Capital: A Critique of Political Economy* Vol. I, Harmondsworth: Penguin, 1976 [1867], pp. 283–90; Karl Marx, *Critique of the Gotha Programme*, Moscow: Progress Publishers, 1960 [1891], p. 11.
6. John Bellamy Foster, Marx and the Environment, *Monthly Review*, July–August 1995, pp. 108–23, esp. p. 114.

7. Karl Marx, *Economic and Philosophic Manuscripts of 1844*, Moscow: Progress Publishers, 1977 [1932], p. 73.
8. Marx, *Capital I*, pp. 125–77.
9. Ibid., p. 247.
10. This question, raised by Marx in *The Poverty of Philosophy*, p. 76, is addressed later, in more detail, in 'The Chapter on Money as Capital' in Karl Marx, *Grundrisse: Foundations of the Critique of Political Economy (Rough Draft)*, Harmondsworth: Penguin, 1973 [1939–41], pp. 239–50.
11. Ibid., p. 248.
12. 'On the Jewish question' in Loyd D. Easton and Kurt H. Guddat (eds) *Writings of the Young Marx on Philosophy and Society*, New York: Anchor Books, 1967 [1843], pp. 216–64, esp. pp. 245–6.
13. Marx, *Economic and Philosophic Manuscripts of 1844*, p. 130.
14. Ibid., p. 131.
15. Marx, *Capital I*, p. 167.
16. Ibid., p. 176.
17. Ibid., p. 173.
18. Karl Marx and Frederick Engels, *The German Ideology*, Parts I and II, New York: International Publishers, 1968 [1845], pp. 35–6.
19. Marx, *Economic and Philosophic Manuscripts of 1844*, p. 97.
20. Antonio Negri, *Marx Beyond Marx: Lessons on the Grundrisse*, New York/London: Autonomedia/Pluto Press, 1991, pp. 23, 33.
21. John Crump, 'The thin red line: non-market socialism in the twentieth century', in Maximilien Rubel and John Crump, *Non-Market Socialism in the Nineteenth and Twentieth Centuries*, London: Macmillan Press, 1987, pp. 35–59.
22. Unless otherwise indicated, all quotes in this section are from E. H. Carr, *The Bolshevik Revolution 1917–23* Vol. 2, London: Penguin, 1966, see pp. 136–50, 247–68 and 343–57. The other primary source informing the discussion in this section is L. N. Yurovsky, 'Problems of a moneyless economy', in Alec Nove and I. D. Thatcher (eds) *Markets and Socialism*, London: Edward Elgar, 1995, pp. 63–87.
23. Leon Trotsky cited in Charles Bettleheim, 'Planification et rapports de production', in his *La Transition Vers l'Economie Socialiste*, Paris, Maspero, 1968, p. 60; and Joseph Stalin cited in Roman Rosdolsky, *The Making of Marx's 'Capital'*, London: Pluto Press, 1977, p. 130.
24. Leon Trotsky, *The Revolution Betrayed: What is the Soviet Union and Where is it Going?*, New York: Pathfinder Press, 1970, p. 65.
25. The pre-history of this subject is covered in a fascinating study by Joan Martinez-Alier, *Ecological Economics*, Oxford: Basil Blackwell, 1987.
26. Vladimir Lenin, 'The role and functions of the trade unions under the New Economic Policy: Decision of the Central Committee of the RCP [Russian Communist Party] (B), 12 January 1922' in his *Collected Works* Vol. 33, 1976, pp. 184–5, cited in Carlos Tablada, *Che Guevara: Economics and Politics in the Transition to Socialism*, New York: Pathfinder, 1989, p. 92 [including Tablada's emphasis].
27. This section draws on various works by Che Guevara, 'Planning and consciousness in the transition to socialism' ('On the budgetary finance system'), in his *Che Guevara and the Cuban Revolution*, Sydney: Pathfinder/Pacific and Asia, 1987, pp. 203–30; Guevara, 'Voluntary work is a school for communist consciousness', in his *Che Guevara and the Cuban Revolution*,

Sydney: Pathfinder/Pacific and Asia, 1987, pp. 231–45; and Guevara 'Economic planning and the Cuban experience', in David Deutschmann (ed.), *Che Guevara – A New Society; Reflections for Today's World*, Melbourne: Ocean Press, 1991, pp. 159–68, as well as commentaries by Michael Löwy, *The Marxism of Che Guevara: Philosophy, Economy and Revolutionary Warfare*, New York: Monthly Review Press, 1973, and Tablada, *Che Guevara.*

28. Löwy, *The Marxism of Che Guevara*, p. 17.
29. Guevara, 'Planning and consciousness', pp. 204–5.
30. André Gorz in 'Contributions in tribute to Ernesto "Che" Guevara' by Italo Calvino *et al.* in Andrew Sinclair, *Viva Che!: The Strange Death and Life of Che Guevara*, Stroud: Sutton Publishing, 2006 (revised edn), pp. 48–134, esp. p. 80.
31. Mora cited in Löwy, *The Marxism of Che Guevara*, pp. 46–7.
32. Bettleheim 'Planification et rapports de production', p. 190.
33. Guevara, 'Planning and consciousness', p. 219.
34. Ibid., p. 214.
35. Che Guevara cited in Löwy, *The Marxism of Che Guevara*, p. 62 from a letter to Jose Medero Mestre in Che Guevara, *Oeuvres III – Textes Politiques*, Paris: Petite Collection Maspero, 1968, p. 317.
36. Löwy, *The Marxism of Che Guevara*, p. 66 cites from a conversation with Che Guevara reported by René Dumont, *Cuba: Socialism and Development*, New York, Grove, 1970 [1964], p. 52.
37. Guevara, 'Voluntary work'.
38. Tablada, *Che Guevara*, esp. Ch. 1.
39. Guevara, 'Planning and consciousness', p. 220.
40. Tablada, *Che Guevara*, p. 128.
41. Ibid., p. 130.
42. Guevara, 'Planning and consciousness', pp. 220–3, esp. p. 223.
43. Fidel Castro cited in Janette Habel, *Cuba: The Revolution in Peril*, London: Verso, 1991, p. 47.
44. Guevara Guevara, 'Planning and consciousness', p. 209.
45. Fidel Castro cited in Habel, *Cuba: The Revolution in Peril*, p. 72, quoted from an interview in *Le Nouvel Observateur*.
46. Bettleheim, 'Planification et rapports de production'.

3
Work Refusal and Self-Organisation

Harry Cleaver

The widespread use of money and financial mechanisms against the working class provides us with great opportunities to elaborate critiques of both the money form of social domination and the possibilities for social organisation beyond exchange value – to critique both the price and money forms, and to open discussion on how to reorganise the genesis and distribution of wealth in society without money, prices or debt.[1]

Stopping short of such discussion traps us in the Proudhonist strategy of monetary reformism. In the nineteenth century, when banks served only business and the rich, that strategy included dreams of mutual credit banks among workers; today it often means pressuring for local 'community-based' banks or creating micro-credit programs. Marx rejected nineteenth century socialist schemes for the democratisation of credit because, he argued, money, credit and debt are capitalist tools of exploitation and control. Rather than trying to appropriate them, they should be destroyed. In today's world of consumer credit and mortgages, we know that we can struggle to use credit and debt for our own purposes at the same time that capital tries to use them to both extract interest and profit and enslave us in an endless cycle of borrowing to buy and working to pay off the debt. Marx showed a clear awareness of the class nature of credit and debt, of the way capital sought to use both against workers. We need an equally clear awareness of how they are still being used to control us, of the degree to which our use of them undermines that control, and of alternatives that move us beyond money, credit and debt altogether.

SOCIALISM?

One of the longest-standing critiques of capitalist development has been that of the socialists. From pre-Marxist analyses through to Karl Marx and Frederick Engels, Rosa Luxemburg, Nikolai Bukharin and Vladimir Lenin to Mao Zedong, Fidel Castro and, most recently, Hugo Chávez, socialists have lambasted the international expansion of capitalist social relations as a process that has brought misery rather than improvements in living conditions to the vast majority of the world's peoples. Rather than 'developing' the Third World, some socialists say, capitalism has 'underdeveloped' much of it – made things worse than they were when it was still 'undeveloped', that is, free from the imposition of capitalist class relations.

Yet, at the same time, socialists have consistently proposed the adoption of an alternative 'socialist development' based on the same processes of investment that put people to work, extract a surplus from that work, and reinvest it to impose more work. The primary difference is that in 'socialist development' *government* plans and organises most of the investment. From the Soviet Union's extraction of an agrarian surplus to finance industrialisation to the current Venezuelan Government's appropriation and reinvestment of oil profits, the process remains approximately the same no matter the rhetoric in which these processes are cloaked.

Some critics, such as Friedrich Hayek in *The Road to Serfdom*, have argued that, even though the concept of socialism can be separated from the experience of self-proclaimed socialist states in the twentieth and twenty-first centuries, the *concept* has always had a totalitarian side to it.[2] That side has derived, they argue, from the misguided notion that investment, economic growth and social development can be planned more efficiently than they can be regulated by the market, which automatically synthesises supply and demand in such a fashion as to best satisfy consumer desires, given the scarce resources available. Planning, they have said, cannot achieve the same results because, first, there are just too many decisions to be made and, second, planning has always meant there must be those with the power to plan, and such a concentration of power must lead, and has always led, to both inept and totalitarian government. This critique, of course, ignores that planning occurs all the time in so-called private enterprise capitalism, at many levels: within and among corporations, by national governments and by supra-national state institutions such as the World Trade Organization. All of these actors, as well as others such as labour movements and consumer groups, have sought to plan the evolution of both supply and demand, the basic components of the market. In short, the 'plan' versus 'market' dichotomy was a fiction that served both ideological sides of the Cold War.

While the concept of socialism has certainly mutated repeatedly over time, meaning many different things to many different people, it seems that within all its history two contradictory meanings struggled with each other. The first is a tradition that honours intentional social and economic planning over the supposedly automatic adjustments of capitalist markets. The second is a tradition that believes human beings can cooperate to jointly determine their collective future in ways far superior to those possible under the regime of capitalist exploitation and the mix of markets and planning associated with it.

For a long time the idea of socialism was a dream that evolved in Western Europe simultaneously with the development of capitalism and its industrial revolution. Dissatisfied with the coexistence of outrageous wealth and abject poverty, appalled by the destruction of traditional communities with all their intimate personal bonds and their replacement by individualism and the competitive war of all against all, offended by ugly cities crammed with dark factories and dank dwellings, dismayed by the displacement of craft skills by a crippling division of labour, many workers and social reformers yearned for a better world.

Struggles to transform their world, either in large, through reform or revolution, or in small, through the founding of experimental communities, were based on such dreams of a better world. Apparently the Frenchman Pierre Leroux, a disciple of Henri de Saint-Simon, first used the term 'socialisme' in 1832 in his journal La Globe. It was also used in the 1830s in Britain by the followers of the reformist mill owner Robert Owen.

From Saint-Simon and Owen onward, socialists condemned the destructive antagonisms and anarchy of free-market competitive capitalism. Rather, they emphasised the naturalness and possibilities inherent in human cooperation and solidarity at the social level. They believed that people could learn to cooperate, to work for each other instead of against each other, to conceive their self-interest more broadly in terms of their community instead of narrowly and egotistically.

Yet, at the same time, even the concepts of Saint-Simon and Owen contained an elitist dimension. Owen was a reform-minded capitalist who theorised and practised 'socialism-from-above'. Saint-Simon's concept of socialism, even more than Owen's, called for centralised, top-down planning by 'those most qualified'. The elitist proclivities of these two founding socialists were not entirely inconsistent with the even more radical communist tradition of the time and the belief in the necessity of highly centralised and tightly controlled governance of their alternative communist society. Even Karl Marx's closest collaborator, Frederick Engels, believed that any complex division of labour demanded a central 'authority' to plan and oversee its operation.

MARX

Marx's own analysis of exploitation and alienation in capitalism led him to believe that the working-class overthrow of capitalism would not only lead to workers' control of production and distribution, but also to the overcoming of all the aspects of alienation inherent in the capitalist use of work as its fundamental mechanism of social control. Exactly how this would be done he did not pretend to know; he merely pointed to existing struggles to see what kinds of changes workers would bring about, for example shorter and safer work time (see Box 3.1).

Marx clearly believed that once workers were in command of the means of production they could transform it so that their products would once again be an expression of their own will (instead of that of their capitalist bosses). Then work itself could become an interesting activity of individual and collective self-realisation (instead of a source of alienation) so that a real flowering of self-organised cooperation would replace the conflicts among workers that has been so much the basis of capitalist control.

At the same time, his understanding of both the role of imposed work in capitalism and the long history of the workers' struggle to reduce it led him to write in his *Grundrisse* that, in post-capitalist society, free time as the basis for the 'full development of individuality' would replace labour as the source of value in society.[3] Thus, post-capitalist society would most likely be characterised, at least in part, by the open-endedness of 'disposable time'; an expanding sphere of freedom would allow the many-sided development of the individual and of society.

The conflict in socialist thought between the desire to foster a new kind of social cooperation and a tendency to turn to elitist methods did not disappear with the development of Marxism but only took on greater ambiguity due to the vagueness of Marx's more abstract discussions of issues of revolutionary power. Marx and Engels had both argued, from their earliest writings, that revolution could bring the abolition of the capitalist subordination of human life to endless work and the tyranny of the market. Their alternative was planning on a social scale of both production and distribution. But what kind of planning? Sometimes they spoke of such planning being accomplished by 'the whole of society', sometimes by 'associated producers'. Sometimes, they called for the takeover and management of various sectors of the economy by the state. However, Marx's analysis of the Paris Commune laid out in *The Civil War in France* emphasised how the ability of workers to recall their representatives and the avoidance of any concentration of military power that could be used against the workers were themselves steps in the abolition of the state.[4]

POST-MARX

The central debate in the Second International (1889–1914), which was a renewed attempt to organise a worldwide socialist movement, was over the best method for overthrowing capitalism. Neither side of this debate – on the one hand, electoral and gradual social reform, and, on the other hand, preparing workers for revolution – called for the socialist party to abdicate its leading role in political struggle. The debate was over *how*, not whether, it should lead.

With the October Revolution and their seizure of power, the Bolshevik party leadership moved with blinding speed to consolidate all power into the hands of the party. While the meaning of the 'dictatorship of the proletariat' may have been ambiguous in Marx, there was no ambiguity at all for the Bolsheviks. Anarchists, such as Emma Goldman, and radical communists, such as Rosa Luxemburg and those who would become known as 'council communists', saw in the dismantling of the workers' factory committees and soviets, the solidification of a Bolshevik state, a reconcentration of power antithetical to their concepts of popular power. The anarchists and radical communists called for democracy and the subordination of the party to the workers' own institutions.

Over the following decades the nationalisation of industry, the police-state imposition of strict industrial labour discipline, the collectivisation of the peasantry and finally the forced labour of the Gulag – all carried out in the name of the people – were the forms taken by Soviet-style socialism. Beneath the veneer of socialist rhetoric was a different method of organising the accumulation of capital, variously referred to as 'state capitalism', 'bureaucratic collectivism', or 'state socialism'.

Every effort to actually construct a socialist society seems to me to have reproduced one of the most fundamental characteristics of the kind of society that it is supposed to replace. That characteristic is the essence of what has always been meant by domination: the imposition of a universal set of rules and the subordination of social diversity to a standard measure. Indeed, when we look closely at the mechanisms socialists have designed for regulating their alternative social systems, we find that their attempts to correct the injustices of capitalism have remained trapped in the capitalist practice of measuring everything in terms of labour and money – in short, in that social reductionism that is so characteristic of capitalism.

At an earlier time, Marx had rejected utopian plans for substituting 'labour chits' (or 'time-chits' or 'labour money') for cash money because, he argued, the substance of money value in capitalism was already labour.[5] Labour chits, therefore, would simply be a primitive form of money and likely to evolve into all too familiar forms. He imagined instead the communist abolition of all kinds of money along with the dramatic reduction of labour time and the substitution of the direct distribution of collectively produced wealth among the producers. However, in the history of post-Marx socialism, the desire to create a new system led many to maintain labour and money as the standards and measures of value. Not surprisingly, they also reproduced the practice of making the very mechanism of domination through endless labour into a virtue, with the socialist version of the work ethic differing from the Calvinist/capitalist one only in its secular trappings.

As the one overarching goal of socialist development became capital accumulation through endless labour, the openness to social, cultural and ethnic diversity that was at least implicit in Marx's notion of the transcendence of labour value by an indeterminate free time has been both ignored and contradicted. Socialism as a homogenous and unified social system became the master narrative. Only later in the twentieth century did some Marxists seek to recuperate and explore the possibilities of real multilateralism in post-capitalist society.

The origins of top-down, centrally planned concepts of socialism lay within the bias of Marxist-Leninists (and the 'critical theorists' of the Frankfurt School) to focus on the power of capital, to see workers as essentially reactive to mechanisms of oppression and, therefore, to think that they depended on some kind of outside leadership (of the party or of intellectuals) to mobilise them for revolution. Such an approach inevitably fails to study our ability to rupture those mechanisms, to throw the system into crisis and to recompose social structures. As a result, even their theoretical understanding has remained one-sided, and more of a paean to capitalist power than a useful tool for us in our struggles.

The political importance of placing *our* abilities at the centre of our thinking about the class conflicts of capitalism, about the dynamics of the development of those conflicts, is revealed by the simple consideration that only on the basis of an accurate appraisal of our existing abilities (and their limits) can we usefully debate how to proceed best in our efforts to transcend capitalism and build new worlds.

For example, outsourcing, or the mobility of fixed capital associated with free trade – production facilities being moved from country A to country B with the products then shipped back to country A – can be seen as another clever capitalist ploy to increase profits by replacing those of us with higher wages by those of us with lower wages. There is obviously truth to this view. However, outsourcing can also be seen as capital *fleeing* the ability of those of us who have been able to impose higher wages and as our ability, in conjunction with the struggles of immigrants who had previously been used against us, to impose rigidities, high costs of production and less work. Seeing things from this latter angle allows us to understand how it was that hundreds of groups of those of us struggling in Canada, the United States of America and Mexico were able to link up quickly in new forms of continental-scale organisation to oppose the North American Free Trade Agreement and to subsequently help form the alter-globalisation movement. This activity, it should be noted, has taken place largely outside traditional trade unions or parties. We should neither be surprised nor attempt to squeeze such organisation into old moulds. On the contrary, a new global class composition calls for us to find new forms of organising.

TRANSCENDING CAPITALISM

There are many different issues involved in the general notion of 'transcending', or going beyond, the current social order. Peter Kropotkin, the deepest and most creative thinker of all the Russian revolutionary anarchists, was acutely aware of both the practical issues of political struggle and the more abstract issue of the character of human social evolution. To provide a general understanding of the latter, Kropotkin pursued research on 'mutual aid' to provide a foundation for his anarcho-communist politics.

He aimed to demonstrate that there was an inherent tendency in human society, as well as in a variety of other animal species, for individuals to cooperate with other members of their species and help each other rather than to compete in a war of all against all.[6] He traced the manifestation of the 'law of mutual aid' down through history. He found it sometimes triumphant, sometimes defeated, by the contradictory forces of competition and conflict but always present and providing the foundation for recurrent efforts at cooperative, self-emancipation from various forms of domination (the state, institutional religion, capitalism). He was able to cut through the rhetoric and the reality of competition to perceive and demonstrate the omnipresence of social cooperation at all levels of society (see Box 3.2).

Various revolutionary tendencies have drawn on Marx's work but insisted on the primacy of the self-activity and creativity of people in struggles against capitalism outside and against the Soviet conversion of revolution into state capitalism and of Marxism into an ideology of domination. They have tended to reconceptualise the process of transcending capitalism in ways similar to Kropotkin's.

AUTONOMIST MARXISM AND SELF-VALORISATION

It was my discovery of a recurrent insistence by some Marxists on the autonomy of working-class self-activity, not only vis-à-vis capital but also vis-à-vis trade unions and the party, that led me to coin the term *autonomist* Marxism to designate this general line of reasoning and the politics associated with it. Autonomist Marxists have argued that the process of revolution is seen either as the work of the people or as being doomed from the start. The emphasis on working-class autonomy has led, in turn, to a reinterpretation of Marxist theory that has brought out the two-sided character of the class struggle and shifted the focus from capital (the preoccupation of orthodox Marxism) to workers, to us.

That shift has led to many new perceptions, such as the recognition that 'working class' is a category of capital, a condition that people have struggled to avoid or to escape. Not only has there been recognition that capitalism seeks to subordinate everyone's life to work – from the traditional factory proletariat to peasants, housewives and students – but also that all those peoples' struggles involve both resistance to this subordination and the effort to construct alternative ways of being. The recognition of such phenomena has led autonomist Marxists to the same kind of research that Kropotkin pursued.

They have developed a systematic Marxist analysis of working-class autonomy that has evolved from a study of how the pattern of capitalist development was determined by working-class negativity (blocking and forcing changes) to the study of the positive content of those struggles (which capital seeks to stem or co-opt). One autonomist Marxist in Italy, Mario Tronti, has reminded us that for Marx capital (dead labour) was essentially a constraint on the working class (living labour).[7] The living, inventive force within capitalism is the imagination and self-activity of workers, not of capitalists. When in the late 1960s and 1970s that creative self-activity exploded throughout the social factory in a myriad of social, cultural and political innovations in Italy, Antonio Negri took a relatively obscure term, 'self-valorisation', which had been used by Marx to talk about the self-reproduction of *capital*, and gave it a new meaning: the self-development of the *working class*.[8]

Negri's term 'self-valorisation' not only gave a name to the positive content of the struggles in Italy but refocused our attention on the ways in which workers not only struggle *against* capital but also *for* a variety of new ways of being. It provided a point of departure for rethinking the content of our struggles and some fundamental issues, such as the nature of revolution and of the 'transition' to post-capitalist society. As Marx had done in his *Economic and Philosophical Manuscripts*, Negri stressed that the creation of communism is not something that comes later but is repeatedly launched by current developments of new forms of working-class self-activity.[9]

There are problems with this term because the self-valorisation of the working class is not homologous with that of capital, and more recently Negri has drawn on both his own and Gilles Deleuze's work on Spinoza to speak in terms of 'constituent power'.[10] But in both cases the point has been to focus attention on the existence of autonomy in the self-development of workers vis-à-vis capital. For too long the development of the working class had been seen by Marxists as merely derivative of the development of capital. Other Marxists (see the online journal *The Commoner*) refer to the activities thus constituted to some identifiable degree outside and beyond capitalist social relationships as forming new dimensions of our 'commons' – harkening back to all the commons (of grazing lands, forests, parks, waters, knowledge, etc.) shared by members of communities that capital has repeatedly sought to enclose and privatise.

Because these terms have been developed in a way that conceptualises self-valorisation or constituent activity not as unified but as diverse, they provide a theoretical articulation of the tradition within autonomist Marxism of recognising the autonomy not merely of the working class but of various sectors of it. To both recognise and accept diversity of self-valorisation, rooted like all other activity in the diversity of the peoples seeking to escape capitalist domination, implies a whole politics, one that rejects traditional socialist notions of post-capitalist unity and redefines the 'transition' from capitalism to communism in terms of the elaboration from the present into the future of existing forms of self-valorisation or commons. Communism is reconceptualised in harmony with Kropotkin's views, not as a some-day-to-be-achieved utopia but as a living reality whose growth needs only to be freed from constraint.

Like Kropotkin's studies, such efforts to discover the future in the present were based not only on a theory of collective subjectivity but also on empirical studies of real workers in action. These researches have explored moments of class conflict and working-class self-activity, such as the workers' councils created during the 1956 Hungarian revolution, students' and women's movements, and the struggles of peasants and the urban poor in Mexico in the late twentieth and twenty-first centuries. In a growing number of cases, the research has focused on new forms of social cooperation. As with Kropotkin, some of the clearest results have come from the study of rural areas, of the self-activity of peasants in their villages. But others have come from urban struggles, for example those of students squatting in buildings to create autonomous centres of youth activism and innovation.

At the same time, networking has provided the means to circulate both information and struggle in ways that extend the notion of community, and therefore of the 'commons', far beyond the isolated locality, even beyond national frontiers. In Mexico, such networks have been called 'hammocks' because, rather than trapping the participant, they are adaptable to the specificities of local needs and projects.

Some Italian and French theorists of working-class autonomy have suggested that a new diversity of subjectivities that rupture capitalist control and continue to defy its present efforts at subordination represents the emergent possibilities of liberation. An early characterisation was that of a new 'tribe of moles', a loose community of highly mobile, drop-out, part-time workers, part-time students, participants in the underground economy, creators of temporary and ever-changing autonomous zones of social life that forced a fragmentation of and crisis in the mass-worker organisation of the social factory. A more recent characterisation is that of 'multitude', also drawn from Spinoza, and used by Michael Hardt and Antonio Negri, and by Paolo Virno.[11]

Whatever concept one uses to talk about our struggles, it has become increasingly clear that within the interpersonal interactions and exchanges of information associated with the 'computer and informational society' is an increasingly collective appropriation of, and control over, communication. Indeed, from almost the beginning, computer communication networks have been constructed by people for their own uses. Originally created and operated to facilitate the development of technology at the service of capital, contemporary networks have been largely constructed by the collectivities that use them. They retain the material stamp of that autonomy in their uncentralised and fluid technical organisation and constitute a terrain of constant conflict between capitalist attempts at appropriation and the fierce allegiance of most users to freedom of use and 'movement' throughout the cyberspace they have created and constantly recreate as moments of their own self-activity, online and off.

A myriad of participants of networks operate from personal or institutional (academic, corporate or state) entry points, using and elaborating the technology in pursuit of their own collective interests. The constitution of a proliferating network of networks – almost totally devoted both to the subversion of the current order and to the elaboration of autonomous communities of like-minded people connected in non-hierarchical, rhizomatic fashion purely by the commonality of their desires – has been striking. Remarkably, the proliferation of the 'personal' computer rapidly evolved into a gateway of communication and mobilisation linking often-isolated individuals into social movements. The modem and the spread of communication nets are providing the sinew of large-scale collective social cooperation in dramatic ways.

NORTH VERSUS SOUTH

Capitalism has always been a global system. The story of imperialism is only very partially the story of the rip-off of wealth, of the opening of markets and of the acquisitions of outlets for capital. All of these are but moments in the global process of turning the world's peoples into workers and then dividing and redividing them with the aim of controlling them all. In the nineteenth century Indian weavers had their thumbs cut off to maintain jobs in British mills. A century later Asian and Latin American workers would be put to work in relocated mills while North American and Northern European textile workers were laid off. These are not just different stages in capitalist development; these are changes in the global class composition in response to changing patterns of our struggles.

We must understand the policies of nation states in terms of the changing balances of class power. Why have some parts of the world been 'developed' while others remained 'undeveloped' or have been 'underdeveloped'? This has happened because an international wage and income hierarchy is necessary for the control of the class globally and in the developed areas some of us could be put to work profitably and in others we could not. What many have repeatedly failed to recognise is how many of us in 'underdeveloped' areas have often *refused* to work for capital on its terms, that is, profitable terms. In such circumstances the absence of capitalist development has been a measure of our strength, not just of our relative weakness (for example, our inability to command a high wage). The international counterpart of seeing those of us working in the North as victims is looking at those of us elsewhere, those of us at the bottom of the international wage and income hierarchy, as simply exploited and oppressed.

Indeed, 'development' and 'underdevelopment' are misleading terms, not only because they designate processes as well as states of being, but also because they designate strategies. De-industrialisation and industrialisation occur as moments in changing rhythms of class struggle, shifting balances of power within a whole as the integrity of that whole is repeatedly threatened by assaults at all levels of the hierarchy. No analysis of the current crisis in capitalist power can be useful that does not grasp the specificities of local variations within the broader context. Capital operates at a global level, so our struggles occur everywhere, and anti-capitalist strategies, like capitalist strategies, must be formulated and implemented globally.

Multinational capital organises itself through the multinational corporation, interstate relations and supranational state forms, such as the International Monetary Fund. None of these are appropriate for us, but we must organise the international circulation of our struggles on a global level. Think globally and act locally is not enough; our local actions must be complementary and that does not necessarily happen automatically. We have achieved complementarities before, for instance the anti-apartheid movement or simultaneous alter-globalisation protests; we must continue to invent ever more effective new approaches.

ZEROWORK; REFUSAL OF WORK

What I have been arguing for some time now is that we get a totally different vision, a different reading of Marxist theory and a different politics of the overthrow and replacement of capitalism, when we focus on the substance of the social relationships of capitalism: work. Capitalism is not just a social system that exploits people through work, such that we can think about ending the exploitation and keeping the work; it is a social system that tends to subordinate all of life to work and, by so doing, alienates those of us forced to work and prevents us from developing our own paths of self-realisation. The subordination of our lives to work means not only that we are we forced to work many intense hours – so many hours that we have little time and energy left over for other activities – but also that those other activities tend to be reduced to the mere recreation of our lives as labour power, so that we are willing and able to work.

For example, the *waged* know that during each day of our usual working week (Monday to Friday for many) most of our waking hours are taken up working directly for capital on the job. But we also find that much of our supposedly 'free' time or 'leisure' time is taken up preparing for work, getting to work, getting home from work, recuperating from work, doing what is necessary so that we can go back to work the next day, and so on. For those of us who are not waged, for example the *unwaged* in the home (usually housewives but often children and sometimes men), 'leisure' time turns out to be mostly dedicated to house*work*, which in turn is not just crafting and reproducing domestic life but involves the work of turning our children into workers and reproducing ourselves as workers.

In other words, women have children but then they (along with husbands sometimes) must rear them to take orders, to curb their desires and spontaneity and to learn to do as they are told (the same work that teachers undertake in schools). As children we are not left free to discover life on our own but are put to school*work*, home*work* and house*work* – the work of turning ourselves into *workers*, as well as reproducing our parents as workers. Similarly, adult housework reproduces labour power daily and weekly through shopping, cooking, feeding, washing clothes and cleaning the house, and the provision of sexual and psychological services (from patching up job-damaged egos to absorbing abuse), all of which is necessary for us to return to work each day without shooting the boss, ourselves or our loved ones. Parallel analyses can be made of the 'free' time on weekends and vacations. In short, I'm arguing not merely that capital has extended its mechanisms of domination beyond the factory but that those mechanisms involve the imposition of work, including *the imposition of the work of reproducing life as work.*

The recognition of how capital has sought to impose work outside waged work must be accompanied by the same understanding of its rule in waged work: namely that imposition always involves struggle. Just as we have resisted the imposition of work inside the factory or office, via slowdowns, strikes, sabotage and *détournement*, so too have we resisted elsewhere the reduction of lives to work. At this point autonomist theory gets beyond the dead end of critical theory. Instead of becoming fixated on capitalist hegemony, on detailing the thoroughness and completeness of capitalist domination, we must recognise, study and then articulate our ability to struggle against our reduction to mere worker. Precisely because capital seeks to intervene and shape all of life, all of life rebels, each nook and cranny of life becomes a site of insurgency against this subordination.

Housewives go on strike in the home or march out of it collectively into the streets. Students take over classes and schools or create 'free universities' of liberated learning opportunities outside the institutions. Peasants refuse to subordinate their production (and thus their work) to the market and collaborate to build networks of mutual aid. The 'unemployed' refuse to look for waged jobs. 'Culture' becomes a terrain of the fiercest struggle between liberating self-activity and its recuperation or instrumentalisation by business. And so on.

What the recognition of all this means is not only that the class struggle is omnipresent but also that *the struggles of those of us who are waged and the struggles of those of us who are unwaged are inherently related through the common refusal of work, that is, the refusal of the reduction of our lives to work, and the struggle for alternative ways of being.* Thus the Old Left definition of the working class as the waged proletariat is obsolete, not only because capital has integrated the unwaged into its self-reproduction, but also because the struggles of the unwaged are integrally related to, and can be complementary to, those of the waged.

Yet at the same time the struggles for alternative ways of being that escape the reduction of life to work are diverse. Unlike the older Marxist notions of replacing capitalism with some kind of homogenous socialism, we must recognise communism as a diversity of alternatives. Revolution involves explosion, the escape from reductionism, rather than the substitution of one unified plan for another. Here is the importance of the autonomy of the struggles of different groups of people seeking to avoid the reduction of their lives to labour.

Most interpretations of Marxist theory, especially of the labour theory of value, fail to recognise how Marx's theory was a *labour* theory not because he worshiped labour as the only source of value in society, but because the universal conversion of life into labour was, and is, the capitalist means of domination. Other class societies involved some forcing of others, such as serfs in feudalism and slaves in many ancient societies, to work, but never had the world seen a society wherein life was redefined as work. Many accurately read Marx's analysis of *alienation* as a critique of the capitalist perversion of work, concluding that socialism and communism involved freeing work from that perversion.

Where they have gone wrong, in my opinion, is that they think Marx focuses on work because he believes unalienated work is the be-all and end-all of human existence, that work defines humanity. Instead, we should see that it made sense for Marx to focus his analysis on work because of its centrality to capitalist domination. He recognised that people struggle against work not merely because it is exploitative but because *there is more to life than work*.[12]

The qualitative transformation of work under capitalism into alienation comes not merely from its organisation but from its *quantitative extension*. The central issue in the transcendence of labour value toward value as disposable time must be the reduction of labour time. Again and again Marx's evocation of post-capitalist society involves the image of the individual and the collectivity doing many things, not just working. The transcendence of alienation can only come with such a quantitative reduction of work that work becomes one, among other, integral aspects of a richly diverse human existence. The liberation *of* work can come only with the liberation *from* work, that is, from the capitalist reduction of life to work. Once we see these things, we are freed from the productivism of all the old socialist illusions; we are free to think about struggle, revolution and freedom in terms of the simultaneous demotion of work from the centre of life and its restoration as one means, among others, of fulfilling human development.

The development of the 'refusal of work' as an explicit demand in Italy in the 1960s was an important reminder that the working class has always struggled against work. Sometimes the reduction of work, the liberation of life from work, has been an explicit demand, as in the fight for the ten-hour or eight-hour day, or for the five-day working week. Between 1880 and 1940 workers' struggles in the United States chopped weekly working hours in half and created the weekend. In the early 1970s in the United States, new demands, this time for a four-day week, surfaced only to be driven from the agenda and replaced by demands for overtime by rising unemployment and falling wages. In Europe, workers have fought for, and won, reductions in weekly working hours from forty or more to thirty-six hours. At other times, especially when the official labour movement has been acting as the labour relations arm of business, such demands have been suppressed and remained hidden from view, observable only in the passive resistance, absenteeism and worker sabotage in everyday life.

A great many social conflicts can be understood in terms of the struggle against work, even when the protagonists have not articulated their demands in those terms. Many student revolts have amounted to a refusal to do the work of creating labour power, mere job training, accompanied by a demand for the time and opportunity to study things that meet student needs rather than the needs of business. Much of the revolt of women can be seen as a refusal to play their traditional roles in the social factory as procreators and re-creators of labour power, accompanied by demands for new kinds of gender and other social relations. The revolts of blacks, or Chicanos, or immigrants in the streets of American cities have not been just a cry of desperation but a rebellion against the roles assigned to them within accumulation: on the margins, as part of the reserve army that made the labour market function, moving in and out of the lowest-paid jobs, living under subsistence conditions, excluded from political participation, and so on. Theirs was a rejection of particular kinds of work, just like that of students and women, but a rejection of work all the same. The struggle against work spreads with its imposition so that it is possible to explore the variety of both refusal and activities that are substituted for work, and thus the changing relationship between work and non-work.

Let's look at this analytically. We know that high rates of unemployment have often been an integral part of capital's response to crisis imposed on it by our struggles, in which the struggle against work has played a critical role. It was a familiar strategy throughout the nineteenth century right up to the 1930s, when an enormous cycle of our forebears' struggles achieved the power to eliminate it for a time. Their struggles forced the generalised adoption of Keynesianism, in which unemployment was demoted to a secondary, marginal tactic, at least in the North. This lasted until my generation undermined Keynesianism in the late 1960s and early 1970s. Unfortunately, the pattern of the development of the crisis has been such that we have *not* had the power to prevent the redeployment of unemployment as a weapon, which was first done massively in the Carter-Volcker-Reagan depression of the early 1980s and is now being done again at the end of the first decade of the twenty-first century. But what kind of weapon is it? When we lose our waged jobs we are not freed from work! We are supposed to go on doing the work of reproducing labour power *and* to make the labour market function by looking for waged jobs.

Part of *our* effort must be to make these dynamics clear so that we can struggle for what we really want, which is a secure income and less work-for-capital so that we have more time to re-craft our lives. Thus, instead of demanding 'full employment' and strenuously searching for new jobs, we can demand less restrictive and more unemployment compensation or even 'citizen wages' independent of jobs. By minimising job searching we can maximise the time we have available to do things more in our own interests. When we return to waged jobs we continue the struggle against work, albeit all too often less intensely because we now have a greater fear of losing the wage. The ability of the unwaged to demand and get income buttresses the ability of the waged to refuse work. As I say, this is an old game: we know the rules, they are pitted against us, but they are not impossible to fight.

When we examine the history of the struggle against work, we discover various ways in which our predecessors have fought. The Luddites smashed the machines that they saw as responsible for their loss of the wage. It didn't work very well, though it wasn't as crazy as some have claimed. Later, workers explicitly linked the struggle against work with the issue of unemployment to demand that all available work and wages should be spread over the entire labour force. A reduction in the working day or week could be the means to spread less work and share wages. Such arguments have been made by Andre Gorz in his *Farewell to the Working Class* and Jeremy Rifkin in *The End of Work*, suggesting that capital has substituted machinery for labour so much that it simply cannot create enough 'full time' jobs to employ everyone.[13] Whatever its limitations, such as not recognising how higher unemployment for the waged has been accompanied by more work for the unwaged, this argument has the virtue of refusing to fall back into the traditional left-wing demand for 'full employment', which just reiterates the fundamentals of capitalism.

Arguments about the need to 'spread the work' played an important role in struggles during the nineteenth century and the 1930s, and helped mobilise support for the reduction of work. The limits of such demands are in the continuing acceptance of the legitimacy of work within capitalism, that is, ignoring its role of domination, rather than being geared to meeting people's needs. Re-situated within a more thoroughgoing critique of all forms of waged and unwaged work, of capitalism and its subordination of desire and of its structuring of life around work, such demands can undermine rather than reinforce capital.

Others have explored self-valorisation in studies of both work and non-work activities. Those studies have borne rich fruit and have provided a wealth of understanding about the diverse experiences of creative struggles that persisted through the crisis, not captured, destroyed or harnessed by capitalist repression or cooptation.

What these concepts of self-valorisation, or of constituent power, or of the creation of new commons do is to draw our attention not only to our ability to limit and constrain capital's domination over us, but also to our abilities and creativity in elaborating alternatives. Just as the concept of the 'refusal of work' helps us to understand how a wide variety of social struggles has undermined capitalist accumulation and repeatedly thrown it into crisis, so too do these concepts help us to understand how our ability to elaborate and defend new ways of being – in our old and new commons – not only against but also beyond capital, is the other side of the crisis.

The power of refusal is our power to carve out times and spaces relatively free from the capitalist imposition of work. The power of self-valorisation is our ability to fill those times and spaces with alternative activities and new forms of sociality – to elaborate our common future in the present. This perspective allows us to recognise and to understand within a political framework the creativity and imagination at work within the so-called 'new social movements' that have always been against the constraints of the capitalist social factory – whether they have articulated their ideas as such or not – and are new primarily in their strength and their imagination.

For example, women's and gay movements have not merely refused the subordination of life to work but have initiated a wide variety of experiments in developing new kinds of gender and family relationships, new kinds of personal and social relations among men and among women. The Green movement has not only attacked the capitalist exploitation of all of nature but has also explored a wide variety of alternative kinds of biocentric relationships between humans and the rest of nature. These movements have overlapped and influenced each other just as they have sought inspiration in various alternative cultural practices, for instance those of Indigenous peoples or those of pre-capitalist European history.

Our political strategy must be to diversify projects of self-valorisation and to avoid being constrained and harnessed within capital by becoming complementary or at least mutually supportive: between us and capital the maximisation of antagonism, among ourselves the elaboration of a politics of difference that minimises or eliminates antagonism. The difficulty is that there is no shortcut, no magic formula, no simple 'unite and fight', not through a particular organisational form, not through an ideology, not even through Marxism (because Marxism provides an antagonistic understanding of capitalist domination but no formula for post-capitalist ways of being). What we want is for our different struggles, against capital and for alternative ways of being, to be complementary and mutually reinforcing. The problem is to find ways of achieving this.

Assuming the accuracy of the kind of analysis I have presented, the struggle against the capitalist reduction of life to work provides one point of commonality to all of us, thus a basis for mutual understanding. Of course, because we are diverse and hierarchically pitted against each other, the imposition of work is experienced differently by different groups of workers so there is nothing simple about organising around the refusal of work. The history of our struggles has made this quite clear.

But it has also made clear that, despite all the differences, people have been able to link up their struggles and make collective gains. Recognising the variation in the ways work is imposed, and the consequent variation in the forms of refusal throughout society, is also useful to be able to recognise the parallels among various kinds of struggles in the present.

When we turn from the struggle against capital to the struggle for a diversity of projects of self-valorisation we have a more difficult problem: how to develop a politics of difference without antagonism. Capital with its essence in command, authority and domination can only conceive of organisation from the top down, by some kind of 'leadership', and can see only chaos in any other kind of order. We, on the other hand, need to be able to perceive and appreciate a variety of kinds of organisations while always evaluating their appropriateness critically. Much of the best of the 'bottom up' history developed over the last 60 years has involved the discovery and making visible of such organisation in popular movements.

SELF-ORGANISATION

Internal organisation by any self-defined group of people in struggle is *self*-organisation. At the same time, because of diversity, any 'internal' organisation, however managed, must also involve the collective organisation of relationships with other groups, in effect the organisation of the *circulation of struggle*. The question, 'How can we build our own power to refuse work or to self-valorise in our own way?' becomes, 'How can we link up with others so that our efforts do not remain isolated but are mutually reinforcing?' All kinds of internally rigid formulae have survived within small groups, but the story of much of the Left has been that such groups have, in part by their own rigidity, and often by their proselytising, cut themselves off and remained isolated from each other. As a result they have stagnated and remained irrelevant to larger social movements where more flexible and adapted forms of organisation have facilitated the circulation of struggle among diverse groups.

All this is true at every level. Everywhere that organisation fails to achieve the circulation of struggle, it fails, whether in a tiny groupescule, in a single city or region or nation. The strength of relatively small groups, such as the Palestinians, the black freedom movements in southern Africa, or the Zapatistas in southern Mexico, has always been largely due to their ability to build networks of alliance to circulate their struggles beyond their specific locales to other groups in other parts of the world. This, of course, is precisely why in every case capital's strategy has been to isolate them, with trade, financial boycotts or travel restrictions so that they could be destroyed. We cannot overemphasise the importance of this experience and must draw the necessary lesson: only through the ever wider circulation of struggle can we hope to achieve the power necessary to destroy the manifold sinews of capitalist domination and to replace them with new social relationships more to our liking.

Today, when the class confrontation is global, our circulation of our own struggles must be organised throughout the world, through every linkage possible. If we understand what is required, we have only to find the means. It is a process that is already under way; it always is. The political problems are: first, the assessment of what is working and what is not, which forms of organisation are facilitating the circulation of struggle and which are hindering it; and, second, building those that are working and abandoning or changing those that are not.

Kropotkin sought to understand the desires and self-activity of people and to articulate them in ways that contributed to both their circulation and their empowerment. In the midst of crisis, let us seek out and support, as he did, the sources of popular innovation and strength while at the same time identifying and combating all obstacles to their development.

Box 3.1   E. P. Thompson on Time and Money

Those who are employed experience a distinction between their employer's time and their 'own' time. And the employer must *use* the time of his labour, and see it is not wasted: not the task but the value of time, when reduced to money is dominant. Time is now currency: it is not passed but spent.

The first generation of factory workers were taught by their masters the importance of time; the second generation formed their short-time committees in the ten-hour movement; the third generation struck for overtime or time-and-a-half. They had accepted the categories of their employers and learned to fight back within them. They had learned their lesson, that time is money, only too well.

Source: E. P. Thompson, 'Time, work-discipline, and industrial capitalism', *Past And Present*, 38, 1967, pp. 57–97, esp. pp. 61, 86.

Box 3.2   Peter Kropotkin on 'Mutual Aid' or Cooperation

For thousands of years in succession, to grow one's food was the burden, almost the curse, of mankind. But it need be so no more. If you make yourselves the soil, and partly the temperature and

▶

the moisture which each crop requires, you will see that to grow the yearly food of a family, under rational conditions of culture, requires so little labour that it might almost be done as a mere change from other pursuits. If you return to the soil, and co-operate with your neighbours instead of erecting high walls to conceal yourself from their looks; if you utilise what experiment has already taught us, and call to your aid science and technical invention, which never fail to answer to the call – look only at what they have done for warfare – you will be astounded at the facility with which you can bring a rich and varied food out of the soil...

... Have the factory and workshop at the gates of your fields and gardens, and work in them. Not those large establishments, of course... but the countless variety of workshops and factories which are required to satisfy the infinite diversity of tastes among civilised men.

Source: Peter Kropotkin, *Fields, Factories and Workshops Tomorrow*, London: George Allen & Unwin, 1974 [1899], pp. 196–7.

NOTES

All italics in quotes are preserved from the originals.

1. This chapter includes revised and updated versions of some passages from previously published work: Harry Cleaver, 'Close the IMF, abolish debt and end development: a class analysis of the international debt crisis', *Capital & Class*, No. 39, Winter 1989; 'Kropotkin, self-valorisation and the crisis of Marxism' in *Anarchist Studies* Vol. 2, No. 2, 1994; and 'Socialism' in W. Sach (ed.) *The Development Dictionary: Knowledge as Power*, London: Zed Books, 1992, pp. 233–49.
2. Friedrich Hayek, *The Road to Serfdom*, London: Routledge, 1944.
3. Karl Marx, *Grundrisse: Foundations of the Critique of Political Economy (Rough Draft)*, Harmondsworth/London: Penguin Books/New Left Review, 1973 [1857].
4. Karl Marx, *The Civil War in France*, New York: International Publishers, 1993 [1871].
5. Marx, *Grundrisse*, pp. 153–8, is one example of several discussions of the various schemes for labour chits, that is, symbols of credit proportional to work hours.
6. Peter Kropotkin, *Mutual Aid: A Factor of Evolution*, New York: Dover, 2006 [1902].
7. Mario Tronti, *Operai e Capitale*, Turin: Einaudi, 1966.
8. Antonio Negri, *Marx Beyond Marx: Lessons on the Grundrisse*, New York/London: Autonomedia/Pluto Press, 1991 [1979].

9. Karl Marx, *Economic and Philosophical Manuscripts*, Moscow: Progress Publishers, 1977 [1844].

10. Antonio Negri, *Insurgencies: Constituent Power and the Modern State*, Minneapolis: University of Minnesota Press, 1999.

11. Michael Hardt and Antonio Negri, *Empire*, Cambridge: Harvard University Press, 2000; Michael Hardt and Antonio Negri, *Multitude: War and Democracy in the Age of Empire*, New York: Penguin Press, 2004; Paolo Virno, *A Grammar of the Multitude: For an Analysis of Contemporary Forms of Life*, New York: Semiotext(e), 2004; Paolo Virno, *Multitude Between Innovation and Negation*, New York: Semiotext(e), 2008. In *Empire*, pp. 102–3, Hardt and Negri distinguish between 'people' and 'multitude' thus:

> *the modern conception of the people is in fact a product of the nation-state*, and survives only within its specific ideological context... We should note that the concept of the people is very different from that of the multitude... The multitude is a multiplicity, a plane of singularities, an open set of relations, which is not homogeneous or identical with itself and bears an indistinct, inclusive relation to those outside of it.

12. Karl Marx, Chapter 10 in *Capital: A Critique of Political Economy* Vol. I, Harmondsworth/London: Penguin Books/New Left Review, 1976 [1867], pp. 340–416.

13. Andre Gorz, *Farewell to the Working Class: An Essay on Post-Industrial Socialism*, London: Pluto Press, 1982; Jeremy Rifkin, *The End of Work*, New York: Tarcher/Putnam, 1996.

4
Money, Markets and Ecology

John O'Neill

This chapter traces parallels in the history of ecological and socialist economic thought and argues that their future is intertwined because both require rethinking of alternatives to market mechanisms for solving environmental and social problems.[1] The analysis of economic debates involving socialist economists, Austrian economists, ecological economists and neo-classical economists informs a discussion of non-market associational forms. The potential and limits of the current surge of forms of deliberative democracy is considered, arguments are made for institutional pluralism within a non-market socialist future and the significance of critical defences of existing non-market orders is highlighted.

ECOLOGICAL AND SOCIALIST THOUGHT

The history of ecological and socialist thought over the last century has been more intertwined than is often supposed. In particular, the socialist calculation debates had an environmental dimension that is often overlooked. The objections that Ludwig von Mises, Friedrich Hayek and other Austrian economists raised against socialism were directed against the tradition of thought that issued in modern ecological economics as well. The precursors of ecological economics – Joseph Popper-Lynkeus, Karl Ballod-Atlanticus, Otto Neurath, Wilhelm Ostwald, Patrick Geddes, Frederick Soddy and Ernest Solvay – were all included among their targets.[2] In particular, two central assumptions of ecological economics were subject to criticism: first, that social choices have to recognise that economic institutions and relations are embedded within the physical world and subject to resource and ecological constraints; and hence, second, that economic choices cannot be founded on purely monetary valuations.

Thus, if the arguments of Mises and Hayek were conclusive against socialism, as many assume, then they have more general implications.

They raise problems with the perspectives on ecologically rational choices that emerged in the tradition of ecological economics. Indeed, while their assumptions are very different from those of the neo-classical economists, and in the case of Hayek more powerful, some of the conclusions drawn by the Austrian tradition parallel neo-classical approaches to environmental problems. For both, the existence of environmental problems is the result of the absence of markets in environmental goods. Their solution lies in the extension of markets to include currently unpriced environmental goods.

The common ground between the ecological and socialist traditions lies in their resistance to this market-based approach to social choice. Mises and Hayek were right to see a common opponent. At the same time, the weaknesses in the argument of Mises and Hayek against the ecological tradition are of more general relevance to socialists. It is not just the history of ecological thought and socialist thought that are intertwined. So also is their future. This is not just because any defensible form of socialism will have to be one that is ecologically sustainable, but also because both require the rethinking of alternatives to market mechanisms for solving environmental and social problems. Recent work within the ecological tradition on the use of non-monetary decision tools, the integration of these with deliberative institutions and the defence of institutional and cultural pluralism, address problems central to future models of socialism. Here, the significance of these institutional claims for the future of socialism in the light of the environmental themes in the history of the socialist calculation debates is considered.

The received story about socialist calculation presents the debate in terms of a conflict between Mises and then Hayek on the one side, and Lange and Taylor on the other. This story is unsatisfactory for three related reasons. First, some of the main characters in the debate are missing, most notably in the context of the ecological themes in the debate Otto Neurath, one of the central figures in the Vienna Circle.

Second, there are more discontinuities in the debates than is often assumed. There were at least two debates that concerned two independent objections to the possibility of socialism. The first debate, to which Mises contributed, was an argument about rational choice and commensurability – specifically the possibility of rational economic action in the absence of a single unit of comparison between alternative economic activities. Neurath's public contribution to the socialist calculation debates was to this earlier phase. The second debate, instigated by Hayek's epistemic objection to socialism, concerned the possibility of planning given the dispersal of knowledge amongst different actors in an economy. While Hayek presents his epistemic argument as a continuation of the first debate it in fact forms a departure from it: indeed, Hayek's own position on the nature of rational choice is closer to that of Neurath than that of Mises.[3] Neurath forcibly highlighted the common ground in their positions in his correspondence with Hayek.[4]

Third, the ecological dimension to the debate has been subsequently missed. The possibility of economic choices that reflect the resource and environmental conditions of economic activity was central to the debates.

INCOMMENSURABILITY, MONEY AND RATIONAL CHOICE UNDER SOCIALISM

Mises's arguments against the possibility of rational choice in socialism were targeted against two opponents: first, those theorists in some Marxist literature who advocated replacing money as a unit of economic calculation with another unit such as labour-time units, and ecological economists, such as Popper-Lynkeus and Ballod-Atlanticus, who advocated energy units; second, Neurath, who denied that rational economic choice required the existence of a single unit of calculation and advocated economic decisions founded on *in natura* calculation in kind.

Mises's arguments against both turn on assumptions about the nature of practical rationality and its dependence on commensurability (having a common measure). Rational economic decision-making involving 'higher order' production goods requires a single cardinal measure on the basis of which the worth of alternative states of affairs could be calculated and compared. Environmental examples were already at the centre of this debate (although more self-consciously so in the work of Neurath than that of Mises – see Uebel).[5] Thus, for example, given the choice 'whether we shall use a waterfall to produce electricity or extend coal and better utilize the energy contained in coal', we need some way of calculating the advantages and benefits of alternatives, and this in turn required a common unit of measurement.[6]

A common cardinal unit of measurement is provided by monetary prices in the market: 'calculations based upon exchange values enable us to reduce values to a common unit'.[7] Prices form, indeed, the only adequate unit of comparison. Comparability between options requires monetary prices that measure exchange values such that one is able to have a determinate answer to the advantages of alternatives by way of simple rules:

> The practical man... must know whether what he wants to achieve will be an improvement when compared with the present state of affairs and with the advantages to be expected from the execution of other technically realisable projects which cannot be put into execution if the project he has in mind absorbs the available means. Such comparisons can only be made by the use of money prices.[8]

On this view, the non-existence of monetary measures in a socialist economy rules out the possibility of rational economic decisions.

Neurath's position is founded on a *rejection* of this account of rational choice. Rational choice does not need value commensurability. No single measure can capture the multidimensional nature of values employed in social choice.[9] The algorithmic view of practical reason that Mises employs exhibits 'pseudorationalism'.[10] Our knowledge that informs decision-making is uncertain and the norms of rationality rarely determine a unique answer, given what is known. A proper rationalist recognises the boundaries of the power of reason in arriving at decisions: 'Rationalism sees its chief triumph in the clear recognition of the limits of actual insight.'[11] It is a mark of the pseudorationalist to believe that there exist technical rules of choice that determine optimal answers to all decisions. Thus, given a choice between alternative sources of energy – say, coal and hydraulic power or solar energy – various ethical and political judgements, for example about intergenerational equity and the distribution of risks, come into play. One cannot make such choices through a purely technical procedure employing some single unit, either monetary or non-monetary.[12]

Neurath did defend the possibility of *in natura* economy and indeed the attempt to realise an economy in kind was central to his socialisation plans in the Bavarian revolution after the First World War. A socialist economy, since it was to consider only the use value of goods, would have to be a non-market 'economy in kind', in which there would exist no role for monetary units to compare options:

> We must at last free ourselves from outmoded prejudices and regard a large-scale economy in kind as a fully valid form of economy

which is the more important today in that any completely planned economy amounts to an economy in kind. To socialize therefore means to further an economy in kind. To hold on to the split and uncontrollable monetary order and at the same time to want to socialize is an inner contradiction.[13]

While physical statistics about energy and material use and so on would be needed in such an economy, there would be no need for a single unit of comparison: 'There are no units that can be used as the basis of a decision, neither units of money nor hours of work. One must directly judge the desirability of the two possibilities.'[14] In the absence of a single unit of measurement for decision-making, choice requires direct comparisons of alternatives. The consequence is that there is no possibility of excluding political and ethical judgements from even 'technical' decisions. In making this claim, Neurath is not only criticising the market, but also socialist alternatives to the market that employ single units in making decisions, be these labour hours or energy units:

> The question might arise, should one protect coalmines or put greater strain on men? The answer depends for example on whether one thinks that hydraulic power may be sufficiently developed or that solar heat might come to be better used, etc. If one believes the latter, one may 'spend' coal more freely and will hardly waste human effort where coal can be used. If however one is afraid that when one generation uses too much coal thousands will freeze to death in the future, one might use more human power and save coal. Such and many other non-technical matters determine the choice of a technically calculable plan ... we can see no possibility of reducing the production plan to some kind of unit and then to compare the various plans in terms of such units.[15]

Neurath's response to Mises focuses specifically on a questioning of the assumptions about economic decision-making that informs Mises's critique: rational practical thinking need not involve any single unit that reduces decision-making to a purely technical procedure of calculation. It requires ethical and political decisions. The socialist responses to Mises, which still require a single unit, were mistaken:

> Even some socialists have agreed with Mises' thesis – without calculation with *one* unit, an economy is *not* possible; socialism

does not acknowledge any calculation with *one* unit; it follows that socialism is impossible – and therefore try to establish that in the socialist society there also can be such a calculation. For us it is essential that *calculation in kind in the economic plan has to be the moneyless basis of socialist calculation of economic efficiency.*[16]

Neurath's arguments against the picture of decision-making that Mises employs turn on specific arguments about the limits of monetary measures and on some more general arguments about the nature of rational choice.

The specific argument on the limits of monetary measures turns principally on the inadequacy of monetary measures – or indeed any single measure – to capture changes in welfare. First, monetary measures cannot capture adequately the multidimensional nature of welfare concepts, such as standard of living or pleasure: 'The attempts to characterize the standard of living are like those which try to characterize the "state of health". Both are multidimensional structures.'[17] Neurath's arguments here go back to a 1912 lecture, 'The Problem of the Pleasure Maximum', in which he criticises the assumption that there is a single scale of value according to which options can be uniquely ordered somewhat surprisingly, from within a hedonist perspective. While Neurath defended a social Epicurean position, which takes the goal of social policy to be the increase of happiness understood as pleasure, he rejected the assumption that differences in distinct pleasures, say of listening to music or contemplating a painting, are themselves comparable in terms of some single unit. Hence there are no units of pleasure on which calculations can be made.[18]

This point about the multidimensionality of the concepts of standard of living is combined with a second, namely the non-separability of those different dimensions: 'We cannot regard [the standard of living] as a weight made up of the sum of the weights of the various parts.'[19] The argument against separability and in defence of a form of holism about values was developed thus by Neurath in an early paper, 'Remarks on the Productivity of Money':

Suppose a civil servant has the choice between two places of residence, A and B. In A, he receives a larger quantity of food and accommodation, in B on the other hand a larger quantity of honour. Is it possible to have a calculus such that it summarises for us food and accommodation as one magnitude, and honour as another? Impossible! We are not able to compute such a complex, containing both pleasure and pain, by first separately establishing the magnitude of pleasure, then the magnitude of pain and finally doing the sum. On the contrary, we can only look at such a complex as a whole. Therefore the conversion into money is of no help in this case... [T]*he calculus of value* reaches its limits, because the value of a sum of goods is not derivable from the sum of the value of the individual goods. Indeed the question may be raised as whether it is possible to ascertain the value of *individual* objects in social life without looking at the social life in its entirety at the same time, that is, whether all goods might be complementary. If this is the case, it is impossible to capture the individual phenomenon by separate calculation, independently of whether one uses monetary calculation or any other kind of calculus.[20]

Given that the value of different goods across different dimensions is not separable, an aesthetic model of ascertaining this is preferred to the bookkeeping model:

[N]either do we compare the artistic achievements of architecture so as to say: this hall is more functional than that one, but less beautiful; let us add up advantages and disadvantages. In comparing two works of art we look at one as a whole and the other as a whole.[21]

HAYEK, EPISTEMOLOGY AND ECOLOGY

Hayek's epistemic criticisms of planning are directed, like Mises's criticisms, not just at socialists but also at attempts in the ecological tradition to understand the ways in which economic institutions are embedded within the physical world and to develop non-monetary methods for economic choices that recognise those physical preconditions. Hayek denied the possibility of non-monetary units for planning economic production. For Hayek the ecological tradition exemplified a 'scientistic objectivism' expressed in 'the characteristic and ever-recurrent demand for the substitution of *in natura* calculation for the "artificial" calculation in terms of price or value, that is, of a calculation which takes explicit account of the objective properties of things'.[22] Neurath became a primary target since his work most clearly combines socialism and *in natura* calculation.

The belief in objectivism and *in natura* calculation for Hayek expresses an illusion about the scope of knowledge that is typified by the social engineer's belief in some purely technical optimal solution to social choices.[23] In holding to the possibility of such an optimum the social engineer is a victim of the illusion of complete knowledge that underpins the project of socialist planning.[24] It exhibits 'Cartesian rationalism', the belief in the omnipotence of reason and the corresponding failure of 'human reason rationally to comprehend its own limitations'.[25]

Cartesian rationalism in the social domain fails to acknowledge the division of knowledge in society, the dispersal of practical knowledge embodied in skills and know-how particular to local time and place. Such knowledge cannot be articulated in propositional form and, hence, cannot in principle be passed on to a central planning body. The market in contrast resolves problems of ignorance by acting as a coordinating procedure, which distributes to different actors that information that is relevant for the coordination of their plans through the price mechanism.[26] Given this view of the price system, to give up prices for calculation in kind is to give up a solution to the problem of ignorance for the illusion of the possibility of complete knowledge based in planning. There is no *in natura* alternative to the monetary measures.

How convincing are Hayek's epistemic criticisms of the underpinning of ecological economics? As a criticism of the doctrine that writers like Neurath held it misses its target. The doctrine that Hayek criticises – that there are some purely physical units, such as units of energy, independent of human use or belief that could be employed for planning – was rejected by Neurath and with it the technocratic idea that there is any 'optimum' solution to social problems. Neurath opposed the technocratic movement, which assumes a single optimum solution 'with its "optimum happiness"', and which 'asks for a particular authority which should be exercised by technicians and other experts in selecting "big plans"'.[27] Neurath's criticisms of technocratic planning start from epistemic assumptions shared with Hayek. Neurath's criticisms of pseudorationalism parallel those of Hayek against rationalism. Both reject the illusion of complete knowledge on which technocratic planning is based.[28]

Of course, Neurath is not alone in sharing this perspective on the socialist side of the debate. Many socialists have taken Hayek seriously not only because there is power in his epistemic criticisms of central planning but also because they share common ground with epistemic arguments offered within the socialist tradition. Hayek's epistemic criticism of centrally planned economies have their counterpart within the history of debates about socialist planning as an argument for democratic and decentralised decision-making and for a proper appreciation of the limits of abstract technical expertise. There is a long tradition of associational socialism that had argued against the possibility of an economy centralised on Fabian or Bolshevik lines.[29]

Similar epistemic themes concerning the importance of local ecological knowledge embodied in particular human practices, the inescapability of social choice in conditions of radical ignorance and the limits of scientific predictability are central to the ecological tradition. These concerns underpin the need for cultural and institutional pluralism, the precautionary principle and the importance of deliberative institutions, which counter the necessary role of the scientific expert. The central question that divides Hayek's position from his socialist and ecological opponents is: how far are specifically market institutions either necessary or sufficient to coordinate practical knowledge? Are there alternatives to market solutions to the coordination of knowledge?

ASSOCIATIONS WITHOUT THE MARKET: THEORY AND PRACTICE

Associational models of socialism tend to be associated with the guild socialist movement. Neurath's route to associational socialism was independent of the British guild socialist movement. However, Neurath had some sympathy with the emphasis they placed on self-government. Thus, in a review he wrote:

In Central Europe we are not sensitive enough to the ideal of self-government. Many people would as much agree to the socialist distribution of housing, food, clothing, education, entertainment and public health by an army of reliable socialist civil servants as to the self-government of these branches of economy.[30]

However, Neurath rejected the model of socialism offered by the guild socialists for two central reasons. First, he rejected their continued acceptance of markets. More generally he followed the traditional Marxist argument that a market economy in which cooperatives would be forced to compete could not realise a socialist economy:

[I]f, after socialisation, the individual economic establishments retain far-reaching autonomous rights and exchange commodities and money between themselves, this will amount to engaging in capitalist economic practices. The capitalism of individuals would then be replaced by 'capitalism of groups'.[31]

Second, and less obviously, Neurath also criticised the statism of the models of socialism they offered. Neurath's associationalism centred more on overlapping functional units of planning, rather than units based on national areas. The focus on function rather than area was introduced in his writings after the First World War in part as a response to the problem of militarism:

> In a world socialist society the fields of life could be linked to each other in the most varied ways, without having to be detachable national units. We might for instance reach a stage... where areas along big navigable rivers would form one administrative unit for building, transport and production, whereas the educational units might depend on language... The national areas might for instance have different boundaries from those of the health areas. Insofar as sharper geographical frontiers of mores, customs, outlook, legal systems etc., show themselves, they need not at all be frontiers of sovereignty under armed protection. Only in this way will the wolfish nature of states be eradicated.[32]

What is significant about Neurath's version is that it retains a clear distinction between the flourishing of associations and the flourishing of exchange relations, a distinction that many recent uses of the term 'civil society' have blurred.[33] He avoids the assumption, which has dogged much twentieth-century political thought and action, that we must choose either state planning or the 'internationalism of the "money-order"'.[34] Indeed, Neurath tends to turn that point around: that the monetary order itself tends to produce certain kinds of uniformity.

The significance of institutional and cultural pluralism in a socialist economy is central to Neurath's defence of associationalism:

> [W]ithin the framework of a deliberately devised economic plan it is possible for forms of economy of various kinds to co-exist without being forced into competition: craft co-operatives, special settlements with shared work, industrial associations. In this way perhaps the intolerance of the market economy will be overcome, which destroyed everything that stood against 'laissez faire' and the wish of expansion for capitalist gain. Manchester liberalism... treated community and guild movements with contempt.[35]

The claims about cultural uniformity of the market are reiterated in a criticism of the lack of pluralism found in many models of socialism:

> Should China, India, Central Africa really get one and the same socialism? Each comparative study of different orders of life teaches us that it was the tendency to organise the economy in all civilisations after the same pattern which made the free market society so much hated. If socialism should bring liberation, it must be joined by tolerance, it must do justice to the differences in civilisations and fit each one into the economic plan and the administrative economy in its own way.[36]

Neurath defended an associational socialism without markets in which unification of the economy was to be married with decentralisation of decision-making:

> The economic plan requires the economy to be unified. This does not mean that all decision-making is centralised, as many Social Democrats wish. It is enough if a central body ensures that independent decisions by various economic groups will fit into the general plan.[37]

Of course, that position raises its own difficulties. Within a non-market setting, how are problems of coordination to be overcome without extensive and excessive centralisation of powers? The problems of combining coordination of activities with their self-administration and of realising institutional pluralism were recurrent ones in Neurath's practical engagement in social action. Neurath was involved in various social experiments, but three in particular are relevant here: the socialisation plans in post-war Bavaria, the housing movement in post-war Vienna and the unity-of-science movement in the 1930s. Each has relevance to Neurath's model of non-market associational socialism. If there is a movement in Neurath's thought it is the movement towards increasing decentralisation, which in turn reflects historical experiences.

Socialisation Plans in Post-War Bavaria

Neurath's first and most direct practical engagement in socialisation was his involvement as director of socialisation in Bavaria during the post-war revolutionary period. Neurath's total socialisation plans were radical in being committed to a rapid movement towards a planned moneyless economy in kind. Indeed, in his Bavarian plans, socialisation in this sense took priority over the abolition of private property.[38] A feature of the plans was the commitment to pluralism in the forms that non-capitalist organisation could take within a general system of central indicative planning:

> The programme of socialisation here discussed makes an attempt at a simultaneous realisation of socialism, solidarism and communism... It provides for co-operatives for peasants and craftsmen, for collectivist settlements on a communist basis and for large-scale socialist production in agriculture and industry to exist side by side, in order to do justice to their different aspirations to realise a collective economy in their own way... Mere majority decision will give way to *an economic tolerance* that can support several non-capitalist forms of economy simultaneously.[39]

The terms 'communism' and 'socialism' here have a particular idiosyncratic meaning, associated with Tönnies's distinction between *Gemeinschaft* and *Gesellschaft*. Communism refers to socialisation within the context of *Gemeinschaft*, in which relations are constituted by habit and custom. A significant feature of Neurath's socialisation plans was the degree to which the habitual and customary were not eliminated. Socialism refers to socialisation within the context of the more formal relations of *Gesellschaft*. Solidarism refers to the various cooperative movements. Central to that institutional pluralism was the role of associations of producers. While Neurath retained the commitment to a planning agency, a central economic administration, the intention was that it left autonomy to lower associations:

> Wherever possible, the realisation of the measures to be taken would be left to non-bureaucratic *associations that administrate themselves*. These associations are to be consulted in the course of determining the economic plan and have a vote in it. They may be of different kinds. *Craftsmen* and *peasants* may be grouped in co-operatives, which take responsibility for the raw materials and additional inputs and ensure that the final product will be available to all people... Special organisations would have to encompass the *big production plants*... [T]he co-operatives of the craftsmen and the associations of industry would, just like the peasant co-operatives and the agricultural associations, be united in *national associations* that control the production

from the raw material till the end product. For instance, the national association for construction works would comprise the production of construction materials, the administration of building land, and the actual construction works.[40]

Alongside these production associations, Neurath also allowed a role for the workers councils within the overall organisations, which, significantly for Neurath, were to include not just factory workers but also representatives of women involved in domestic labour and those unable to work.

Neurath's socialisation plans during the Bavarian revolution were never realised. However, his subsequent reflections on the experiences engaged with issues of planning without centralisation of knowledge and decision-making.

The Housing Movement in Post-War Vienna

A second major activity, which is reflected in his many references to the example of construction and housing in his socialisation writings, was his involvement in the housing movement in post-war Vienna.[41] On returning to Vienna after the failure of the Bavarian revolution, Neurath became secretary of the Research Institute for Social Economy, which aimed to gather information for the development of socialist economy. Through the institute's activities, Neurath become secretary-general of the League of Settlers and Small Gardeners in 1921. The settlement movement grew during the food shortages at the end of and just after the First World War, when many in the urban population established small gardens for food and livestock at the outskirts of the cities. Through local organisations of mutual aid these grew into small garden cities. In 1916 it had only 2000 members in 13 local organisations. In Neurath's first report on the movement it had 30,000 members in 230 local organisations, later growing to a movement of some 50,000. While the statutes of the movement stated that it 'excluded' party politics, it contained various socialist, anarchist, communist and conservative forces, often in conflict with each other. The social democratic party, after an initial period of scepticism, was supportive and the city administration provided support through leases on land, the provision of water and the like. The experiment was successful, although eventually incorporated into the larger social-democratic housing projects in post-war Vienna.

A feature of Neurath's role in the organisation is that he argued for maintaining historically given cooperatives and associations of farmers and workers within the larger central socialist organisation that would coordinate the movement. The problem was one of coordinating activities that were self-managed, while maintaining social ownership against tendencies within the movement towards privatisation, and maintaining some degree of discipline in the coordination of the various activities that rendered it a cooperative movement. Clearly, it differed from the larger socialisation plans of the Bavarian republic in its scale. It involved coordination of cooperatives with specific housing and land-use aims, not the coordination of an entire economy. However, such associational orders for Neurath formed the basis for a wider non-market socialisation of the economy.

The Unity of Science Movement in the 1930s

The concern with sustaining coordination with self-organised activities also pervaded the third social movement in which Neurath was centrally involved, that for the unity of the sciences. To call the Unity of Science movement a social movement might look an oddity, and that is certainly not how the movement has been normally portrayed. Subsequent accounts of the movement have tended to present the program as a form of positivistic reductionism, which died with one of the last publications of the International Encyclopaedia of Unified Science, Kuhn's *The Structure of Scientific Revolutions*. The image is in error.

While reductionism was not absent among all those involved in the Unity of Science movement, it was already rejected by many, in particular Neurath: '[W]ould it not be preferable to treat all statements and all sciences as co-ordinated and to abandon for good the traditional hierarchy: physical sciences, biological sciences, social sciences and similar types of "scientific pyramidism"?'[42] Neurath also rejected a second doctrine, which was often part of the subsequent image of the movement: the belief in a single unified method for the sciences. While Neurath rejected the view that there were fundamental differences between the natural and social sciences, he was a pluralist about methods in the sciences. The belief in the existence of a single method in science was a form of pseudorationalism: hence his opposition to both falsificationism and verificationism. Finally, there is far less of a break between the sociology of science associated with Kuhn and the earlier sociological accounts of Neurath than is often supposed.

The central project of the unity of science movement was a social project, that of coordinating the activities and output of the scientific community, both as a part of a general democratic movement for social change and as a means of coordinating knowledge for social planning. The intent of the project was the realisation of the coordination of different disciplines. The project addressed two social problems. The first is what Neurath calls the 'democratisation of knowledge' that was central to Neurath's work from the cultural education movements of red Vienna; his work on museums and visual education through isotypes belonged to the same social project.[43] The second problem is the way that decisions about particular states of affairs draw on different sciences. This problem is central to any possibility of social planning that calls on various forms of knowledge. Neurath's response to the problem was a defence of a unity of language for the sciences, specifically of physicalism – the view that all statements in science be controllable by sentences containing terms that refer only to spatio-temporal particulars.

In the work of Neurath the orchestration of the sciences is taken to illustrate 'how much unity of action can result, without any kind of authoritative integration'.[44] Science is integrated without any pyramidic organisation. The model of orchestration of the kind one finds in the sciences reflects Neurath's vision of planning, particularly in his later writings, as a possible 'future order based not on "state pyramidism", if this term may be accepted, but on "overlapping institutions", which do not coincide with any "hierarchic" world pattern.'[45] And whatever the plausibility of that vision there is an important point here – the scientific community is an example of an international non-market order within existing economies. It offers one of the many examples of non-market coordination of knowledge and activities within existing market societies. It is a social achievement to which Neurath is right to draw attention.

DELIBERATION, PLURALISM AND THE INSTITUTIONS OF SOCIALISM

The shared assumption of both Austrian and neo-classical economics, that rational choice requires the use of market mechanisms and monetary measures, remains at the core of current debates in environmental economics. The standard critical response to market solutions has been the shift from the market to the forum, to experiments in deliberative institutional frameworks for social choice. Deliberative models of democracy have recently enjoyed a justifiable revival. Against the market picture of democracy as a procedure for aggregating and effectively meeting the given preferences of individuals, it offers a model of democracy as a forum through which judgements and preferences are formed and altered through reasoned dialogue.[46] In the context of public environmental choice it has had particular power in criticism of market-based approaches to environmental choice.

Market-based approaches to the resolution of value conflicts about the environment are reason-blind. The strength and weakness of the *intensity* of a preference as measured by a person's 'willingness to pay' at the margin for their satisfaction do count in a decision; the strength and weakness of the *reasons* for a preference do not. Preferences are treated as expressions of mere taste to be priced and weighed one with the other. Market approaches offer conflict resolution without rational assessment and debate. However, because environmental conflicts are open to reasoned debate, which aims to change preferences (not record them), it follows that different institutional forms are needed for their resolution.

Where conflict is open to reasoned adjudication, discursive institutions are the appropriate form for resolving the conflict. In practice the revival of deliberative democracy has been expressed in the development of 'new' formal deliberative institutions, which are often presented as experiments in deliberative democracy. These include citizens' juries, citizens' panels, in-depth discussion groups, consensus conferences, round tables and, more problematically, focus groups.[47] At the same time, at the level of decision-making tools, there have been attempts to develop multi-criteria decision aids that recognise the irreducibility of different dimensions of value involved in social choices. Where such multi-criteria decision aids have tended to be technocratic and expert-based in the past, the recent move has been to find ways of integrating them into deliberative institutional contexts.[48]

How far can such experiments inform a model of a future socialist society? To the extent that these experiments in deliberation are offered as purely political solutions in the absence of changes to economic institutions there are two grounds for scepticism from socialists. The first appeals to well-worked socialist arguments against the purely formal equality involved in liberal institutions. While 'new' deliberative institutions are often presented as 'facilitating' 'inclusive' 'dialogue' between equals, dialogue takes place against the background of large asymmetries of social, institutional and economic power. This has implications for the ways deliberative forums can operate. Within formal deliberative forums the capacity and confidence to speak differs across class, gender and ethnicity. Just as willingness to pay is unevenly distributed, picking up inequalities of income, so also is willingness to say.

Moreover, deliberative institutions are open to being used strategically. Some of the new 'deliberative' institutions, in particular focus groups, are often employed in political practice to gather information of likely responses to different policies, not in order to foster public deliberation but rather to anticipate and forestall it. The origin of the focus group technique lies after all in market research. Where deliberation is public, power is exercised in the framing of issues before discussion and in the choice of the constituency for debate. If effectively captured by powerful institutions, deliberative institutions provide strong legitimation tools. The purely formal equality of liberal institutions is not sufficient for the proper working of deliberative institutions. A rough equality in economic and social power is a necessary condition, and such equality requires shifts away from current patterns of ownership and control. This argument from deliberative ideals to the need for economic and social equality strikes me as entirely right. In the context of social and economic equality, a more Athenian model of democracy in which deliberative institutions are chosen by lot, such as the citizens' jury, could play a wider role in economic and political life. It offers the possibility of a social order of equals in which each takes turn in positions of power where, in the phrase of Aristotle, 'they rule and are ruled in turn'.[49]

A purely political model of deliberation is also open to a second objection concerning the split between citizen and market actor that it assumes. One version of this is in Karl Marx's 'On the Jewish question'.[50] In the perfected democratic constitution the individual lives in two worlds and two roles – as a citizen in the communal world of democracy and as a self-interested agent in the world of the market. Social emancipation requires the transformation of the economic realm of bringing the communal citizen down to earth in his everyday life 'when the real, individual man re-absorbs in himself the abstract citizen'. The division that Marx criticises – between 'citizen' and 'market agent' – is assumed by many who advocate a deliberative response to environmental problems. Consider, for example, the distinction between the preferences that an individual has in the role of consumer and those that she has as a citizen drawn by Sagoff in his influential *The Economy of the Earth*. As a consumer an individual expresses 'personal or self-regarding wants and interests'; as a citizen she expresses her 'judgements about what is right or good'. For Sagoff, it is in the role of citizen that the individual deliberates about environmental goods.[51]

The mistake of market approaches to environmental problems is that they transform an issue that requires public deliberation by citizens into one to be resolved by consumer preferences. Sagoff's use of the distinction between citizen and consumer takes for granted the institutional contexts of different preference orders. That split is problematic. It is unclear just where and what the boundary of the political and the market is supposed to be, because there are very few economic decisions that do not have environmental consequences. Within the economic sphere itself, to leave the allocation of most resources to the market is incompatible with the realisation of environmental goods. The market responds only to those preferences that can be articulated through acts of buying and selling. Hence the interests of the commercially inarticulate, both those who are contingently so (the poor) and those who are necessarily so (future generations and non-humans) cannot be adequately represented. Moreover, a competitive market economy is necessarily oriented towards the growth of capital, and therefore is incompatible with a sustainable economy. The idea that we can simply live in two worlds with the kind of preference schizophrenia that Sagoff assumes is untenable. Public deliberation needs to be taken into the economy itself.

This case for bringing deliberative institutions into the economic realm is, however, open to two major objections. The first is a version of Hayek's epistemological criticisms of planned economies, which has recently been deployed by Hodgson against the possibility of a predominantly non-market economy coordinated by deliberative institutions.[52] If there are forms of tacit or practical knowledge that cannot be passed on to a central planning system because they are not open to articulation, then neither will they be open to articulation in a deliberative setting. Hence models of socialism that rely purely on deliberative institutions to coordinate activities will be open to some of the same objections made to the epistemic case against planning. The argument runs to the conclusion that any coordination of dispersed tacit knowledge requires mechanisms that 'rely to some significant extent on the market and the price mechanism'.[53]

These epistemological arguments do point to limits to deliberative institutions as processes of social coordination and choice. However, they are not conclusive as arguments for a market as against deliberative institutional framework within economic life. First, social coordination does not require specifically market institutions.

Indeed, the very examples that are normally employed to illustrate the significance of practical knowledge highlight this point. When Hodgson illustrates the role of practical knowledge, he turns (as did Hayek) to Polanyi's claim that 'all scientific advances and technological innovations are bound up with tacit knowledge'.[54] Hodgson is right to do so.[55] The coordination of scientific knowledge, both tacit and articulated, is one of the institutional achievements of the modern world. However, as support for the need for markets and prices to coordinate tacit knowledge, the example fails.

The public scientific community is one of the great examples of a predominantly non-market social order within the modern world. The danger in the current introduction of market mechanisms into public science is that it will reduce rather than increase the rate of innovation. Conflicts around the development of new intellectual property regimes centre on the control of knowledge crucial to innovation. More generally, the coordination of knowledge, tacit and articulated, is a ubiquitous problem that exists at all points in the social and economic order. As knowledge has come to the centre of economic life in the modern world, the management of the distribution of unarticulated knowledge throughout organisations of various kinds without its loss has become an increasingly important task. The market is not needed for coordination and, as the case of science shows, can become a hindrance. There exist various levels of coordination throughout the economy in different institutional forms, our knowledge of which is often practical and unarticulated. While it may be true that deliberative institutions *alone* cannot realise coordination, deliberation clearly can have a coordinating role within a wider context of practically and institutionally embodied knowledge – consider again the case of the scientific community. Just as the market is not needed for coordination, neither is there reason to assume that dialogical forms of coordination necessarily reduce the use of local and tacit knowledge.

A second, and more powerful, objection to the position Marx defends in 'On the Jewish question' is the institutional monism it involves, a monism that has been a feature of much socialist thinking over the last century. Whatever the specific problems with market economies, the assumption that the division between the private person and the public citizen is one that should simply be overcome is problematic.[56] However, the criticism of institutional monism also cuts in the opposite direction.

The recognition of the need for institutional pluralism has been a central point in ecological criticism of the market economy.

Ecological knowledge is embodied in particular practices and traditions that cannot be articulated and that globalised markets undermine.[57] This point appeals to an argument for pluralism within the socialist tradition that recent resistance to globalisation has brought back to the fore. Thus, for example, a rejection of the monism of both free-market liberalism and technocratic models of socialism was central to Neurath's work and, hence, Neurath's defence of '*economic tolerance* that can support several non-capitalist forms of economy simultaneously'.[58] There are good epistemological reasons for such tolerance – different forms of knowledge are embodied in different social practices and institutions. There are also reasons to do with the nature of different goods. For example, given their different natures, health, love and the recognition of the worth of a scientific achievement should not be distributed by identical institutional principles: the first follows need, the second the fortunes of kinship and affection, the third merit. While market mechanisms are inadequate, neither is there a single socialist principle of distribution that applies to all.[59]

The defence of institutional pluralism needs stressing in current debates. There is a tendency among socialists to think in terms of some single model of social relations, and this is as true for decentralised planning as it is for centralised planning. There is a pluralism of non-market forms of social and economic relations, such as gifts, public networks of recognition, scientific communities, kin relations and cooperatives. It is a mistake in considering the future of socialism after the failure of centralised state economies to look for *the* new model. Given the knowledge embodied in human traditions and practices there are good epistemological grounds for scepticism about the attempt to reorganise all human activities on the basis of some general set of rational principles. As Hayek and Neurath both note, reason sees its maturity in the recognition of its own limits.

Conversely, the significance of non-market orders that exist within contemporary society need to be recognised, and defended against market encroachment while remaining critical of their internal forms of power. Globalisation has seen the geographical spread of commercial norms into communities, which retain non-market economic relations employing common property, mutual aid and gift, and for whom markets previously existed on the margins of their economic life. At the same time in advanced market economies there has been an expansion in the domains of goods and relations falling under market norms. Domains that were previously outside market norms, such as public science, access to information, control of agricultural and natural biodiversity, and bodily integrity are being redefined as potential spheres of market exchange that are coming under new property rights regimes. Environmental goods are increasingly coming under the norms of market exchange in both these senses.[60]

A link exists between current resistance to the spread of market norms and property rights – keeping knowledge free, sustaining islands of cooperative activity, maintaining access to environmental goods – and the possibility of a socialist future. The significance of the recent anti-capitalist movement against neo-liberal globalisation has been the defence of non-market institutional and cultural forms against the spread of market norms. Socialists need not just recreate utopian visions, but build on existing non-market orders – to remind ourselves of the existence of social relations and networks, both local and global, that have developed outside market norms.

The future of socialism is not ultimately compromised by the possibility of feasible alternatives to the capitalist economy, although the unattractiveness of the putative alternatives in Eastern Europe and Asia that went under the title of socialism has left its legacy. The problems come increasingly from a form of social lock-in – that the capitalist market order survives because it becomes so tied into all human relationships that construction of an alternative becomes increasingly difficult to build or even imagine. In that context the defence of existing non-market orders becomes part of the project of maintaining the possibility of an alternative.

NOTES

All italics in quotes are preserved from the originals.

1. This chapter developed out of a revised version of 'Socialist calculation and environmental valuation: Money, markets and ecology', *Science and Society*, Vol. 66, No. 1, 2002, pp. 137–51, complemented by edited extracts from 'Socialism, associations and the market', *Economy and Society*, Vol. 32, No. 2, 2003, pp. 184–206 and from 'Ecological economics and the politics of knowledge: the debate between Hayek and Neurath', *Cambridge Journal of Economics*, Vol. 28, No. 3, 2004, pp. 431–47.
2. Joan Martinez-Alier, *Ecological Economics*, Oxford: Blackwell, 1987.
3. John O'Neill, 'Who won the socialist calculation debate?', *History of Political Thought*, 27, 1996, pp. 431–42.
4. Otto Neurath, 'Physicalism, planning and the social sciences: Bricks prepared for a discussion *v.* Hayek', *The Otto Neurath Nochlass in Haarlem*, Vol. 202, K56, 26 July 1945.

5. T. Uebel, 'Incommensurability, ecology, and planning: Neurath in the socialist calculation debate, 1919–1928', *History of Political Economy*, 37, 2005, pp. 309–42.

6. Ludwig von Mises, *Socialism: An Economic and Sociological Analysis*, Indianapolis: Liberty Press, 1981, p. 98.

7. Ibid., p. 99.

8. Ludwig von Mises, *Human Action*, Chicago: Henry Negnery, 1966 [1949], p. 208.

9. Otto Neurath, 'Inventory of the standard of living', *Zeitschrift for Sozialforschung*, Vol. 6, 1937, pp. 140–51, esp. p. 146.

10. Otto Neurath, 'The Lost Wanderers of Descartes and the Auxiliary Motive' [1913], in R. S. Cohen and M. Neurath (eds) *Otto Neurath: Philosophical Papers*, Reidel: Dordrecht, 1983.

11. Ibid., p. 8.

12. Otto Neurath, 'Personal life and class struggle' [1928], in M. Neurath and R. S. Cohen (eds), *Empiricism and Sociology*, Riedel: Dordrecht, 1973, p. 263.

13. Otto Neurath, 'Through war economy to economy in kind' [1919], in Neurath and Cohen (eds), *Empiricism and Sociology*, 1973, p. 145.

14. Ibid.

15. Otto Neurath, 'Personal life and class struggle' [1928], p. 263.

16. Otto Neurath, 'Economic plan and calculation in kind' [1925], in Cohen and Uebel (eds), *Otto Neurath*, p. 430.

17. Otto Neurath, 'Inventory of the standard of living', p. 146.

18. Otto Neurath, 'The problem of the pleasure maximum' [1912], in Cohen and Neurath (eds), *Otto Neurath*.

19. Otto Neurath, 'Inventory of the standard of living', p. 143.

20. Otto Neurath, 'Remarks on the productivity of money' [1909], in Cohen and Neurath (eds), *Otto Neurath*, pp. 243–4.

21. Ibid., p. 294.

22. Friedrich Hayek, *The Counter-Revolution of Science*, Indianopolis: Liberty Press, 1979, p. 170.

23. Ibid.

24. Ibid., p. 173.

25. Ibid., p. 162.

26. Friedrich Hayek, *Individualism and Economic Order*, London: Routledge & Kegan Paul, 1949.

27. Otto Neurath, 'International planning for freedom' [1942], in Neurath and Cohen (eds), *Empiricism and Sociology*, pp. 426–7.

28. Otto Neurath, 'Physicalism, planning and the social sciences'.

29. D. Schecter, *Radical Theories*, Manchester: Manchester University Press, 1994; H. Wainwright, *Arguments for a New Left: Answering the Free Market Right*, Oxford: Blackwell, 1994.

30. Otto Neurath, 'Von der Gildenfront', *Der Kampf*, 14, 1921, pp. 416–20.

31. Otto Neurath, 'Economic plan and calculation in kind' [1925], in Cohen and Uebel (eds), *Otto Neurath*.

32. Otto Neurath, 'Personal life and class struggle' [1928], p. 271.

33. John O'Neill, *Ecology, Policy and Politics* London: Routledge, 1993, Ch. 10.

34. Otto Neurath, 'International planning for freedom' [1942], in Neurath and Cohen (eds), *Empiricism and Sociology*, p. 434.

35. Otto Neurath, 'Total socialisation' [1920] in Cohen and Uebel (eds), *Otto Neurath*, p. 397.
36. Ibid., p. 402.
37. Ibid., p. 388.
38. Ibid., Section 2.
39. Otto Neurath, 'A system of socialization' [1920] *Archiv for Sozialwissenschaft and Sozialpolitik* 48, pp. 44–73, translated in Cohen and Uebel (eds) *Otto Neurath*, 354–5.
40. Ibid., pp. 362–3.
41. P. Neurath, 'Otto Neurath (1882–1945) – life and work' in Elisabeth Nemeth and Friederich Stadler, *Encyclopedia and Utopia: the Life and Work of Otto Neurath (1882–1945)*, Dordrecht: Kluwer, 1996, pp. 21–3.
42. Otto Neurath, *Foundations of the Social Sciences*, Chicago: University of Chicago Press, 1944, p. 8.
43. Otto Neurath, 'Visual education: humanisation versus popularisation' in Nemeth and Stadler, *Encyclopedia and Utopia*, pp. 245ff.
44. Otto Neurath, 'The orchestration of the sciences by the encyclopedism of logical empiricism' [1946], in Cohen and Uebel (eds), *Otto Neurath*, p. 230.
45. Otto Neurath, 'Planning or Managerial Revolution' (Review of J. Burnham *The Managerial Revolution*) [1943], in Cohen and Uebel (eds), *Otto Neurath*, p. 536.
46. S. Benhabib (ed.), *Democracy and Difference*, Princeton: Princeton University Press, 1996; J. Cohen, 'Deliberation and democratic legitimacy', in Robert Goodin and Philip Pettit (eds), *The Good Polity*, Oxford: Blackwell, 1989; J. Dryzek, *Discursive Democracy*, Cambridge: Cambridge University Press, 1990; J. Elster, 'The market and the forum: Three varieties of political theory' in J. Elster and A. Hylland (eds), *Foundations of Social Choice Theory*, Cambridge: Cambridge University Press, 1986; J. Elster (ed.) *Deliberative Democracy*, Cambridge: Cambridge University Press, 1998; D. Miller, 'Deliberative democracy and social choice', *Political Studies*, 40, 1992, pp. 54–67.
47. M. Jacobs, 'Environmental valuations, deliberative democracy and public decision-making institutions' in J. Foster (ed.), *Valuing Nature?*, London: Routledge, 1997; M. O'Connor (ed.), *Ecological Economics*, 34 – Special Issue: Social Processes of Environmental Valuation, 2000, pp. 165–282; K.P. Rippe and P. Schaber, 'Democracy and environmental decision-making', *Environmental Values*, 8, 1999, pp. 75–88.
48. B. De Marchi, S. Funtowicz, S. Casio and G. Munda, 'Combining participative and institutional approaches with multicriteria evaluation', *Ecological Economics*, 34, 2000, pp. 267–82.
49. Aristotle, *Politics II*, Indianapolis: Hackett, 1998, Section II, Part ii.
50. Karl Marx, 'On the Jewish question', in L. D. Easton and K. H. Guddat (eds), *Writings of the Young Marx on Philosophy and Society*, New York: Anchor Books, 1967, pp. 216–64.
51. M. Sagoff, *The Economy of the Earth: Philosophy, Law and the Environment* [2nd edn], Cambridge: Cambridge University Press, 2007.
52. G. Hodgson, *Economics and Utopia: Why the Learning Economy is Not the End of History*, London: Routledge, 1999, pp. 48–9.
53. Ibid., p. 49.
54. Ibid.
55. Cf. John O'Neill, *The Market: Ethics, Knowledge and Politics*, London: Routledge, 1998, pp. 150ff.

56. R. Keat, 'Individualism and community in socialist thought' in J. Mepham and D.-H. Ruben (eds), *Issues in Marxist Philosophy* 4, Brighton: Harvester Press, 1981.

57. Joan Martinez-Alier, 'The merchandizing of biodiversity', *Capitalism Nature Socialism*, 7, 1996, pp. 37–54; O'Neill, *The Market*, Ch. 10.

58. Otto Neurath, 'A system of socialization', *Archiv for Sozialwissenschaft and Sozialpolitik*, 48, 1920, pp. 44–73; translation in Cohen and Uebel (eds) *Otto Neurath*, p. 355.

59. M. Walzer, *Spheres of Justice*, Oxford: Blackwell, 1983.

60. John O'Neill, 'King Darius and the environmental economist', in John O'Neill and T. Hayward (eds), *Justice, Property and the Environment: Social and Legal Perspectives*, Aldershot: Avebury, 1997.

5
The Value of a Synergistic Economy

Ariel Salleh

The global crises – environmental and economic – have governments and United Nations agencies scurrying for solutions. But the international capitalist ruling class is reluctant to let go of its wealth, privilege and control. The realist mantra insists that 'there is no alternative' and Al Gore's plan for a sustainable America highlights the dilemma.[1] Gore envisages congressional incentives to reduce deforestation and support solar, wind and geothermal spots in the southwestern deserts of the United States of America. There will be a national low-loss underground grid, plug-in hybrid cars, retrofitted buildings and conservation advice for households. Gore hopes to replace the Kyoto Protocol with a treaty that caps carbon emissions ready for trade.

The trouble is that the construction of Gore's new high-tech cities in the Southwest will consume vast amounts of front-end fuels in welding turbines and grids, road-making, water supply, component manufacture for housing, and air-conditioning for supermarkets and schools. Furthermore, what is offered is another mortgage – borrow now, pay later. Beyond this, another fragile biodiversity will be damaged and humans will weather the psychological costs of mass resettlement. The new urbanisation will mean a loss of farmland, possibly to be replaced by foreign agricultural leases. If that happened, how would the displaced peasants of Central America survive and how much heat pollution would be generated by haulage of food to US markets?

This chapter examines capitalism from the point of view of Indigenous peoples and economies of the global South. It addresses the need for food and energy sovereignty, discusses the destructive humanity–nature metabolism of capitalist practices (contrasting them with polycultures and synergistic economies), and lists the environmental and social benefits of a non-monetised society–nature metabolism.

FOOD AND ENERGY SOVEREIGNTY

Clearly the mainstream capitalist economy is not a rational model. But are there ways of meeting human needs without the collateral damage of toxins and carbon? Is money really essential to production? Who might have alternatives to bring to the table? In April 2009, the Indigenous Peoples' Global Summit in Anchorage called for a new economic template, a compact for self-managed local communities based on food and energy sovereignty (see Box 5.1). They demanded that the United Nations Framework Convention on Climate Change acknowledge the ecological debt notched up by affluent societies as the main contributors of greenhouse gas. And they proposed that the United Nations hold regular 'Technical Briefings by Indigenous Peoples on Traditional Knowledge'.[2]

The global North does not give due credit to the capacities of peoples on the margins of capital. Rather, the common rhetoric emphasises the South's 'need for development'. It is a convenient line, one that coincides with capital accumulation based on economic extraction from the periphery. This same ethnocentrism also shapes the standard modelling assumptions of the Intergovernmental Panel on Climate Change. Some might call it environmental racism, but, in any event, it is about letting others pick up the tab, such as when Mexican corn is exported to the United States of America for biofuel rather than saved for tortillas, nuclear tests displace Aboriginal communities from their country, a nation from the North signs off on a United Nations Reducing Emissions from Deforestation and Forest Degradation in Developing Countries scheme, or the land of poor farmers in Kalimantan is converted into a carbon sink for coal-based consumer lifestyles.

True, the United Nations and big non-government organisations express concern that peasants and fisher-folk will suffer badly from rising sea levels, but racism appears again when conservationists claim that the populations of India and China are the biggest threat to global warming. In fact, ecological footprint studies show that consumption per capita in China is negligible compared with the average individual footprint in Australia or the United States of America.[3]

The ecological footprint indicator should help keep policy on track, but measurement alone does little to shift the supposition that a capitalist model of production is the only viable way. Thus, the current focus on adjusting input/output parameters simply delays a more thoughtful response to the question of sustainability or, rather, to the question of sustainability with justice. Clearly the international capitalist economy is not a democratic one, dependent as it is on consuming the life-world of others elsewhere. The current crises signify that it is time to stand back and ask why the globalising North has configured its humanity–nature metabolism so badly.

THE HUMANITY–NATURE METABOLISM

Metabolism is the process by which humans take from nature, digest and give back in return, and cultures across the world have devised different ways of managing it. One pioneering ecological economist, Nicholas Georgescu-Roegen, made the society–nature metabolism the centrepiece of his new discipline. Against the grain, he introduced an awareness of biological systems and thermodynamic principles into economic reasoning.[4] Yet today this would-be sustainability science largely deals with the tip of the production iceberg. Most transfers between humans and nature are 'meta-industrial', outside of any money economy and, in fact, not even named as economic (see Box 5.2).[5] But it is just these non-monetised production practices at the interface with nature that merit a closer look. Indigenous and peasant societies have found 'synergistic' ways of meeting human needs, that is, simultaneously satisfying a multitude of daily use values, including cultural ones, while protecting the ecosystem as the material bottom line.[6]

Meanwhile, the capitalist economic cycle of extraction → manufacture → transport → market → consumption → disposal creates and maintains a chasm between humans and nature. US Marxist John Bellamy Foster identifies the 'metabolic rift' between town and country as the source of this impoverished ecological understanding. Corporate globalisation and free trade export this rift across the face of the earth. British sociologist Peter Dickens describes the alienated modern consciousness as an outcome of the division of labour. The more technologically mediated daily life is, the more people lose a feeling for their own organic embodiment as nature. Ecofeminist Silvia Federici uses the word 'amnesia' to describe this psychological splitting, which environmental abuse expresses.[7]

The split between humanity and nature is clear in the methods of some ecological economists for whom 'scarcity' is an ontological constant rather than a man-made anomaly. Living systems are pulverised into dead matter for turning into commodities. Natural metabolic flows are pulled apart and treated as linear variables. There is little grasp of active human co-evolution with the environment, bypassing the historically gendered, class and racialised origins of economics, to leave a distancing pseudo-scientific vocabulary of 'human capital' and 'natural capital'. The psychology of nature externalisation is assisted by all kinds of quantifying devices, and this in the face of overwhelming qualitative incommensurables on the ground. This lack of reality testing is exacerbated by the capitalist prioritisation of exchange value and adoption of money as the standard of comparison.

Another distancing technique is the fantastical projection of the economy as an engine. Former US Society for Ecological Economics President Robert Costanza says that the machine runs on four kinds of measurable capital – built, human, social and natural – all readily substituted one for another in production. Furthermore, the achievement of human satisfaction or 'quality of life' depends on getting the balance of these calculable components right.[8] Presumably what follows is a number-crunching laboratory exercise whose conclusions are to be dispensed across the population by Environmental Protection Authority decree.

The dualism of humanity versus nature is slowly being challenged in mainstream economics. For example, innovative moves have been made by ecological economist Herman Daly, albeit from the World Bank. Alongside the canon of efficiency, he has introduced 'environmental sustainability and social justice'. Alongside the Gross National Product, he advocates a Genuine Progress Indicator. Beyond short-term productivism, Daly knows that biological time and reproduction is slower than economic time and production, and that intergenerational equity will call for thinking with a long time horizon. He points to the origin of the word 'economics' in *oikos*, the study of households, the ecosystem being like a human household writ large.[9] But this insight remains in the realms of metaphor as long as domestic labour is not examined in its materiality and not accorded value.

The functionalist heritage of neoclassical economics is still active in Daly's work and this cancels out its more progressive implications. The abstract and indeed fetishised character of capital as such goes unquestioned. The mandatory mathematical modelling is there and the focus on 'sustainable scale', 'just distribution' and 'efficient allocation' resonates all too easily with green business and the triple bottom line. Moreover, Daly's core variables – scale, distribution and allocation – operate in an *ad hoc* system whose imaginary boundaries are never justified. His use of cybernetic analogies reifies the economy much as the 'hidden hand' of market liberalism does. Economic functions described in the passive voice create an impression of inevitability that deflects people's belief in their own capacity for taking responsibility and making change.

The transformative potential of academic disciplines is simply latent as long as sociological bias in the formulation of its analytic tools passes unnoticed. Thus, Daly and many of his confreres do not ask: Who decides on scale? Who distributes to whom? Who is entitled to make allocations? And, why is this so? True, conferences in ecological economics now include sections on peasant and Indigenous societies and, sometimes, even host a feminist symposium. But all too often they appear as marginal strands added on, 'problem areas', examples of 'distributional conflicts', or 'externalities' waiting to be assimilated into the master map. If the amnesia of industrialisation could be shaken off, perhaps then it would be respectable to explore other ways of satisfying human needs: Economies beyond money? Kinds of society–nature metabolisms that do not cause collateral damage?

POLYCULTURES AND SYNERGISTIC ECONOMIES

Recent and quite exhaustive research by Catherine Badgley and colleagues concludes that organic farming could feed an even larger global population than currently exists, so minimising environmental and health costs of agricultural production.[10] In fact, the greater part of food consumed is already produced organically through peasant cultivation and local fishing, while healthy hunter-gatherer economies exist in the global South as well. As the Food and Agriculture Organisation noted in its Rome 2007 report, unlike agricultural monocultures favoured by business, these polycultures foster biodiversity and water security, naturally sequester carbon, and are resilient to infestation and climatic disturbance.[11] In short, they demonstrate Georgescu-Roegen's economic principle of dovetailing human activities with metabolic flows in nature. More than this, polycultures are synergistic economic practices.

Is it not precisely these marginals and their people's science that can show us how to build an alternative, sustainable and democratic, global economy? Where would such a claim fall in the white middle-class masculine discourses of the Group of Eight, the World Bank, the International Monetary Fund, and the World Trade Organisation? The Indian historian Ramachandra Guha and his Barcelona colleague Joan Martinez-Alier have written a magisterial review of ecological knowledge in grassroots communities at the global economic periphery.[12] But conventional wisdom, and a comforting attitude of racial superiority in some quarters, is surely tested by the call to value these meta-industrial economies. In standard International Monetary Fund reckoning, the rhetoric of 'incapacity' in the global South eases the psychology of colonial domination: non-industrial peoples must fall to the inexorable wheel of progress and bank loans are essential to get them onto the bottom rung of the 'development' ladder.

Under this patronising yet self-serving development paradigm, common land, water, biodiversity, labour and loving relationships are pulled away from an autonomous web of eco-sufficiency.[13] People are turned into 'human capital' and their habitat quantified as 'natural capital'. All this primarily benefits an international class of entrepreneurs and their government hangers-on because, as noted above, capital cannot expand profits without consuming its metabolic periphery. For centuries, First Nation peoples from Africa to Oceania to South America have struggled against appropriation of their livelihood resources. But are ecological economists on their side? Or does their sustainability science support the colonising mindset by default?

Economists are comfortable measuring what they call productivity but have a hard time with the idea of reproductivity. Few ecological economists stay focused on the energetics of regenerative cycles. However, the celebrated ecofeminist Vandana Shiva does just this in her accounts of meta-industrial labour among Indian forest-dwellers.[14] Here it is women who manage the integrity of ecological and human cycles. As healers, they gather medicinal herbs among the trees and, as catalysts of fertility, they transfer animal waste to crops, returning the by-products to animals as fodder. Their daily round – protecting natural sustainability and human sustenance – is an exemplar of scientific complexity in a synergistic economy. Shiva is describing a compact whereby people self-manage their resources with a sophisticated ethic of mutual cooperation and sharing. Money plays no part in these society–nature transactions (see Box 5.3).

Similarly, Indigenous peoples – from Borneo to Peru – practise a kind of eco-systemic 'holding' that facilitates both conviviality and metabolic exchanges. Aboriginal Australians too make their seasonal walk through country with deliberation and disciplined harvesting in the knowledge that it will replenish. Three hours' work a day suffices in this bioregional economy.[15] According to

John Gowdy, a student of Georgescu-Roegen, the hunter-gatherer rarely extracts more matter/energy than is needed for maintenance.[16]

NON-MONETISED SOCIETY–NATURE METABOLISM

The methodological features of a non-monetised society–nature metabolism, which follow, contrast sharply with the incoherent regime of commodity production.[17]

- The *consumption footprint is small* because local resources are used and monitored daily with care.
- *Closed loop production* is the norm.
- Scale is intimate, maximising responsiveness to matter–energy transfers in nature, so *avoiding disorganisation and entropy*.
- Judgements are built up by trial and error, using a *cradle-to-grave assessment* of ecosystem health.
- Meta-industrial labour is *intrinsically precautionary* because it is situated in an intergenerational time frame.
- *Lines of responsibility are transparent* – far from the confusion of small decisions that often impairs corporate or bureaucratised economies.
- Where social organisation is less convoluted than in urban centres, the efficiencies of *synergistic problem-solving* can be achieved.
- In farm settings and in wild habitat, *multi-criteria decision-making* is common sense.
- Regenerative work patiently *reconciles the time scales of humans and other species*, and readily adapts to disturbances in nature.[18]
- This is an economic rationality that *knows the difference between stocks and flows*; no more is taken than is needed.
- It is an *empowering work process*, without a division between the worker's mental and manual skills.
- The *labour product is immediately enjoyed or shared*, whereas the industrial worker has no control over his or her creativity.
- Such provisioning is eco-sufficient because it *does not externalise costs on to others as debt*.
- Autonomous local economies imply *food and energy sovereignty*.

These production techniques display an exacting empiricism and closely match principles of sustainability advocated by good environmental consultants in the global North. The trouble is that in capitalist societies committed to economic growth governments under pressure from business often shelve such expert advice. Then again, administrations may be so unwieldy that official endorsements fail to translate across to the appropriate social groups. By contrast, among meta-industrial communities – at least where livelihood resources are free from development impacts – sustainability is already in action.

Over and above these concerns, the way that Indigenous economic models satisfy multiple needs all at once is impressive. To paraphrase the Chilean economist Manfred Max Neef: they are not only sovereign and independent but also environmentally benign and creatively social.[19] Besides achieving subsistence, eco-sufficient economies foster learning, participation, innovation, ritual, identity and belonging (see Box 5.4). Conversely the engineered satisfiers of capitalist societies, such as bureaucracies or cars, use up much energy and time, sabotaging the very convenience they were designed for. An economics governed by exchange value and capital accumulation exploits workers, diminishes the contribution of mothers and caregivers, and fails to instil any sense of belonging in the young.

Capitalism is not synergistic. In fact, the logic of markets generates many random consequences. A plethora of international programs exist to mitigate the side effects of capitalism, such as climate change, biodiversity loss and chemical or nuclear emissions, but taxes and subsidies, green engineering, and bioethical formulae simply paper over an unfair system tailored to individual gain. The leaders of the Group of Eight find themselves in a strange double bind as they steer the crises of capitalism from the soft upholstered seat of a black limousine. Consider the future vision outlined by Germany's Federal Minister for the Environment:

> The lynchpin of a model of sustainable development has to be a 'third industrial revolution', at the centre of which is energy and resource efficiency ... If China becomes the 'world's workbench', India casts itself as the 'global service provider', Russia develops into the 'world's filling pump', and Brazil as the 'raw materials warehouse' and 'global farmer' provides Asia's industrial and service companies with iron ore, copper, nickel and soybeans, Germany should then assert and strengthen its position in the global division of labour as 'the responsible energy-efficient and environmental technician'.[20]

This 'economic reason' floats in a material void. The metabolic costs of a global division of labour reliant on transcontinental trade are blocked out, displaced, externalised onto nature and the bodies of others. In this 'third industrial revolution', Germany as 'the responsible energy-efficient technician' would actually be living on credit, buoyed up by an invisible ecological debt. Meanwhile, the cultural integrity of peoples in Asia or South America is sacrificed as the life-world of their regions is given over to a narrow internationally specified production role.

The self-deceptions of capitalism and its illusory ideology of progress are challenged by compact economic models. In Karl Marx's vision, 'A non-exploitive relation of people to nature requires a "real social communality" among people themselves, supported by property that is simultaneously individual and social'.[21] For life on earth to flourish, the rule of capitalist industry and exchange value will have to be overturned. In this context, it is encouraging to find Olivier de Schutter, United Nations Special Rapporteur on the Right to Food, advising the 17th Session of the United Nations Commission on Sustainable Development that what is more critical than the size of aid budgets is an awareness of 'different models of agricultural development which may have different impacts and benefit various groups differently' – a small but sound step in the direction of public consciousness raising. The peasant movement *Via Campesina* endorses de Schutter with a further comment that:

[M]assive land takeovers or acquisitions meant for agro-fuel production, animal feed, tree plantations to produce pulp and paper and for wood and mining projects are taking from indigenous peoples, fishermen and small farmers the possibility of accessing these resources ...

Clearly, there are key actors that militate against food sovereignty, like the export-oriented production model led by big transnational corporations ... the World Bank, the International Monetary Fund (IMF) and regional development banks, along with multilateral organisations promoting free trade like the World Trade Organization (WTO) ... the United States and European Union ...[22]

The economy of permanent consumption and 'green conversions' not only fails the thermodynamic test, it is blindly ethnocentric. In a time of ecological crisis and capitalist collapse, technical briefings by

Indigenous peoples on traditional knowledge can be a salve to global confusion and despair by showing that there are well-established alternative ways of configuring the society–nature metabolism. This is not to say that everyone should head for the hills, but to argue that the epistemology of meta-industrial production provides indispensable 'capacity-building' for a global North staring blankly at a 'wrong way, go back' sign. And this capacity-building is not only about protecting sustainability, recognising the value of a synergistic economy is essential to a democratic globalism based on mutual respect. The worldwide majority is not 'costing the earth', although the mists of environmental racism can make this hard to see. What costs the earth and wastes its peoples is the begetting of money by money.

Box 5.1   From the Anchorage Declaration, April 2009

We are deeply alarmed by the accelerating climate devastation brought about by unsustainable development. We are experiencing profound and disproportionate adverse impacts on our cultures, human and environmental health, human rights, well-being, traditional livelihoods, food systems and food sovereignty, local infrastructure, economic viability, and our very survival as Indigenous Peoples.

Mother Earth is no longer in a period of climate change, but in climate crisis. We therefore insist on an immediate end to the destruction and desecration of the elements of life.

Through our knowledge, spirituality, sciences, practices, experiences and relationships with our traditional lands, territories, waters, air, forests, oceans, sea ice, other natural resources and all life, Indigenous Peoples have a vital role in defending and healing Mother Earth. The future of Indigenous Peoples lies in the wisdom of our elders, the restoration of the sacred position of women, the youth of today and in the generations of tomorrow.

Calls For Action...

11. We call on States to recognize, respect and implement the fundamental human rights of Indigenous Peoples, including the collective rights to traditional ownership, use, access, occupancy

▶

and title to traditional lands, air, forests, waters, oceans, sea ice and sacred sites as well as to ensure that the rights affirmed in Treaties are upheld and recognized in land use planning and climate change mitigation strategies. In particular, States must ensure that Indigenous Peoples have the right to mobility and are not forcibly removed or settled away from their traditional lands and territories, and that the rights of Peoples in voluntary isolation are upheld. In the case of climate change migrants, appropriate programs and measures must address their rights, status, conditions, and vulnerabilities.

12. We call upon states to return and restore lands, territories, waters, forests, oceans, sea ice and sacred sites that have been taken from Indigenous Peoples, limiting our access to our traditional ways of living, thereby causing us to misuse and expose our lands to activities and conditions that contribute to climate change.

13. In order to provide the resources necessary for our collective survival in response to the climate crisis, we declare our communities, waters, air, forests, oceans, sea ice, traditional lands and territories to be 'Food Sovereignty Areas,' defined and directed by Indigenous Peoples according to customary laws, free from extractive industries, deforestation and chemical-based industrial food production systems (i.e. contaminants, agro-fuels, genetically modified organisms).

Source: Indigenous Peoples' Global Summit on Climate Change, The Anchorage Declaration, 24 April 2009 [accessed 28 August 2011], at http://www.indigenousportal.com.

Box 5.2   Ariel Salleh on 'Meta-Industrial'

Most analyses of capitalism have tended to treat workers as waged white men, whereas reproductive labour is deemed the province of the unwaged – women domestics and carers, peasant farmers, and indigenous hunter-gatherers. However, the latter meta-industrial groupings, nominally outside of the economic

▶

system, actually constitute the majority of workers in 21st century global capitalism.

The case for recognizing meta-industrial workers as 'a class', and even as 'agents of history' in the current conjuncture, rests on at least six interlocking assumptions.

- Dominant discourses from religion to economics are culturally hierarchical, and devalue meta-industrial workers, by ideologically positioning reproductive labour at the lowly interface of humanity with nature.
- Meta-industrials reproduce necessary biological infrastructure for all economic systems, but under capitalist globalization this labour is undertaken at ever increasing cost to that material base and to the reproduction of their own lives.
- A phenomenological analysis of meta-industrial practices, whether household, farming, or hunter gathering, highlights their ecologically benign quality, as forms of human provisioning which sustain metabolic linkages in nature.
- This hands-on reproductive labour interaction with habitat creates lay knowledges of an economic and ecological kind. It represents a thoroughly reality tested and 'embodied materialism'.
- Observation of anti-globalization movements and forums indicates that despite cultural differences, reproductive labour groupings have a common material stake in challenging capitalist notions of development.
- A shared meta-industrial class perspective can provide a basis for unifying socialist, feminist, postcolonial, and ecological concerns. This politics is synergistic, addressing class, race, and gender, injustices, as well as species and habitat, simultaneously.

Source: Ariel Salleh, 'Globalisation and the meta-industrial alternative' in Robert Albritton, Shannon Bell, John R. Bell and Richard Westra (eds), *New Socialisms: Futures Beyond Globalization*, London: Routledge, 2004, pp. 201–11, esp. pp. 201–2.

Box 5.3   Vandana Shiva on Scientific and Commercial Forestry in India

There are in Asia today two paradigms of forestry – one life-enhancing, the other life-destroying. The life-enhancing paradigm emerges from the forest and the forest communities – the life-destroying from the market. The life-enhancing paradigm creates a sustainable, renewable forest system, supporting and renewing food and water systems. *The maintenance of conditions for renewability is the primary management objective of the former.* The maximizing of profits through commercial extraction is the primary management objective of the latter. Since maximizing profits is consequent upon destruction of conditions of renewability, the two paradigms are cognitively and ecologically incommensurate. Today, in the forests of Asia the two paradigms are struggling against each other. This struggle is very clear in the two slogans on the utility of the Himalayan forests, one emanating from the ecological concepts of Garhwali women, the other from the sectoral concepts of those associated with trade in forest products. When Chipko became an ecological movement in 1977 in Adwani, the spirit of local science was captured in the slogan:

What do the forests bear?
Soil, water and pure air.

This was the response to the commonly accepted slogan of the dominant science:

What do the forests bear?
Profit on resin and timber.

The insight in these slogans represented a cognitive shift in the evolution of Chipko. The movement was transformed qualitatively from being based merely on conflicts over resources into involving conflicts over scientific perceptions and philosophical approaches to nature. This transformation also created that element of scientific knowledge which has allowed Chipko to reproduce itself in different ecological and cultural contexts. The slogan has become the scientific and philosophical message of the movement, and has laid the foundations of an alternative forestry science, oriented to

▶

the public interest and ecological in nature. The commercial interest has the primary objective of maximizing exchange value through extraction of commercially valuable species. Forest ecosystems are therefore reduced to the timber of commercially valuable species.

'Scientific forestry' in its present form is a reductionist system of knowledge which ignores the complex relationships within the forest community and between plant life and other resources like soil and water. Its pattern of resource utilization is based on increasing 'productivity'...

Forest movements like Chipko are simultaneously a critique of reductionist 'scientific' forestry and an articulation of a framework for an alternative forestry science which is ecological and can safeguard the public interest. In this alternative forestry science, forest resources are not viewed as isolated from other resources of the ecosystem. Nor is the economic value of a forest reduced to the commercial value of timber.

The industrial materials standpoint is the capitalist reductionist forestry which splits the living diversity and democracy of the forest into commercially valuable dead wood and destroys the rest as 'weeds' and 'waste'. This 'waste' however is the wealth of biomass that maintains nature's water and nutrient cycles and satisfies needs of food, fuel, fodder, fertilizer, fibre and medicine of agricultural communities.

The Green Revolution has displaced not just seed varieties but entire crops in the Third World. Just as people's seeds were declared 'primitive' and 'inferior' by the Green Revolution ideology, food crops were declared 'marginal', 'inferior' and 'coarse grained'. Only a biased agricultural science rooted in capitalist patriarchy could declare nutritious crops like *ragi* and *jowar* as inferior. Peasant women know the nutrition needs of their families and the nutritive content of the crops they grow. Among food crops they prefer those with maximum nutrition to those with a value in the market. What have usually been called 'marginal crops' or 'coarse grains' are nature's most productive crops in terms of nutrition.

Source: Vandana Shiva, *Monocultures of the Mind*; *Perspectives on Biodiversity and Biotechnology*, London: Zed Books & Third World Network, 1993, pp. 19–21, 21, 24, 24–5.

> **Box 5.4   David Suzuki on the Wisdom of Subsistence Farming and Unity in Diversity**
>
> Air binds us together as a single living entity extending through time and space.
>
> Subsistence farmers show the same responsibility for the soil they till, feeding and tending their land so that it in turn will feed their families over the long term. In every region the lore of the land is a local compendium of wise ways to coax a harvest from the soil – when to plow, which plant species to combine, how to protect the soil from the weather so that the forces that put it together cannot take it apart. The farmer must artfully fit human needs into the natural systems he (or, more usually, she, in most parts of the world) is tapping into – the local web of life, adapted to local conditions, designed by the place over a long period of time. It is only now in the 'developed' world that we seem to believe we can improve on nature and rewrite the rules.
>
> Just as genetic diversity within a species and the variety of species within an ecosystem allow single species of whole ecosystems to survive in the face of changing conditions, so diversity of traditional knowledge and culture have been the main reason for our success. We have adapted to environments as diverse as the Arctic tundra, deserts, tropical rain forests, prairie grasslands and modern megacities. If variation of genes in a species that is adapted to local conditions provides a buffer against catastrophic change, then cultural diversity has been just as crucial to humanity's continued vigour and success in a variety of ecosystems.
>
> Source: David Suzuki with Amanda McConnell, *The Sacred Balance: Rediscovering our Place in Nature*, St Leonards: Allen & Unwin, 1997, pp. 50, 103, 138.

NOTES

All italics in quotes are preserved from the originals.
All URL addresses were accessed on 20 October 2010.

1. Sharon Astyk, 'A New Deal or a war footing? Thinking through our response to climate change', *The Chatelaine's Keys* [blog], posted 11 November 2008 at http://sharonastyk.com.

2. Indigenous Peoples' Global Summit on Climate Change, *The Anchorage Declaration*, 24 April 2009, at http://www.indigenoussummit.com.
3. Mathias Wackernagel and William Rees, *Our Ecological Footprint: Reducing Human Impact on the Earth*, Gabriola Island, BC: New Society, 1996; for national comparisons, see the Global Footprint Network at www.footprintnetwork.org.
4. Nicholas Georgescu-Roegen, *The Entropy Law and the Economic Process*, Cambridge, MA: Harvard University Press, 1971.
5. On 'meta-industrial', see Ariel Salleh, *Ecofeminism as Politics: Nature, Marx and the Postmodern*, London: Zed Books, 1997, pp. 164–6 and 175–8; Ariel Salleh, 'Globalisation and the meta-industrial alternative' in Robert Albritton, Shannon Bell, John R. Bell and Richard Westra (eds), *New Socialisms: Futures Beyond Globalization*, London: Routledge, 2004.
6. On the term 'synergistic', see Manfred Max-Neef, *Human Scale Development: Conception, Application and Further Reflections,* New York and London: Apex Press, 1991.
7. John Bellamy Foster, *Marx's Ecology*, New York: Monthly Review Press, 2000; Peter Dickens, *Reconstructing Nature*, London: Routledge, 1995; Silvia Federici, *Caliban and the Witch*, New York: Autonomedia, 2004; Ariel Salleh, 'Body logic: 1/0 culture' in *Ecofeminism as Politics,* London: Zed Books, 1997.
8. Robert Costanza, R. B. Fisher, S. Ali, C. Beer, L. Bond, R. Boumans, N. L. Danigelis, J. Dickinson, C. Elliott, J. Farley, D. E. Gayer, L. MacDonald Glenn, T. Hudspeth, D. Mahoney, L. McCahill, B. McIntosh, B. Reed, S. A. T. Rizvi, D. M. Rizzo, T. Simpatico and R. Snapp, 'Quality of life: an approach integrating opportunities, human needs, and subjective well-being', *Ecological Economics*, Vol. 61, No. 2, 2007, pp. 267–76.
9. Herman Daly, Jon Erickson and Joshua Farley, *Ecological Economics: A Workbook for Problem Based Learning*, Washington: Island Press, 2005.
10. Catherine Badgley, Jeremy Moghtader, Eileen Quintero, Emily Zakem, M. Jahi Chappell, Katia Aviles-Vázquez, Andrea Samulon, and Ivette Perfecto, 'Organic agriculture and the global food supply', *Renewable Agriculture and Food Systems*, Vol. 22, No. 1, 2007, pp. 86–108, esp. p. 86.
11. Food and Agriculture Organisation, International Conference on Organic Agriculture and Food Security, Rome, May 2007; Anthony Furnell, 'Not cheap, just frugal!', *Future Tense*, ABC Radio National, 2 April 2009, transcript at http://www.abc.net.au/.
12. Ramachandra Guha and Joan Martinez-Alier, *Varieties of Environmentalism: Essays North and South*, London: Earthscan, 1997.
13. Ariel Salleh (ed.), *Eco-Sufficiency & Global Justice: Women Write Political Ecology*, London and New York/Melbourne: Pluto Press/Spinifex Press, 2009.
14. Vandana Shiva, *Staying Alive*, London: Zed Books, 1989, p. 45. Also see Veronika Bennhold-Thomsen and Maria Mies, *The Subsistence Perspective*, London: Zed Books, 1999.
15. Deborah Rose, *Nourishing Terrains,* Canberra: Australian Heritage Commission, 1996.
16. John Gowdy (ed.), *Limited Wants, Unlimited Means: A Reader in Hunter-Gatherer Economics and the Environment*, Washington: Island Press, 1998.
17. Adapted from Ariel Salleh (ed.), *Eco-Sufficiency & Global Justice*, London and New York: Pluto Press, 2009, pp. 302–3.
18. Barbara Adam, *Timescapes of Modernity*, London: Routledge, 1998.

19. Max-Neef, *Human Scale Development*.
20. Bundesministerium für Umwelt [Federal Minister for the Environment], 'Naturschutz und Reaktorsicherheit, Ökologische Industriepolitik. Memorandum für einen "New Deal" von Wirtschaft, Umwelt und Beschäftigung [A New Deal for the Economy, the Environment and Employment]', Berlin, 2006, cited by Judith Delheim, 'Seven Theses for a Discussion on Energy Policy and Social-Ecological Conversion', unpublished manuscript, Berlin, 2007, pp. 9–10.
21. Paul Burkett, 'Nature in Marx Reconsidered', *Organization & Environment*, Vol. 10, No. 2, 1997, pp. 164–83, citing Karl Marx, *Grundrisse*, New York: Vintage Books, 1973, p. 267.
22. La Vía Campesina and Friends of the Earth International, Pambazuka, 'Food Sovereignty: A New Model for a Human Right', 18 May 2009, at Share the World's Resources [website], http://www.stwr.org.

6
The Gift Economy

Terry Leahy

The 'gift economy' might seem like a crazy anarchist delusion, yet I believe that sooner or later we will see that it is the only thing that will actually work. In this chapter I present a sociologist's view of contemporary relations between people and with nature and how I became drawn to the utopian model of the gift economy. I look at anarchist strategies for living right now, how we would like to live after the revolution and reformist strategies for cobbling together 'hybrids' of the gift economy and capitalism. I argue that both are inevitable. (For anarchist Alexander Berkman's view of 'anarchism', see Box 6.1.)

UTOPIA

Currently, utopian schemes have a tenuous legitimacy in the social sciences. I defend utopian writing as no more fantastical than ideas underpinning every other social order. I agree with Cornelius Castoriadis that the imaginary is a central and inevitable feature of all societies.[1] Everyday life and political acts that result in social change are never lived in total clarity and sober realism but are inevitably suffused with fantasies and daydreams. They are the New Age therapist's 'affirmations', statements intended to shift unconscious blocks to change.

In researching attitudes to environmental politics with a focus group of unemployed young adults in the Hunter Valley region (Australia) in the 1990s, I was particularly interested in their visions of our long-term future. One, let us refer to him as 'Jason', drew on a television documentary when suggesting a utopia:

> Yeah, we're all going downhill... So we've gotta try and save this planet... Man's greed for the dollar is, they'll just take more and more and not give anything back to the environment. But if we put it back into the forests... We should use our shit. We should

recycle excrement... if man didn't stuff up we'd have the land of milk and honey and... live like the Ituri forest people [Africa]. All right, they do as little work as possible, a bit of hunter-gathering work 'cause it's a really good area, they can just keep moving on. Then they dance and sing to the gods, smoke hemp through their pipes and umm walk on stilts, play games with bows and arrows. They just play games the rest of the time.[2]

I was struck by parallels with my own daydreams and utopian model, also inspired by ethnographic descriptions of stateless societies – a society free from alienated labour, and relocated in a desired future. In high school, I was fascinated by accounts of Central Australian Aborigines and made artefacts of Aboriginal tools and ceremonial objects from the photos. Jason's utopia is a society without commodities, wage labour or money – a 'gift economy', a term appropriated from Marcel Mauss by the Situationists.[3] In a gift economy, products are either consumed directly by producers or made available to others as gifts.

An idealised picture of pre-colonial stateless societies may ignore competitive political struggles between men and a patriarchal division of labour and social status. To be consistent with anti-patriarchal politics, men and women would share domestic responsibilities and public power equally in a gift-economy utopia of the future.

Jason's utopia is preoccupied with a new relationship between humans and nature, abandoning agriculture as a laborious extraction of products from nature. He has an Edenic vision of nature paralleling 'permaculture', which is the 'conscious design and maintenance of agriculturally productive ecosystems, which have the diversity, stability and resilience of natural ecosystems.'[4] Permaculture is achieved by replacing monocultures based on plough cultivation of staple cereal crops with polycultures of trees, shrubs and perennial vines supplemented by gardening for root crops, vegetables and legumes. This holistic organic gardening system deals with pests by companion planting, relies on mulch and composting to fertilise, encourages species diversity and carefully chooses suitable perennials for each site. Vast distant acreages producing meat now would be replaced with locally produced small animals fed with excesses of locally grown fruit and nut crops. (See Box 6.2 for permaculture design principles.)

As in Jason's vision, permaculture is set up to produce food and other useful products without constant attention, yet it does require work. Permaculture has been most successful where fuel, machinery and fertiliser were not readily available because of poverty or trade embargoes, such as in Vietnam and Cuba. The labour of establishing permaculture is considerable: growing trees and shrubs, earthworks to catch water, and harvesting fruit and nut crops. But modern commercial agriculture requires considerable work in manufacturing inputs to farming and in distributing outputs – efforts that are vastly reduced in localised permaculture economies.

Arguably, the labour cost of food produced by permaculture today is higher than that bought on the market. However, it offers a viable strategy for undermining the market economy. As an element in an envisaged gift economy it has the advantage of being a system of sustainable agriculture and food production as creative gardening versus the monotonous work associated with monocultures. Permaculture links people immediately and sensuously to the natural world, on which they depend for their subsistence, creating a basis for localised independent food production as a foundation for political autonomy. Unlike Jason, I do not envisage a future without modern technology, material wealth and the sociality of global communication. Modernism opens up social and material possibilities beyond small austere self-sufficient communes.

I asked residents in the Hunter whether or not alternative economic and political structures could solve environmental problems better than representative democracy and capitalism. While doubting that such systems could work in reality, 'Prawn' spontaneously produced the basic outline of the utopia that I call the gift economy:

> If money was, say, totally meant nothing, right, and we said to each other, righto, now Matt, you bloody drive a good boat... and Barry you're good on splicing and knots, you're good at what you do. Everyone. We've all got our little bit to do, you know. And we said, righto. Well, let's all just do it that way... Instead of working for money... the people who grow the fruit, we'll bring in the fertiliser and... you got people who make cars... So everyone, the whole world, is just self-sufficient with each other.[5]

The project of creating an environmentally sustainable economy is difficult within the framework of global capitalism, consumerism and representative democracy. Change is necessary for environmental reasons alone, which I argue in more detail below.

I favour a mode of production in which we have abolished capitalism, state socialism, remnant feudalism, wage labour and money, and have a gift economy instead. Mostly, people would operate according to an ethic of maximising pleasure and giving useful services and products to others. All production would be voluntary and organised to satisfy the immediate needs of producers or would be given away to meet others' needs, like a vast extension of voluntary forms of organisation that already exist. Conduct could not be regulated by denying livelihood to any section of society, since all people would be supplied by gifts from a multiplicity of independent collectives of producers. The gift economy society would be socially, racially and sexually egalitarian. Armed forces would depend on various producers' collectives for provisions and arms.

This system would be more compatible with ecological imperatives than capitalism is because useless production would be reduced. In a gift economy it makes no sense to work hard and without enjoyment, producing useless items that no-one else needs, whereas in capitalism it makes sense to entrepreneurs to produce any marketable commodity, however unnecessary, to make a profit. Those producing such commodities have no choice regarding their work, which is dictated by superiors, and purchasing useless goods seems sensible as compensation for forced labour.

My gift economy would not mean dividing into self-sufficient communes. Instead, people would participate in multiple networks of overlapping productive activities. Coordination would be achieved by voluntary organisations advising other voluntary organisations of problems of shortages, waste, future requirements and so forth. People would need to be motivated by generous and sympathetic benevolence to others. In a gift economy, producers in all sectors would decide what to produce and how to distribute it based on the needs of other groups. The status of the givers would depend on genuine needs being met by the gift. Producers in each sector would be aware of their dependence on the services of other sectors. To produce without considering the needs of others would undermine the social ethic guaranteeing services from others.

My gift economy is neither a communalist utopia nor is it 'bioregional' (like the one sketched in Chapter 11).[6] It is organised into networks of producers' collectives that geographically overlap. It is not a return to some pre-industrial tribal society, but there would be no state. Coordination of adequate production and fair distribution could be achieved by:

- Independent and multi-pronged collectives – including media, research and administrative workers – keeping the other producer collectives up to date with what is required by whom and for what.

- The will of the various producers' collectives to ensure that outcomes of distribution are equitable.

Together, these collectives would secure a fair share and sort out problems. Fine-tuning would result from informal gift links between consumers themselves.

The gift economy described here is one kind of anarchist stateless utopia drawn from the writings of Situationists, and consistent with the thinking of Murray Bookchin (see Box 6.3) and Graham Purchase.[7] Multiple gift networks would provide the standard of living.[8] A gift economy would make it easier to transform technology and infrastructure for sustainability and to accept the sacrifices of material consumption needed to retrofit existing society for sustainability. Work would be the key arena for creativity and participation. Ownership of all means of production would be shared fairly equally and vested in producers, meaning choice about what to produce and for whom, whether we are talking about food, housework, transport and housing, songs and artworks, or sex and friendship.

The permaculturist David Holmgren discusses classless societies as typically reliant for subsistence on crops gathered in different seasons from trees grown over a wide area.[9] Wildernesses of classless societies are dominated by tree species useful to, and encouraged by, humans. A typical tactic in breaking the resistance of these societies has been to burn and fell these forests, forcing the population to depend on annual cereal crops that are easily controlled by armies and given and withheld by ruling classes and their enforcers.

The gift economy is a reversal of key aspects of capitalism and class societies in general. A selfish interest operates in the gift economy. Gifting can be a self-centred desire for pleasure, a way to enjoy social prestige and affection. Producing focuses on use for oneself or known others, whether locals, kin or friends – or those connected through networks of electronic communication and shared enthusiasms. The structure pays off as a total system to benefit all of us. Gifts are necessary for everyone to live well. It is treasured as a system that works better than alternatives, which have already been tried with such calamitous effects.

SOCIALISATION FOR A GIFT ECONOMY

A cultural shift must take place for a gift economy to work. However, the keys to socialisation for a gift economy are gradually occurring already. Three aspects are essential:

- Being indulged one's infant and childhood needs allows one to become a generous adult who feels confident that other people will meet their needs.
- The involvement of men in the direct care and succour of young children is necessary to prevent boys from becoming anxious, competitive and insecure adults who seek to gain advantage to establish their masculinity.
- Childhood experience of familial adults as equal partners negotiating daily life is necessary if people are to grow up without always expecting someone to be the boss.

First, traditional Western child-raising practices have emphasised denial and self-control to prepare for adulthood and work. Annette Hamilton argues that being indulged one's infant and childhood needs allows one to become a generous adult who feels confident that other people will meet their needs.[10] She concludes that Western adults tend to become extremely and continuously anxious that other people will not meet their needs, thus amassing and hoarding consumer goods and property to stave off these anxieties. However, we are seeing a gradual process of reversal of these aspects of socialisation in Western societies.

Second, men caring for young children prevents boys from becoming anxious, competitive and insecure adults who seek to establish their masculinity by gaining advantage. Nancy Chodorow argues that a universal feature of patriarchies is that men avoid childcare, leaving it to mothers.[11] Initially, boys identify with mothers and have a close emotional link with women. But to be 'men' in a patriarchy that stops intimate daily company with adult males, boys deny their ties to women and reject the qualities of female nurture. Instead, they develop abilities to compete for status among other men to prove their masculinity competitively with adult males. These psychological conditions of competitive masculinity work against a gift economy but could be undone by men's developing close nurturing relationships with their children.

Third, childhood experience of family life in which adults are equal partners negotiating daily life is necessary if people are to grow up without expecting someone to be boss. Following Freud and Reich, Shulamith Firestone suggests a connection between authority in the family and the widespread acceptance of authoritarian social structures.[12] A father becomes the psychological model for an authoritative figure who demands love and obedience. In class societies, leaders find it easy to represent themselves as 'fathers' of society, an ideology concealing exploitation. To overturn this mass psychology of hierarchy and submission it is necessary to support the feminist goals of equal power for men and women in the interrelated realms of domestic life and the wider economy.

Later, I show the significance of socialisation in the case of revolutionary Spain. Here it suffices to point out that any gift economy set up today would be most likely an interim measure if it did not complete the feminist revolution already begun. Yet a gift economy could well support cultural diversity that included liberal and mystical religious traditions and their new age rivals. Nevertheless, patriarchy is inconsistent with the economic logic of the gift economy. In a patriarchy, women's labour is exploited. In capitalism, men's control over money is a key structure of patriarchy although there have been patriarchies without money. For the work that women do to become part of a gift economy, feminist issues have to be pushed for their own sake.

Furthermore, many actions of social movements today can be seen as part of a transition to a gift economy. For example, the permaculture movement inspires food forests, community gardens and aid projects as strategies to address pending environmental catastrophe, thereby promoting a benevolent and harmonious interaction between humans and the natural world. These strategies avoid two unsatisfactory alternatives: suppression of the natural environment for the sake of survival, or catastrophe in which nature 'takes revenge' by threatening human survival.

CAPITALISM CANNOT SURVIVE GLOBAL WARMING

Today capitalism could come to a sticky end despite the absence of a revolutionary proletariat because a growth economy is impossible to reconcile with a finite environment. Change necessary to halt global warming cannot be contained within capitalism. The changes required imply a drastic reduction in material production and consumption. Revolution is possible if the environmental crisis causes widespread disaffection. Whatever is done to resolve the environmental crisis, we are not going to end up with capitalism. Quite a likely outcome is the collapse of civilisation.

Current emissions from burning fossil fuel burning are 6 gigatonnes per year. A very generous estimate of the maximum concentration of carbon dioxide that we would have to aim at to avoid catastrophic effects – blocking the Gulf Stream and consequently freezing Europe and the United States of America, or the ocean floor, releasing methane and permafrost, creating a warming feedback loop – is 400 parts per million. A much more sensible figure to aim at is 320 parts per million.[13] However, even the larger figure seems politically impossible at present – it's pretty close to the current 380 parts per million, up from an average 280 parts per million over the 750,000 years or so before the twentieth century. Yet, to maintain 400 parts per million, we would have to cut emissions to 0.5 gigatonnes per year by 2040 and subsequently extract carbon from the atmosphere – a reduction to one tenth of present emissions. This is extreme enough.

In per capita terms, the problem is more drastic. If this target were shared equally between 9 billion people in 2050, it would imply 1 to 2 per cent of current rich-world per capita use. Even if we kept the use of fossil fuels below 2 per cent of our current per capita use in developing countries, we would have to reduce our own use to the same level.[14] This fossil fuel energy cannot be readily replaced by any feasible alternative technology.[15] The consequence would be a drastic reduction in material consumption. Whether it would be experienced as impoverishing is debatable.

A capitalist economy expands continuously by virtue of competitive private ownership and a politics that constantly promises increased consumption to those who are on the receiving end of exploitative bad deals. Yet, as Ted Trainer points out, a continuing world growth rate of 3 per cent per annum would mean four times the output of products by 2050 and eight times by 2075, and 4 per cent growth would mean a sixteen-fold increase.[16] Arguably, this implies drawing almost all our current energy from renewable sources and providing, say, seven to 15 times as much again for 'healthy' capitalism.

However, this ignores expanding consumption in developing countries where, for instance, India and China might continue to expand at up to 8 per cent each year. So, we will have to persuade them that it is in their interests to re-tool. Without using military force, we would need to show them that we can be affluent and comfortable without pumping carbon dioxide into the atmosphere. Renewable alternatives currently are more expensive than fossil fuels. We would need to cut production and consumption to a sustainable level and keep it there. The implication is negative growth. Within the ownership regime of capitalism, this implies political restraint on the owners of capital that fundamentally alters the mode of production.

Comparing this and other crises of accumulation in capitalism is misleading. Often other crises were resolved by developing new accumulation strategies, providing either new goods or services, or old ones at a fraction of their former cost (for example, expansion of railways, automobiles and electricity). A switch to green energy does not remotely resemble this. It is about substituting cheap energy sources with expensive ones, which is why the capitalist class is dragging its feet. Meanwhile our future survival is threatened. Thus, I envisage two broad possibilities.

First, the capitalist class agrees to direct most productive capacity to saving the planet. It redistributes some wealth, reduces and fairly distributes work hours. However, greater leisure undermines the bosses' authority. It would amount to a negotiated change to a new mode of production: people would have much more control over their work; there would be far fewer hours of necessary work; most importantly, goods and services would need to be allocated on the basis of need; developing countries and rich countries would end up at a similar level of affluence; and we would all look after the planet and other species. All very attractive, but everything that made a capitalist economy function is abolished by degrees. Second, these problems are resolved coercively by fascism or, perhaps, technocratic feudalism, which would not solve environmental problems in the long term and might end in technological stagnation.

There is no path out of the present crisis that leaves the capitalist mode of production intact. A reformist approach of the kind envisaged by business optimists is a path to end capitalism. Another possibility is that envisaged by Jared Diamond, where we end up like past civilisations that undermined their environments with a flurry of grand projects and expensive wars and an inevitable collapse in food production and, thus, a declining population.[17] Yet another possibility is that an ungrateful populace would massacre the ruling class.

In contrast to capitalism, a gift economy could lead to benign outcomes for the environment. Taking farming as an example, producers would see no advantage in overusing their land. They would seek to conserve their agricultural and environmental resources so as to live well in the future and to ensure continual social recognition by giving farm produce to the community. In a capitalist economy entrepreneurs market anything that can be sold and consumers purchase these goods because they are tied to a life of forced labour, leading to overproduction and overuse of land and other resources. In a gift economy, people's productive efforts would be tempered by the desire to enjoy a leisured existence and beautiful healthy environments.

Material wealth would depend on the desire of others to give. Creativity and choice, which now focus in the sphere of leisure, would inform productive processes and an environmentally benign society. For example, creating a permaculture forest amounts to both an enjoyable appreciation of nature's bounties and a sustainable mode of production. In terms of values, the gift economy operates with an ethic of generosity and egalitarianism. Giving to those in need results in pleasure. This ethic also applies to the natural world, with other species having value and respect and benefiting from the gifts of care and concern.

FOOD PRODUCTION

Capitalist agricultural practices have eroded the environment on which we rely for food. For instance, agricultural production depends on key soil nutrients, chiefly compounds based on nitrogen, phosphorus and potassium. Some of these elements become embodied in plant and animal products and are lost to local soils as products are exported from the country to cities, or other countries, without nutrient recycling. The scientific and commercial solution to nutrient loss is replacement with artificial fertilisers, which are very expensive, ultimately destroying soil humus and agricultural productivity as well as polluting waterways.

Modern agriculture depends massively on cheap fossil fuel for food transport, artificial fertilisers, pesticides and herbicides. The Intergovernmental Panel on Climate Change has argued that we need to cut carbon dioxide emissions and fossil fuel use by 60 to 80 per cent to stabilise greenhouse gas emissions or we risk devastating climatic changes that would increase the costs of agriculture and ruin certain useable agricultural sites. Furthermore, we are likely to run out of accessible oil reserves within ten to 20 years. So, it would be sensible to use the latitude that cheap oil provides to set up the physical and social structures necessary to live in an agricultural economy that does not depend on oil.[18]

Certain leguminous plants can fix nitrogen from the air, storing it in their roots. This property is used in organic and other sustainable agricultures, and in much commercial agriculture. Leguminous plants are grown in rotation with pasture or grain crops to improve soil humus and add nitrogen. However, the low cost of fertiliser makes it cheaper than nitrogen replacement through 'green manure' crops, which need planting and slashing. Phosphorus presents a more intractable problem in Australia. Without phosphate ores the one way to replace phosphates removed through crops and animals exported from the farm is by recycling nutrients from animal and human waste, as practised in many ancient societies.

Creating scenarios for Sweden, Gunther has recommended small rural villages a kilometre or so apart supplied with food by diverse farms of 40 hectares.[19] More labour would be required for nutrient recycling, growing leguminous crops and producing animal feed, but villagers would not be working to pay for transport, packaging and distribution. Villagers would supply human manure, phosphorus would be recycled locally, and distributors, transporters, processors and retailers would be unnecessary. The energy costs of producing artificial fertilisers would vanish, and the energy costs of redistributing and recycling phosphorus would be negligible compared with those currently incurred in treating sewage and manure.

In Australia, the consequences of such ruralisation would be extremely disruptive but, ultimately, much less than if current practices continue and the price of oil escalates. Ruralisation in small hamlets of, for example, 200 people, might appear as death to the intellect. But people could visit, stay in other households and move between villages on solar-powered trains, using bicycles, sailing ships and airships, and electronic communication. There would be much to enjoy living in landscapes less dense than urban ones, with safe sustainable farms, wildlife living in parks and agroforestry zones.

People often argue that environmental damage is inevitable because high-input agriculture is necessary to feed a large population. Yet much recent research supports low-input agriculture and shows that yields and even economic returns from more sustainable farming are also good, and quite sufficient for our global population.[20]

In contrast, capitalism works against environmental sustainability, with non-human nature privately owned, its use often depending on what is profitable in the short term. Other barriers to moving to a sustainable agriculture include increases in the costs of labour-intensive techniques, new information and technology, and new crops, even though organic agriculture is seen as avoiding falling yields and having lower costs because of reduced inputs.[21] Capitalist cultural and political pressures favour unsustainable trends as political instability seems to follow any decrease in market growth or growth in unemployment. Expensive, well-packaged and exotic foods remain moral rewards for a life of otherwise thankless labour.

Nevertheless, sustainable agricultural production is increasing despite such hurdles.[22] Often these kinds of developments are what I call 'hybrids' *of the gift economy and capitalism*. By hybrids, I mean beneficial changes embodying some control of production by producers or the community at large and/or some giving, that is, forms of distribution that follow from a different logic than simply gaining the highest profit.

HYBRID STRATEGIES

Hybrids are strategic reforms that express care and concern for the natural world and future humans and/or involve gifts to the planet. Examples are: voters who support environmental taxes, consumers who decide to pay a higher price for more environmentally friendly produce, farmers and marketers who farm sustainably as an expression of their love for the natural world, and volunteers who engage in non-market sustainable farming in community gardens or alternative lifestyle farms. Hybrids such as volunteering tap into people's need for meaningful creative work. Hybrids such as 'fair trade', which aims to be environmentally and socially sustainable, can prefigure alliances and networks of participatory democratic structures that would organise production and distribution in a gift economy.

In short, hybrids offer useful ways to frame strategies that fit within, and move beyond, capitalism by pointing to the gift economy. They might be symbiotic with capitalism, ameliorating some of its excesses, but also must be antithetical to the culture and economy of capitalism in certain ways. Hybrid modifications to capitalism are radical in as much as they are embryos of a new social order. It is not helpful to expect hybrids to be pure gift economy enclaves. Instead they further the goals of left-wing social movements even while inflected by aspects of capitalist economy and culture. Given time and enough proliferation of hybrids, they will develop further to replace capitalism.

In contrast, traditional anarchist strategies, such as direct action, are purist – living now in the way we would like to live after the revolution. For instance, in direct action, people take an aspect of daily life or production out of the control of capitalists and bureaucrats. Activities such as 'reclaim the streets' and 'critical mass' rallies are revolutionary in defying capitalist legal structures and state ownership. They follow the Situationists, who encouraged rioters and looting of consumer goods.[23] Temporary seizures are fun and filled with an adrenaline rush of risk-taking. However, while they offer a sense of controlling the means of production, and might help achieve some reformist victories, they rarely lead to effective long-term control. If we take a purist line and validate these kinds of actions as the *only* legitimate political strategy then the most romantic political actions can be futile heroic gestures. There is a danger that risky self-sacrifice becomes a token of political credibility that gives undemocratic power to social movement leaders sanctified by their sacrifices.

However, Situationists accurately argued that experiences that might create a demand for capitalist alternatives are systematically closed off. We do not experience the joy of egalitarian social contact, engaging with others in freely chosen creative projects, or giving. Instead, our employers own what we produce and socially appropriate giving is a commodity bought in a shop. In this context the gift economy seems stranger than science fiction because we have so few experiences that embody its principles of operation. The Hakim Bey strategy of 'immediatism' evolved from an analysis of the Situationist concept of mediation. In what Bey calls 'too-late capitalism', all life and relationships are mediated so that there is no space for real social ties.[24] The immediatist strategy makes use of time outside paid work.

All that immediatism requires is to meet regularly with other people who want to be part of 'the game' and engage in some creative pastime. Bey's favourite example is a working bee, where people together make a quilt. Face-to-face work is not mediated (by connections such as the Internet and post), costs are shared, and products of creative labour are given away, preferably to group members. All spectators must be performers also. There are three problems: the difficulty of meeting, resisting the temptation to bend the group's efforts to commercial purposes, and the possibility of state surveillance and interference. But Bey hopes that links between such groups can eventuate in change to a new kind of society.

Like other forms of direct action, immediatism appropriates the social space for this action from areas of social life normally controlled by capitalism. This is odd if we regard leisure as free time outside capitalist work. However, Bey – like Cleaver in Chapter 3 – argues that leisure is already social space colonised by capitalism. Capitalism depends on leisure for consumption and refreshment for further work. The least politically threatening forms of leisure in capitalism are socially isolating and unproductive – like watching television – so your only experience of production is in your job. Immediatism reappropriates leisure time for social and productive arrangements following a gift economy, thus politically contradicting capitalism.

Immediatism is an example of a more general strategy developed in an earlier work by Bey, *T.A.Z.: The Temporary Autonomous Zone*.[25] The premise of the temporary autonomous zone (TAZ) is the recognition of insurrections as moments of intensity, as festivals of creativity. As distinct from a TAZ – a small island of commendable anti-capitalist practice isolated from the global economy – 'hybrids' occur where aspects of capitalist economic, political and social structures mix with aspects of a gift economy. While I regard them as politically useful, Bey denigrates partial and piecemeal strategies for daily life, such as the aforementioned hybrids. Advocating hybrids is definitely reformist anarchism but speaks directly to new-age critiques of 'political' strategies, which criticise sacrificing 'the now' to long-term goals instead of making the most of the present. Hybrids are practised in many social movements, such as feminism, queer politics, environmentalism, anti-racism and non-government development organisations.

THE TRANSITION TO A GIFT ECONOMY

The traditional concept of a revolution suggests popular unrest and secret organisations planning mass demonstrations in city centres of a country or even a continent. If that worked and demonstrations were a success, further steps would depend on whether or not the police and armed forces sided with the demonstrators. Following this, parties of interested people would occupy and run all enterprises, ignoring any instructions from former bosses. Products would be given away and coordination achieved by voluntary collectives. Either the police and armed forces would dissolve, giving their weapons to community groups, or their members would form collectives to protect popular appropriations from violent opposition.

Alternatively, a revolution via parliament could be initiated by declaration by a majority party, with a majority vote inviting people to take over the means of production according to their interests and passions. The army would be asked to facilitate this process, either forming themselves into democratic committees or turning their arms over to popular community groups. Developments would depend on the degree of popular disaffection with capitalism, the level of popular support expressed on the street and on reactions of the armed forces. Presuming all went well, a parliamentary announcement and accompanying actions in society would effectively terminate parliamentary democracy.

A 'revolution by stealth' might happen as the pervasiveness and influence of hybrid organisations came to dominate the economy, nationally, regionally or internationally. Hybrid organisations could combine capitalist forms (money, property and wage labour) with decision-making structures and cultural norms of a gift economy – local democratic control, gift distribution and creative participation. The capitalist class might realise their interest in fostering creative participation. Alternatively, the capitalist class might be increasingly frozen out of the economy by 'subordinate' classes investing savings in hybrid organisations and building them to the point where nothing capitalists tried to market would be sold and no-one could be induced into capitalist work. Both tendencies could happen together. Money might be distributed to the poor so that producers' collectives could be paid to distribute gifts, and eventually abolished (to be replaced by contracts, promises and agreements). Despite the diversity of cultures, it is not entirely ridiculous to imagine a gift economy taking over globally. It could operate in just one country, but a successful example could galvanise opposition to capitalism in other places. Most likely any gift economy would have to achieve either a near universal spread or the military capacity to defend attacks from capitalist forces.

A gift economy would complete the feminist revolution and would depend on men feeling comfortable with gender equality and abandoning patriarchal control over women. A gift economy would provide reliable subsistence through chains of donors and recipients linked by promises and agreements. Committed local community members would provide housing and food security. Other volunteers would replace them if they wanted to move to other work. If needed, they would be helped to perform adequately.

The gift economy would empower local producers' collectives to avoid environmental damage at source and producers making gifts would be appreciated for their environmentally friendly practices.

This gift economy revolution is not sparked off by generosity; its essential requirement is a widespread desire for us to take over and do a better job. Generosity comes after that, as people discover that it is the only way for exchange, modern technology and localised control to happen all at once. Modern technology and the limited affluence of a green economy depend heavily on sharing products between producer groups. A train service could not run in a barter economy, but it could run as a gift to the community.

By the late 1950s the workers in rich countries were clearly becoming more bored and frustrated with meaningless work only compensated by passive, individualised consumer affluence. Paul Cardan foresaw a revolutionary struggle premised on the demand for creative work, for work controlled by workers and for more excitement in daily life.[26] While globalisation threatens continued growth in affluence for workers in rich countries, there are valid aspects of Cardan's analysis. Demands for participation still undermine cultures of passivity and routinised obedience. Attempts to control workers by bureaucratic surveillance have grown. Frustration still drives demands for excitement, creative pleasure and social connection while the capitalist class channels these demands into consumerism.

In short, capitalism encourages the very cultural forces – hedonism, sociability, creativity and autonomy – that undermine its long-term rule. These 'permissive' tendencies contradict the work ethic, puritanism and discipline, which are central cultural requirements for a work force based in alienated labour. In this context, the psyche swings wildly between sexual conservatism, guilt, work addiction, individualised status competition, abstinence and 'realism' through to sexual and gender experimentation, and attempts to make life fun, autonomous and meaningful, fantasy, drugs and spirituality, along with desires for egalitarian social connection, care, friendship and communication locally and globally. These contradictions appear both in the affluent rich countries and in the Third World, expressed variously within and between countries. Ideally, by the time hybrids and the environmental crisis have created the conditions necessary for a revolutionary change, we will also have seen the cultural forces of late capitalism triumph over the cultural foundations of class society.

On the one hand, it is hard for anarchists to come up with any convincing account of what to do while 'waiting' for the revolution, which is why hybrid strategies make sense. On the other hand, environmentalists have no workable utopia. They mistake today's hybrids for the future utopia. They envisage a capitalist economy in which local money and right livelihood, community banks and sustainable land cooperatives replace big companies motivated solely by greed. They retain money, wage labour and a state, thinking a simple change in culture and personnel will overcome the environmental and social weaknesses of capitalism. They do not understand that hybrids have a transient role and make no sense in any utopia that would realise an ethics of sharing and caring between people and with nature. They find it difficult to understand why land-sharing cooperatives get taken over by greedy, manipulative power-hungry individuals. Why do labour exchange trading systems (LETS) and cooperatives fade from lack of interest? (See Chapter 7 for an explanation.) Why do eager proponents of right livelihood end up doing something unthinkable? Half the time these schemes crumble because capitalism reclaims their resources and personnel.

Environmentalists blame human nature and capitalist culture: a lack of moral purity, a failure of will, a lack of strength to make the necessary sacrifices. They ask people to tighten their belts, invoking a puritan moral position that has little credibility in postmodern society. People are scared, few voting for their solutions. It is hard for environmentalists to say, 'The problem is capitalist structures'. Instead they criticise capitalists' greed and ordinary peoples' selfish ignorant consumerism, believing the way forward is to spread alternative economic structures within capitalism. But community banks, right livelihood and land-owning collectives are paradoxical and dissolve within capitalism. For instance, right livelihood is about how to make an ethical and interesting living *within the capitalist economy*, doing something that brings in a reasonable income. In other words, it is a strategy premised on markets. So, if the market fails, it cannot work. What point is there in an ethical avocado farm if no-one has money to buy avocadoes or if ethical avocado growers swamp the market?

In fact the only circumstances in which a gift economy can become dominant and survive is as capitalism is *replaced* and, with it, hybrids! If the kind of ethical production and distribution that environmentalists favour took hold, then money would be irrelevant and, so too, hybrids such as community banks. We would have achieved a gift economy. The ethical avocado grower would apply avocado skills in interesting ways useful to others and give to those who could benefit most from their largesse. You could call this new behaviour 'right livelihood' if you wanted, but it is a radically different life strategy in this new gift economy.

We tend to think of capitalism as a set of legal rules and regulations: the means of production is owned privately and labour power is a commodity bought and sold. Yet, in reality, it is our behaviour that defines capitalism as a social structure. The power of hegemony does not derive from some sovereign point, be that a legal system or the capitalist class as a conspiratorial clique.[27] It is created through a multiplicity of everyday actions in which people think and behave predictably. The strategy of hybrids works on this premise to create a vast multitude of behaviours that contradict capitalism.

To emphasise the points made so far in this chapter, I conclude with an analysis of the anarchist experiment in Spain in the mid-1930s.

THE GREAT ANARCHIST DISASTER IN SPAIN

In many parts of Spain, a popular revolution took control in 1936. It was the longest and largest anarchist experiment to date, as pointed out by Sam Dolgoff:

> The Spanish Revolution of 1936–39 came closer to realizing the ideal of the free stateless society on a vast scale than any other revolution in history, including the aborted Russian Revolution of 1917. In fact, they were two very different kinds of revolution. The Spanish revolution is an example of a libertarian social revolution where genuine workers' self-management was successfully tried. It represents a way of organizing society that is increasingly important today. The Bolshevik revolution, by contrast, was controlled by an elite party and was a political revolution. It set the doleful pattern for the authoritarian state capitalist revolutions in Eastern Europe, Asia (China, Korea, Vietnam), and Latin America (Cuba).
>
> The Spanish revolution thus marks a turning point in revolutionary history.[28]

The key mistaken strategy occurred when the leaders of the anarchist federation became participants in a left-wing coalition government in Madrid. Subsequently, the central government unwound local control achieved by workers' and peasants' councils. The willingness of the party faithful and ordinary workers to trust their leadership was largely responsible for the failure to maintain local control. They all too willingly gave up control of production when the leadership said it was necessary 'for the sake of the revolution'.

Class society sets up habits of obedience and worship of authority. These are long-standing psychological dispositions that will not evaporate overnight in a 'revolution'. The most likely outcome of such a revolution is that the revolutionary masses consent to replacing the ruling class with a faction of the revolutionary leadership, paving the way for the reintroduction of class control and alienated labour. This happened in Spain: continued use of money and wage labour implied control from above and necessitated distribution and planning from above. In turn, top-down distribution and planning required money and wage labour.

Why did the workers take any notice of their leadership? Willing sacrifice embodied in a leader who inspires others to the same behaviour is a key psychological foundation of patriarchal authority structures and was entrenched in Spain. There is no point in a revolution organised only by a minority. Coups by extremist minorities provide ideal conditions for revolutionary leaders to become a new ruling class. This suggests that the revolutionary appropriation of the means of production must take place after, not before, the psychological and cultural foundations of egalitarian society have been laid.

It is tempting to try to derive lessons from the disaster in Spain. Most anarchists conclude that they should never have abandoned their principles and become representatives in a statist executive body.[29] The events in Spain reinforce their belief that anarchists should not support parliamentary initiatives or political parties. Even though I am an anarchist, I find this unpalatable and my theory of hybrids suggests that such a strong line is not really useful.

In the mainstream anarchist analysis, the central issue is the failure of the leadership to enact anarchist principles. What is left out of this narrative is the insignificance of such failures if the rank and file had abandoned its leadership and anarchist organisations the minute they had impeded the social revolution. When the mass of people had military control of the streets and control of the factories, they could have maintained and consolidated their control in the form of a gift economy. They could have treated all attempts to initiate a new system of paid police as counter-revolutionary and forced them down. Economic organisation and order could have come from negotiating producers' agreements to supply materials and distribute products.

Attempts to continue a wage and money economy while taking over the means of production was a central mistake at all levels. Real economic power remained with the government – or, for those businesses that had not been collectivised, with private interests – not factory committees. Most significantly the historical legacy of Spanish class society, the psychology of dominance and submission, expressed in ordinary people continuing to look to great leaders and immortal organisations for solutions, impeded the revolution.

ANOTHER WAY

As an alternative, let us imagine a future scenario for a country like Australia, where the Greens had become an anarchist party in the sense of advocating an anarchist solution – the gift economy – as the only way out of problems of social injustice, coercive work and environmental disaster. Alternatively, anarchists had formed a party and were contesting elections. The following principles would make sense.

First, anarchists in a parliamentary minority should never consent to become members of a government and should always vote according to their true views. They should not do deals with major parties in exchange for concessions. If they voted for motions that fell short of the anarchist agenda they would have to explain to voters why they thought these motions would effect reform and were the best current parliamentary option.

Second, if anarchists had a parliamentary majority they should declare a gift economy and invite the army and police to distribute their weapons to local workers' committees. They should declare the end of money and private property and invite the population to take over control of the means of production, with each unit governed by those working in it and distributing its product according to their wishes. They should declare the parliament a house of discussion. These would be simple pronouncements; for a successful social revolution there could be no parliamentary legislation or monopoly of force in future. The anarchist or green organisation should warn people that this is what they would do if they gained a majority, explaining that the social revolution would depend ultimately on military force, with the army or police supporting the revolution: 'If you are not prepared for this outcome or doubt that the revolutionary forces can win, don't vote for us.'

The revolution in Spain was different from either of these two scenarios. The republican government did not have the power to control economic and military life. To do this they invited anarchist representatives to become members of various governmental executive committees, in a sense to become effectively members of a governing cabinet of ministers. There was no new election and no electoral process to reflect popular support for the anarchist left. Instead, the republican leaders claimed legitimacy as the most recently elected government and invited anarchist and socialist leaders into the government as part of an emergency coalition in 'a government of national unity' representing all parties.

As representatives of the popular movement, the anarchist leaders should have explained to the right-wing republican parties that the people had taken over the economy and should be allowed to get on with it. Most anarchist writers agree that the leadership should never have been inveigled into sharing government power with the forces of the right; there was a real chance of exercising power at the level of production. Instead the leaders negotiated with liberal and reformist forces to attempt a new structure of government and wage labour that would combine workers' control with capitalist or nationalist state ownership of production. This might best be described as workers' participation in management. While that might be a useful and progressive strategy in some circumstances, in Barcelona at that time, this participation strategy was a *retreat* from the reality on the streets, a failure to recognise the specificity of the social revolution as a complete abandonment of wage labour. The idea that you can have workers' control, wage labour, money and government coordination of the economy is an illusion.

A key issue for the leadership was their unwillingness to see the 'stake' of the anarchist (and socialist) unions gambled away for a social revolution that might not happen. They were scared that, without the support of the liberals and right-wing socialists, there would be no chance of defeating Franco. With their support, they envisaged some kind of consolidation of anarchist power after Franco's defeat.

What was missing in the anarchist analysis at this time was Bey's perspective: that numbers of radical risings have been unsuccessful in overthrowing class society and can be regarded as TAZs carved out of the space of class society.[30] In Spain it should have been possible to push the TAZ scenario as far as it would go because the initial takeovers of factories and barracks laid a strong basis. Sure, the chances are that the anarchist autonomous zone would not have been permitted to infect other countries. The fascist armies of Germany and Italy, or even the 'democratic' governments, would have conquered Spain. But it would have been inspiring if Catalonia and other provinces had held out, for even a few years more, by operating a gift economy.

What were ordinary people and leaders really feeling beneath their macho posturing? In Spanish anarchist culture at the time, it would not have been easy to express fear, to reject the social revolution because that was more likely to lead to mass death than the more middle-of-the-road alternatives. A successful gift economy TAZ in a major European country might have scared fascists and capitalists into genocidal frenzy. Instead, after Franco's victory, Spain even avoided participation in the Second World War. Maybe a guilty sense of relief buried anarchism in Spain. It certainly never recovered from these events.

I have a sense, too, of anarchists choking at the point of social revolution like athletes do at tennis matches. The wrong lesson to draw from all this is that anarchists should have been more militant, more selfless, more courageous, more true to their principles. Very 'old soldier'. Perhaps they should have been a lot more open about what they feared and been prepared to initiate this experiment like a TAZ with the open proviso of abandonment once it cost more lives than was worth the candle.

In conclusion, I would like to see a rapprochement between anarchists, environmentalists and other social activists. Anarchists have a strong sense of the capitalist causes of environmental crises. A gift economy is a more practicable and workable utopia than anything coming out of the broader left and environmental movements today. Regulated capitalism and a mixed economy with world government are neither practicable nor attractive. The social actions we can work on most readily today are hybrids of the gift economy and capitalism. Ultimately we can hope to see these culminate in the gift economy, the only form of social organisation that can maintain modern technological knowledge and embody it in an environmentally sustainable civilisation.

Box 6.1 Alexander Berkman on Anarchism

I must tell you, first of all, what anarchism is *not*.
It is *not* bombs, disorder or chaos.
It is *not* robbery and murder.
It is *not* a war of each against all.
It is *not* a return to barbarism or to the wild state of man.
Anarchism is the very opposite of all that.

▶

Anarchism means that you should be free; that no one should enslave you, boss you, rob you, or impose upon you.

It means that you should be free to do the things you want to do; and that you should not be compelled to do what you don't want to do.

It means that you should have a chance to choose the kind of a life you want to live, and live it without anybody interfering.

It means that the next fellow should have the same freedom as you and that every one should have the same rights and liberties.

It means that all men are brothers, and that they should live like brothers, in peace and harmony.

That is to say, that there should be no war, no violence used by one set of men against another, no monopoly, and no poverty, no oppression, no taking advantage of your fellow-man.

In short, anarchism means a condition of society where all men and women are free, and where all enjoy equally the benefits of an ordered and sensible life.

Source: Alexander Berkman, *ABC of Anarchism*, London: Freedom Press, 1977 [1929], p. 2.

Box 6.2   David Holmgren on Permaculture Design Principles

1. Observe and interact.
2. Catch and store energy.
3. Obtain a yield.
4. Apply self-regulation and accept feedback.
5. Use and value renewable resources and services.
6. Produce no waste.
7. Design from patterns to details.
8. Integrate rather than segregate.
9. Use small and slow solutions.
10. Use and value diversity.
11. Use edges and value the marginal.
12. Creatively use and respond to change.

Source: Adapted from David Holmgren, *Permaculture: Principles & Pathways Beyond Sustainability*, Hepburn: Holmgren Design Services, 2002, p. viii.

Box 6.3   Murray Bookchin on an Anarchist Utopia

If humanity is to live in balance with nature, we must turn to ecology for the essential guidelines of how the future society should be organized. Again we find that what is desirable is also necessary. Man's desire for unrepressed, spontaneous expression, for variety in experience and surroundings, and for an environment scaled to human dimensions must also be realized to achieve natural equilibrium. The ecological problems of the old society thus reveal the methods that will shape the new. The intuition that all of these processes are converging toward an entirely new way of life finds its most concrete confirmation in the youth culture. The rising generation, which has been largely spared the scarcity psychosis of its parents, anticipates the development that lies ahead. In the outlook and praxis of young people, which range from tribalism to a sweeping affirmation of sensuousness, one finds those cultural prefigurations that point to a future utopia.

Source: Murray Bookchin, *Post-Scarcity Anarchism*, Berkeley: Ramparts Press, 1971, p. 27.

NOTES

All italics in quotes are preserved from the originals.

1. Cornelius Castoriadis, *The Imaginary Institution of Society*, Cambridge: Polity Press, 1997.
2. Quote originally cited in Terry Leahy, 'Sociological Utopias and Social Transformation: Permaculture and the Gift Economy' at The Gift Economy, Anarchism and Strategies for Change [website], accessed 20 October 2010, at http://www.gifteconomy.org.
3. Raoul Vaneigem, *The Revolution of Everyday Life*, London: Left Bank Books & Rebel Press, 1983; Marcel Mauss, *The Gift: The Form and Reason for Exchange in Archaic Societies*, London: W.D. Halls, 1990, [1923–24, French].
4. Bill Mollison, *Permaculture: A Designers' Manual*, Tyalgum: Tagari, 1988, p. ix.
5. Quote originally cited in Terry Leahy, 'The Australian Public, Developing Countries and the Environment', at The Gift Economy, Anarchism and Strategies for Social Change [website], accessed 20 October 2010, at http://www.gifteconomy.org.
6. Kirkpatrick Sale, *Dwellers in the Land: Bioregional Vision*, Philadelphia: New Society, 1991.

7. Murray Bookchin, *Post Scarcity Anarchism*, San Francisco: Ramparts Press, 1971; Graham Purchase, *Anarchism and Environmental Survival*, Tucson: See Sharp Press, 1994.

8. Vaneigem, *The Revolution of Everyday Life.*

9. David Holmgren, 'Aboriginal land use', in *Collected Writings 1978–2000*, Hepburn: Holmgren Design Services, 1992.

10. Annette Hamilton, *Nature and Nurture: Aboriginal Child-Rearing in North-Central Arnhem Land*, Canberra: Australian Institute of Aboriginal Studies, 1981.

11. Nancy Chodorow, 'Family structure and personality', in M. Z. Rosaldo and L. Lamphere (eds), *Woman, Culture and Society*, Palo Alto: Stanford University Press, 1974.

12. Shulamith Firestone, *The Dialectic of Sex: The Case for Feminist Revolution*, London: Paladin, 1972.

13. David Spratt and Phillip Sutton, *Climate Code Red: The Case for Emergency Action*, Melbourne: Scribe Publications, 2008.

14. Ted Trainer, *Renewable Energy Cannot Sustain Consumer Society*, Dordrecht: Springer, 2007, p. 2.

15. Ibid.; Ted Trainer, *The Conserver Society; Alternatives for Sustainability*, London: Zed Books, 1995.

16. Ted Trainer, *Renewable Energy Cannot Sustain Consumer Society*, pp. 115, 128.

17. Jared Diamond, *Collapse: How Societies Choose to Fail or Survive*, Camberwell: Penguin, 2005.

18. David Holmgren, *Permaculture: Principles & Pathways Beyond Sustainability*, Hepburn: Holmgren Design Services, 2002.

19. F. Gunther, 'Fossil energy and food security', *Energy and Environment*, Vol. 12, No. 4, 2002, pp. 253–75, esp. p. 266.

20. J. Pretty, *The Living Land: Agriculture, Food and Community Regeneration in Rural Europe*, London: Earthscan, 1998; J. Pretty, *Regenerating Agriculture: Policies and Practice for Sustainability and Self-Reliance*, London: Earthscan, 1999; J. Pretty, *Agri-Culture: Re-Connecting People, Land and Nature*, London: Earthscan, 2002.

21. Pretty, *The Living Land*; Pretty, *Regenerating Agriculture.*

22. Pretty, *Agri-Culture.*

23. K. Knabb (ed.), *The Situationist Anthology*, Berkeley: Bureau of Public Secrets, 1981.

24. Hakim Bey, *Immediatism*, Edinburgh: AK Press, 1994.

25. Hakim Bey, *T.A.Z.: The Temporary Autonomous Zone: Ontological Anarchy, Poetic Terrorism*, New York: Autonomedia, 1991.

26. Paul Cardan, *Modern Capitalism and Revolution*, London: Solidarity, 1974.

27. M. Foucault, *The History of Sexuality Vol. I*, New York: Vintage Books, 1980.

28. Sam Dolgoff (ed.), *The Anarchist Collectives: Workers' Self-Management in the Spanish Revolution 1936–1939*, New York: Free Life Editions, 1974, p. 5.

29. Vernon Richards, *Lessons of the Spanish Revolution*, London: Freedom Press, 1972.

30. Fredy Perlman, *Against His-story, Against Leviathan!*, Detroit: Black & Red, 1983.

Part II

Activism and Experiments

7
Non-Market Socialism

Adam Buick

I first became critical of capitalism while still at school towards the end of the 1950s. At first I thought that the alternative was what existed in Russia. After all, they called themselves 'socialist', the opposite of capitalism. But then I read Milovan Djilas's book, *The New Class*, which came out in 1957 and showed that Yugoslavia, Russia and so on were not the classless societies they claimed to be (see Box 7.1).[1] At the same time, I read left-wing Labour Party politician Aneurin Bevan's book, *In Place of Fear*, which had come out earlier, in 1952, and which convinced me that not only did socialism have to be democratic but also could only be established by democratic (electoral, parliamentary) means.[2]

After reading these two books I was convinced that countries such as Russia were not socialist and that socialism could only be democratic. As the Labour Party – and the Trotskyists who were then 'boring from within' it – never had any attraction for me, I looked around for an organisation that was left of Labour but not the Communist Party. In Britain I approached five parties: the Independent Labour Party, the Socialist Party of Great Britain, the Socialist Labour Party of Great Britain (a UK affiliate of the Socialist Labor Party of America), the Fellowship Party (a pacifist party) and the Fife Socialist League (a breakaway from the Communist Party in Scotland).

The two parties that particularly interested me were the Socialist Party of Great Britain and the Socialist Labour Party because, basically, they advocated only socialism as they understood it and, unlike the others, nothing else. It so happened, though I did not fully realise it at the time, that both of them argued that socialism involved the abolition of money – although the Socialist Labour Party wanted to replace it with 'labour-time vouchers' (discussed later in this chapter). The Socialist Party of Great Britain is a 'companion party' of the World Socialist Movement. (Box 7.2 outlines the distinguishing principles of the World Socialist Movement today.)

A MONEYLESS SOCIETY

Any party that advocates only 'socialism' inevitably must have a lot to say about what socialism would or could be like. As I read through the past and current literature of the Socialist Party of Great Britain, I realised that right from its formation in 1904 it had insisted that socialism had to involve the abolition of money. I was introduced to and read the two classics of a moneyless society, Thomas More's *Utopia* and William Morris's *News from Nowhere* (see Box 7.3). In the end I was convinced that the alternative to capitalism had to be a moneyless society. Further reading led me to the understanding that this was the position of Karl Marx and Frederick Engels, despite the claims of the Russian government and its supporters.

Looking back, I think that what attracted me to the idea of a moneyless society was disgust at the methods used by sellers to obtain money. I always used to say (and still would) that an evening watching the advertisements on commercial television (introduced into Britain in 1955) should be enough to put anyone off capitalism, with its tricks, half-truths and patent lies devised to try to sell you things.

In college I studied, among other things, economics and could see that I was being taught an intellectual defence of buying and selling. Economics was defined as the study of the allocation of scarce resources amongst competing needs, with money as the best way to do this. In fact, because needs were assumed to be infinite, scarcity and money were seen as natural phenomena that could never be abolished. I did not agree but that was what I was taught, and what, as far as I know, economics students still learn.

The fallacy put forward by the writers of these textbooks was to beg the question. By defining scarcity in relation to infinite needs they made it impossible to overcome. But this is not a normal definition of 'scarcity' and its opposite 'abundance', which are more normally defined in relation to some actual needs, which are never infinite. But once it is conceded that needs are not infinite (as they are manifestly not) then the whole intellectual structure of economics collapses. Whether or not scarcity – and money – can be abolished becomes a question, not of definition, but of fact. Could or could not enough of the things actually needed be produced? On the basis of statistics produced by such organisations as the United Nations Food and Agriculture Organisation and the World Health Organisation, and with the elimination of the waste that capitalism involves, not just in arms but in the whole money system, I was convinced that it could be. Therefore, a moneyless socialist society was possible.

WILD CAPITALISM

In the 1980s there was a change in the intellectual atmosphere, as reflected with the coming into office of Ronald Reagan in the United States and Margaret Thatcher in Great Britain. Keynesianism and the idea of government intervention to help people went out and were replaced by the harsh doctrine of unregulated, wild capitalism. The old ideas of Ludwig von Mises that a moneyless, socialist society was impossible were resuscitated. In 1920, in his article *Economic Calculation in the Socialist Commonwealth*, Mises had argued that, while a moneyless society might be able to decide what it wanted to produce, it would not be able to work out the most efficient way to do this; only a system with market-determined prices could.[3] If attempted, a moneyless society would sooner or later collapse into economic chaos. This became known as the 'economic calculation' argument against socialism. Mises had been criticising the ideas circulating at the time (and earlier) inside the German and Austrian Social Democratic parties about how to organise the production and distribution of wealth in a non-capitalist society, in particular the view put forward by Otto Neurath (later a noted philosopher) that money would not be needed, as calculations could be done directly in kind. (See detailed discussion of these debates in Chapter 4.)

However, the latter-day followers of Mises had a problem: there was no longer anybody around defending these ideas since the Social Democratic and Labour parties had long since abandoned any idea of abolishing the market, arguing merely for government intervention to regulate it. The only people prepared to take Mises head-on were the Socialist Party of Great Britain; in the 1980s and early 1990s, I spent some time arguing in the columns of *Free Life* (the journal of the Libertarian Alliance) and *Libertarian Student* (its student publication) that the production and distribution of wealth could be sustainably organised without money.[4]

I have to admit, though, that the latter-day followers of Mises forced us to think more about how this could be done and to sharpen our arguments. They accused us of standing for a centralised, command economy that implied that all decisions about the production and distribution of wealth would be taken by some central planning office. This is, I suppose, theoretically possible if it required a very powerful computer but, in the end, we came to the conclusion that it would not be necessary.

PRODUCTION FOR USE

The alternative was a self-regulating system of moneyless production for use, which would be responding to real demand (that is, to what people decided they wanted for their individual consumption) as opposed to only 'effective' demand (that is, what people were prepared to buy with money). If a system worked for effective/ paying demand, as Mises and other defenders of the capitalist market system claimed, why would it not work for real demand? Much of the work on this alternative system of self-regulating production for use was done by Pieter Lawrence, who drafted the 1994 Socialist Party of Great Britain pamphlet *Socialism As A Practical Alternative*.[5] Another contributor to elaborating this alternative system was Robin Cox.[6] John Crump and I outlined such a system, in 1986, in the final chapter of our book, *State Capitalism; The Wages System under New Management*:

> Since the needs of consumers are always needs for a specific product at a specific time in a specific locality, we will assume that socialist society would leave the initial assessment of likely needs to a delegate body under the control of the local community (although, once again, other arrangements are possible if that were what the members of socialist society wanted). In a stable society such as socialism, needs would change relatively slowly. Hence it is reasonable to surmise that an efficient system of stock control, recording what individuals actually chose to take under conditions of free access from local distribution centres over a given period, would enable the local distribution committee (for want of a name) to estimate what the need for food, drink, clothes and household goods would be over a similar future period. Some needs would be able to be met locally: local transport, restaurants, builders, repairs and some food are examples as well as services such as street-lighting, libraries and refuse collection. The local distribution committee would then communicate needs that could not be met locally to the body (or bodies) charged with coordinating supplies to local communities.
>
> Once such an integrated structure of circuits of production and distribution had been established at local, regional and world levels, the flow of wealth to the final consumer could take place

on the basis of each unit in the structure having free access to what is needed to fulfil its role. The individual would have free access to the goods on the shelves of the local distribution centres; the local distribution centres free access to the goods they required to be always adequately stocked with what people needed; their suppliers free access to the goods they required from the factories which supplied them; industries and factories free access to the materials, equipment and energy they needed to produce their products; and so on.

Production and distribution in socialism would thus be a question of organising a coordinated and more or less self-regulating system of linkages between users and suppliers, enabling resources and materials to flow smoothly from one productive unit to another, and ultimately to the final user, in response to information flowing in the opposite direction originating from final users. The productive system would thus be set in motion from the consumer end, as individuals and communities took steps to satisfy their self-defined needs. Socialist production is self-regulating production for use.

To ensure the smooth functioning of the system, a central statistical office would be needed to provide estimates of what would have to be produced to meet people's likely individual and collective needs. These could be calculated in the light of consumer wants as indicated by returns from local distribution committees and of technical data (productive capacity, production methods, productivity, etc.) incorporated in input–output tables. For, at any given level of technology (reflected in the input–output tables), a given mix of final goods (consumer wants) requires for its production a given mix of intermediate goods and raw materials; it is this latter mix that the central statistical office would be calculating in broad terms. Such calculations would also indicate whether or not productive capacity would need to be expanded and in what branches. The centre (or rather centres for each world-region) would thus be essentially an information clearing house, processing information communicated to it about production and distribution and passing on the results to industries for them to draw up their production plans so as to be in a position to meet the requests for their products coming from other industries and from local communities.[7]

This is still my position.

MARX

The first article that Karl Marx wrote after becoming a socialist in 1843 was a criticism of a book on the Jewish question, which was published in the *Deutsch-Franzoische Jahrbucher* in Paris in 1844. It is important because it showed a clear understanding that the establishment of socialism involves the disappearance of both the state and money, a view Marx held for the rest of his life but which has been largely forgotten by the great majority of those who call themselves Marxists, who in fact stand for a state capitalism in which money would continue to exist.[8]

The first part of Marx's article 'On the Jewish question' supports the granting of full political rights to religious Jews (as non-Christians) within existing society, but argues that political democracy is not enough as it does not amount to 'human emancipation', which can only be achieved 'when man has recognised and organised his "forces propres" [own powers] as social forces, and consequently no longer separates social power from himself in the shape of political power'.[9]

The second, shorter, part applies the same sort of reasoning to money: 'emancipation from... money', Marx wrote, 'would be the self-emancipation of our time'.[10] It is basically an attack on money and a call for the establishment of a moneyless society as the way to achieve 'human emancipation'. It has not been given the same circulation as some of Marx's other writings of the same period. In a sense this is a pity because some of Marx's strongest denunciations of money and its effects on relations between people are to be found in it:

Practical need, egoism, is the principle of civil society, and as such appears in a pure form as soon as civil society has fully given birth to the political state. The god of practical need and self-interest is money. Money is the jealous god of Israel, in face of which no other god may exist. Money degrades all the gods of man – and turns them into commodities. Money is the universal self-established value of all things. It has therefore robbed the whole world – both the world of men and nature – of its specific value. Money is the estranged essence of man's work and man's existence, and this alien essence dominates him, and he worships it.

Selling is the practical aspect of alienation. Just as man, as long as he is in the grip of religion, is able to objectify his essential nature only by turning it into something alien, something fantastic, so under the domination of egoistic need he can be active practically, and produce objects in practice, only by putting his products, and his activity, under the domination of an alien being, and bestowing the significance of an alien entity – money – on them.[11]

In some notes made in 1844 after reading James Mill's *Elements of Political Economy* – which marked the beginning of what was to become a life-long study and critique of political economy – Marx argued that, in private property society, people produce with a view to exchanging their products for money, so that what they produce becomes a matter of indifference to them as long as they can sell it, which mean that money will dominate their lives:

> Within the presupposition of division of labour, the product, the material of private property, acquires for the individual more and more the significance of an *equivalent*, and as he no longer exchanges only his *surplus*, and the object of his production can be simply a *matter of indifference* to him, so too he no longer exchanges his product for something directly *needed* by him. The equivalent comes into existence as an equivalent in *money*, which is now the immediate result of labour to gain a living and the *medium* of exchange.

> The complete domination of the estranged thing over man has become evident in money, which is completely indifferent both to the nature of the material, i.e., to the specific nature of the private property, and to the personality of the property owner. What was the domination of person over person is now the general domination of the *thing* over the person, of the product over the producer. Just as the concept of the *equivalent*, the value, already implied the *alienation* of private property, so *money* is the sensuous, even objective existence of this *alienation*.[12]

In these same notes on Mill, Marx explained in more detail how human beings came to be dominated by the products of their own labour, while at the same time giving us a glimpse of how things would be different in a moneyless society:

> The essence of money is not, in the first place, that property is alienated in it, but that the *mediating activity* or movement, the *human*, social act by which man's products mutually complement

one another, is *estranged* from man and becomes the attribute of money, a *material thing* outside man... Owing to this *alien mediator* – instead of man himself being the mediator for man – man regards his will, his activity and his relation to other men as a power independent of him and them. His slavery, therefore, reaches its peak.[13]

This is still fairly philosophical, but the meaning is clear enough: in a 'truly human' society (to speak like Marx at this time) human beings would produce things to satisfy their needs, and their products would 'mutually complement one another'; this movement of products from the producer to those who needed them would not take place via money but would be directly organised under conscious human control; in addition, the value of a product would be the value humans put on it in terms of usefulness or capacity to give pleasure. With private property and production for money, on the other hand, this cannot happen: not only does the movement of products from producer to consumer come to be 'mediated' by money, but the value of a product comes to be judged not in human terms but in terms of a sum of money; finally, the whole process of the production and distribution of wealth escapes from human control and is dominated by an alien force, money.

In his now well-known *Economic and Philosophical Manuscripts of 1844*, and in what could be regarded as a prophetic vision of the sort of commercial advertisers' world we have to suffer today, Marx expanded on the point about the pursuit of money becoming the main aim of life in private property society:

The need for money is therefore the true need produced by the economic system, and it is the only need which the latter produces. The quantity of money becomes to an ever greater degree its sole effective quality. Just as it reduces everything to its abstract form, so it reduces itself in the course of its own movement to quantitative being. Excess and intemperance come to be its true norm.[14]

Nobody reading such passionate denunciations of money can be left with any doubt that Marx stood for a moneyless society. Wages were a direct consequence of estranged labour, and estranged labour was the direct cause of private property. He never abandoned his view that money should be abolished through the establishment of a society based on common ownership and production directly for human need.

BORDIGA

In 1975, a pamphlet called *Un Monde Sans Argent: Le Communisme* [*A World Without Money: Communism*] was published in France. The authors argued for the immediate establishment of a moneyless, communist society:

> Communism does not overthrow capital in order to restore commodities to their original state. Commodity exchange is a link and a progress. But it is a link between antagonistic parts. It will disappear without there being a return to barter, that form of primitive exchange. Mankind will no longer be divided into opposed groups or into enterprises. It will organise itself to plan and use its common heritage and to share out duties and enjoyments. The logic of sharing will replace the logic of exchange.

The pamphlet was published by a group called Les Amis de 4 Millions de Jeunes Travailleurs [The Friends of the 4 Million Young Workers], who were influenced by Situationists and, above all, the later writings of Amadeo Bordiga (1889–1970).[15]

Bordiga had been, before the First World War, an active and prominent member of the 'intransigent' wing of the Socialist Party of Italy. Intransigents opposed reformist trends within the socialist party. Bordiga pointed out that, for Marx and Engels, socialist society involved the disappearance of money, buying and selling, wages, the market and all other exchange categories.

Marx distinguished three stages after the capture of political power by the working class: a transition stage, a lower stage of communism and a higher stage of communism, the last two of which were both to be non-commercial and non-monetary. For Bordiga, both stages of socialist and communist society (sometimes distinguished as 'socialism' and 'communism') were characterised by the absence of money, the market and so on, the difference being that in the first stage labour-time vouchers would be used to allocate goods to people, while in full socialism this could be abandoned in favour of full free access.

Bordiga was adamant that socialism did not mean handing over control of the use – and thus effective ownership – of individual factories and other places of work either to the people working in them or to the people living in the area where those factories or places of work were situated: 'the land will not go to peasant associations, nor to the class of peasants, but to the whole of society'.[16] Schemes for 'workers control' were not socialist demands. Socialism, Bordiga always insisted, meant the end of *all* sectional control over separate parts. Social classes and the political state would eventually, in the course of a more or less long transition period, give way to 'the rational administration of human activities', nonetheless 'a stateless economy'.[17] Bordiga took the view that administrative posts were best filled by those most capable of doing the job, not by the most popular; similarly, what was the best solution to a particular problem was something to be determined scientifically by experts in the field and not a matter of majority opinion to be settled by vote.

Bordiga was a vigorous critic of all forms of so-called 'market socialism', whether this took the form of the state's replacing private capitalists but retaining the enterprise form (as in Russia) or of various schemes for 'workers control' of enterprises:

> A system of commercial exchange between free and autonomous enterprises... is even a step backward compared with numerous sectors already organised on a general scale in the bourgeois epoch, as required by technology and the complexity of social life. Socialism, or communism, means that the whole of society is a single association of producers and consumers.[18]

Instead, Bordiga saw production in socialist society as being organised through a plan established by the central administration and drawn up and executed exclusively in physical quantities of useful things without having recourse to any general equivalent, neither money nor labour-time. Bordiga expected that in socialism the level of production would eventually become relatively stable, which would make planning routine. Production would probably even decrease, as compared with capitalism.

Only goods that could be consumed more or less rapidly would be made available (obviously without charge) for individual consumption; all other goods would remain social, to be used in accordance with the arrangements society would make for their use. In socialism, houses would not be owned, but simply occupied by those who lived in them. Bordiga preferred to speak of consumption being social in socialism rather than individual. Although individuals would be free to choose which particular goods to take, not even in full socialism would individuals be able to consume whatever they might feel they wanted to; they would only be able to consume whatever society had decided should be available for individual consumption.

The description of future society given here evidently earns Bordiga a place amongst those advocating a non-market society to replace capitalism but, in view of the 'non-democratic' character of the administrative structure which he envisaged future society as having, the question of the extent to which it can be regarded as socialist must be seriously faced. Bordiga does not seem to have realised the extent to which restricting decision-making to a minority within society, even to an elite of well-meaning social and scientific experts, conflicted with his definition of socialism as the abolition of private property.

The technocratic aspects of Bordiga's 'description of communism' were ignored by most of those influenced by him. Thanks in part to the writings of Bordiga, the realisation that socialism is neither state ownership nor workers' control of enterprises engaged in profit-and-loss accounting (whether in money or labour-time) has been encouraged, particularly in France, Italy and Spain.

WHERE LETS FAILS

If you listen to the enthusiasts they can recreate communities, cure unemployment, undermine the multinationals and even provide an alternative to the global capitalist economy. What can? LETS or Local Exchange and Trading Systems can.[19] This is what the enthusiasts said when they became popular. First, from Haverfordwest in Wales, Harry Wears:

> I'm really enthusiastic about LETS. I think it's the most exciting mechanism for social change I have ever come across. In LETS, debts don't accrue interest and there is no pressure to pay. A LETS cheque can't bounce, nor a LETS business go bust. LETS sees money as a symbol but, unlike sterling, it can't be manoeuvred to the detriment of the people using it.[20]

Then, from Southwark in London, Donnachadh McCarthy:

> It is a system to recreate a community economy which we were losing because of multinational companies and big supermarkets. Money which comes into Southwark is used once and then leaves via the banks which use it to finance projects elsewhere.[21]

And Ed May of the New Economics Foundation:

> With mass unemployment in Britain many people have the time but not the cash. LETS gives them access to things they would not otherwise have.[22]

Finally, commentator John Vidal:

> The implications, say the theorists, are enormous. In a cash-starved economy (one in five British households is severely in debt), despite the existence of wealth in the form of skills and resources, traditional exchange is hijacked by a lack of cash. With local currencies, as long as people make their goods and skills available, their exchange can go round and round. 'The community therefore becomes richer,' says Paul Ekins, a green economist.[23]

It is, of course, absurd that people who need things should go without even though the skills and resources to provide for them exist. I can go along with the LETS enthusiasts in denouncing this scandal of unmet needs alongside unused resources. The difference is that, while both of us criticise money, LETS enthusiasts answer 'yes' to the question, 'So, you want to go back to barter?' while I would answer 'no'. They want to retain exchange and trading with some new kind of money; I want a society based on common ownership geared to producing things directly for people to take and use in which exchange and trading, and money as the means of exchange, would be redundant. (Box 7.4 outlines ways that labour vouchers function, and the World Socialist Movement's position on labour vouchers.)

Return to Barter

LETS are essentially local barter clubs. A group of people with varying skills get together and agree to exchange services that they can provide with any other member without using money. Records, however, have to be kept. Each member has an account and when one member's services are used their account is credited with the exchange value of that service while that of the user is debited by the same amount. What normally happens is that each member is given a sort of chequebook, which they can use to pay for other members' services either at a published price or as agreed between the two. Clearly, for all this, a unit of account is needed. Some

NON-MARKET SOCIALISM   151

schemes define this unit in terms of labour time. Others tie it to the pound. The accounts could in fact be done in pounds but generally the unit is given a special name. In Britain, in Bath, it is an 'oliver', in Brixton it is a 'brick', in Reading a 'ready', and so on.

Do LETS really allow people, as is claimed, to bypass money and so have 'access to things they would not otherwise have'? Two unemployed people with different skills can always barter their services. Thus an unemployed plumber can repair an unemployed electrician's central heating in exchange for some rewiring by the electrician. A LETS is merely an extension of this: the plumber or electrician joins a barter club and gains access to a wider range of potential clients as well as access to a wider range of reciprocal services. Too often, though, services include things like aromatherapy, holistic massage, tarot reading and other such New Age fads not normally needed by the unemployed. So, it's an alternative to placing cards in newsagent's windows or relying on the grapevine to learn about work opportunities. As such, like the black economy, it's a way of surviving in the capitalist jungle but that's all. But, do not LETS help create a 'local community spirit'? Maybe, but no more than any other local club.

Small is Small

The trouble is that the idea has been hijacked by all sorts of currency cranks and funny money theorists who see it as the basis for an 'alternative money' and an 'alternative economy'. They overlook two important facts.

First, the activities covered by LETS, such as repairs and personal services, can all be carried out by a single individual and in the normal money economy could be done by self-employed people working on their own. In fact, from an economic point of view, LETS club members are acting as self-employed; a LETS is a club in which self-employed individuals barter their services. It could never extend beyond this to productive activities that require expensive equipment and plant and a large workforce – such as, precisely, the manufacture of the things that LETS members and the self-employed repair.

Second, there are definite limits to the size a LETS can attain. The biggest in Britain has only 300 members. If it got much bigger than this the administrative work of recording all the transactions would grow and could no longer be done by voluntary or part-time labour; people would have to be employed to do it, which would add to the running costs of the scheme and have to be shouldered by the members. The membership fees and transaction charges already levied by the scheme would rise. At a certain point this would cancel the advantages of being in the scheme and members would find it more convenient to re-enter the money economy and resort to newsagents' windows and contacts.

Funny Money

What most of the currency cranks who have latched on to the LETS idea envisage is converting the units of account the schemes use (such as olivers, bricks and readies) into a real money that would circulate. In fact most commentators, such as the journalist John Vidal, refer to the LETS units of account as 'currencies', but this is misleading.[24] They are not money; they do not circulate. They only exist on paper or computer disk as a record of transactions. In fact LETS are more cumbersome than using money. After all, with a real money that circulates, an individual account of a person's exchange transactions does not have to be kept.

Some of the advantages claimed for LETS units also apply to cash. So when Harry Wears says (in the quote above) 'a LETS cheque can't bounce', this is true, but neither can cash. Similarly, when it is argued that people have an incentive to use LETS credits – and that when they do accumulate them this does not give them any power to manipulate other people – as they do not pay interest, the same applies to cash. A large LETS credit balance is no more useful than a hoard of cash.

What is being advocated as the ideal is a money that cannot be accumulated and cannot be lent at interest, with LETS units being seen as the formula to achieve this. But such an 'alternative money' is never going to come into being because it would be worse than existing money. If you have an exchange economy (which LETS enthusiasts accept, as in the full name Local Exchange and Trading System) then conventional money is the best means of exchange. Not only does it allow many more exchanges to take place than barter or a modified form of barter like LETS, but also the payment and receipt of interest facilitates more exchange.

Banks are not, as some LETS theorists (along with the traditional currency cranks) suggest, villains who interrupt the normal circulation of money and goods by not making money available to match needs and resources unless they are paid a tribute in the form of interest. Banks are financial intermediaries, who borrow money from people who do not want to spend it immediately and lend it those who have something to spend money on but no money of their own. Naturally banks take precautions to ensure that they are going to get back any money they lend, but the overall result is that they help keep money circulating and exchange going. To want to keep exchange but do away with banks and the taking of interest is unrealistic in the extreme.

The way to end the scandal of unmet needs alongside unused skills and resources is not to retain the exchange economy while trying to get rid of some of its effects by reforming the money system. It is to get rid of the exchange economy altogether by establishing a society based on the common ownership of productive resources where goods and services would be produced directly for people to take and use and not be exchanged, or bought and sold, at all.

The Environment

A monetary economy gives rise to the illusion that the 'cost' of producing something is merely financial; indeed the word 'cost' is so associated with financial and monetary calculation that we are obliged to put it in inverted commas when we want to talk about it in a non-monetary sense. But the *real cost* of the pencil I'm using to write this is not 50 pence, but the amount of wood, graphite, labour, energy, and wear and tear of machines used in producing it. This will continue under socialism. Goods will not grow on trees, but will still require expenditure of effort and materials to produce them.

The point is that under socialism this expenditure of effort and materials will be estimated and calculated exclusively in kind, directly in terms of wood, graphite, machinery wear and tear, electricity, and so on (including working time). Socialism is concerned with conserving resources and will select productive methods that, other things being equal, use fewer materials and less energy. However, this will be only one factor taken into account in deciding which technical method of production to adopt.

The argument between monetary calculation and calculation in kind is not merely a technical argument about how to calculate and what units to use for this, but is an argument about the real meaning of words like 'value' and 'worth'. In socialism it is not the case that the choice of productive method will become a technical choice that can be left to engineers but that this choice too will be made in terms of the real advantages and disadvantages of alternative methods and in terms of, on the one hand, the utility of some good or some project in a particular circumstance at a particular time and, on the other hand, of the real 'costs' in the same circumstances and at the same time of the required materials, energy and productive effort.

To advocate monetary calculation is to advocate taking only one consideration into account when producing goods and making decisions about which productive methods to employ. This is patently absurd but it is what is imposed by capitalism. Naturally, it leads to all sorts of aberrations from the view of human interests, in particular ruling out a rational, long-term attitude towards conserving resources, and it imposes on the actual producers intolerable conditions – such as speed-ups, pain, stress, boredom, long hours, night work, shift work and accidents.

Socialism, because it will calculate directly in kind, will be able to take into account these other, more important, factors than production time. Naturally, this will lead to adopting different, often quite different, productive methods than under capitalism. Certain methods will be ruled out altogether. The fast-moving production lines associated with the manufacture of cars would be stopped forever (except perhaps in a museum of the horrors of capitalism); night work would be reduced to the strict minimum; particularly dangerous or unhealthy jobs would be automated or completely abandoned. Work can, and in fact must, become enjoyable and safe.

Since materials and energy, and work to the extent that it is not interesting and creative but only routine, are real 'costs', the aim will be to minimise them. Methods of production too will only change slowly. This will make decision-making about production much simpler. The alternative to monetary calculation in terms of exchange value is calculation in kind in terms of use values, of the real advantages and real costs of particular real alternatives in particular real circumstances.

The death of the commodity will be the beginning of a truly human society existing in harmony with the rest of nature.

Box 7.1   Milovan Djilas, Ex-Vice President of Yugoslavia, on Communist Workers and Plans

Compulsory labour in the Communist system is the result of monopoly of ownership over all, or almost all, national property. The worker finds himself in the position of having not only to sell his labour; he must sell it under conditions which are beyond his control, since he is unable to seek another, better employer.

▶

There is only one employer, the state. The worker has no choice but to accept the employer's terms. The worst and most harmful element in early capitalism from the worker's standpoint – the labour market – has been replaced by the monopoly over labour of the ownership of the new class. This has not made the worker any freer.

When the USSR became the first country to embark upon national planning, its leaders, who were Marxists, connected this planning with Marxism. The truth is this: although Marx's teachings were the idealistic basis of the revolution in Russia, his teachings also became the cover for later measures taken by the Soviet leaders...

Although leaning heavily on Marx in the beginning, Communist planning has a more profound idealistic and material background. How can an economy be administered other than as a planned economy when it has or is going to have a single owner?

Source: Milovan Djilas, *The New Class: An Analysis of the Communist System*, London: Unwin Books, 1966 [1957], pp. 103, 108.

Box 7.2   On the World Socialist Movement

The World Socialist Movement:

- claims that socialism will, and must, be a wageless, moneyless, worldwide society of common (not state) ownership and democratic control of the means of wealth production and distribution.
- claims that socialism will be a sharp break with capitalism with no 'transition period' or gradual implementation of socialism (although socialism will be a dynamic, changing society once it is established).
- claims that there can be no state in a socialist society...
- claims that only the vast majority, acting consciously in its own interests, for itself, by itself, can create socialism.
- opposes any vanguardist approach, minority-led movements, and leadership, as inherently undemocratic (among other negative things).

▶

- promotes a peaceful democratic revolution, achieved through force of numbers and understanding.
- neither promotes, nor opposes, reforms to capitalism.
- claims that there is one working class, worldwide.
- lays out the fundamentals of what a socialist society must be, but does not presume to tell the future socialist society how to go about its business...

Source: 'How the WSM is different from other groups', accessed at the World Socialist Movement site, 1 March 2010, at http://www.worldsocialism.org.

Box 7.3 Conversation from William Morris's Utopian Novel *News From Nowhere*

'It is clear from all that we hear and read, that in the last age of civilization men had got into a vicious circle in the matter of production of wares. They had reached a wonderful facility of production, and... they had gradually created (or allowed to grow, rather) a most elaborate system of buying and selling, which has been called the World-Market; and that World-Market, once set a-going, forced them to go on making more and more of these wares, whether they needed them or not. So that while (of course) they could not free themselves from the toil of making real necessaries, they created a never-ending series sham or artificial necessaries, which became, under the iron rule of the aforesaid World-Market, of equal importance to them with the real necessaries which supported life. By all this they burdened themselves with a prodigious mass of work merely for the sake of keeping their wretched system going.'

'Yes – and then?' said I.

'Why, then, since they had forced themselves to stagger along under this horrible burden of unnecessary production, it became impossible for them to look upon labour and its results from any other point of view than one – to wit, the ceaseless endeavour to expend the least possible amount of labour on any article made, and yet at the same time make as many articles as possible. To this "cheapening of production", as it was called, everything was sacrificed: the happiness of the workman at his work, nay, his

▶

most elementary comfort and bare health, his food, his clothes, his dwelling, his leisure, his amusement, his education – his life, in short – did not weigh a grain of sand in the balance against this dire necessity of "cheap production" of things, a great part of which were not worth producing at all. Nay, we are told, and we must believe it, so overwhelming is the evidence, though many of our people scarcely *can* believe it, that even rich and powerful men, the masters of the poor devils aforesaid, submitted to live amidst sights and sounds and smells which it is in the very nature of man to abhor and flee from, in order that their riches might bolster up this supreme folly. The whole community, in fact, was cast into the jaws of this ravening monster, "the cheap production" forced upon it by the World-Market.'

Source: William Morris, *News From Nowhere*, London: Routledge & Kegan Paul, 1970 [1890], pp. 79–80.

Box 7.4   The World Socialist Movement on 'Labour Vouchers'

What are Labour Vouchers?

Labour vouchers (or labour cheques, labour certificates, labour-time vouchers) are a device suggested to govern demand for goods in 'socialism', much as money does today under capitalism. Those who support labour vouchers have several different approaches or definitions of them. We try here to clarify what labour vouchers are ... we use the words 'paid', 'earned', 'purchase' and similar words to mean actions in 'labour voucher socialism' that would be similar to what those words mean today.

Most labour voucher supporters agree that:

1. Labour vouchers are paid for hours of labour performed.
2. Labour vouchers are not money.
3. Labour vouchers are used to purchase goods and services.

But they disagree with each other on the following points.

1. How are labour vouchers apportioned?
a. Each worker gets the same quantity for each hour worked. If the agreed upon rate is 100 labour vouchers for 1 hour, everyone who works for one hour gets 100 labour vouchers.

▶

b. The number of labour vouchers paid per hour depends upon the difficulty or desirability of the work performed.

2. *Temporary or Permanent?*

a. Labour vouchers are a temporary measure. The general feeling here seems to be that people are used to money now and need time to wean themselves from it.

b. Labour vouchers will be permanent. These advocates say that society needs some method to restrict access to goods, and/or that without them there is no way to determine what items should be produced in what quantity when there are conflicting desires for goods.

3. *What about those who do not or cannot work?*

a. Basic necessities should be free to all.

b. Enough labour vouchers should be given out to those who do not work (or don't work enough) to ensure that they can afford basic necessities (and perhaps more).

c. Enough labour vouchers should be given out to those determined (by someone or some group) to be needy, or justifiably unable to work, to ensure that they can afford basic necessities (and perhaps more).

4. *What about non-traditional work, or work not paid today? (housework, art, etc.)*

a. Pay for housework, art etc. on an hourly basis like any other work (possibly including difficulty factors, etc.).

b. Pay for art based upon desirability: how many people go to see it or some such measure.

c. Straight exchange: art is purchased with labour vouchers for whatever the buyer and seller agree upon.

5. *Can labour vouchers circulate?*

a. No. Once a purchase is made the labour vouchers are either destroyed, or must be re-earned through labour.

b. Yes. It appears that there are few who believe that labour vouchers should circulate like money, but there are those who believe that they can be 'invested' (although not for profit, proponents assure), or that when something is purchased, the seller could use them for their own purchases.

▶

> *Why the World Socialist Movement Opposes Labour Vouchers*
> ... Labour vouchers would tend to maintain the idea that our human worth is determined by how much or how many goods we can own (or produce). Labour vouchers require administration... Labour vouchers imply that someone must police who takes the goods produced by society... a waste of human labour in socialism...
>
> Source: 'Labour Vouchers' at the World Socialist Movement (WSM) site, accessed 1 March 2010, at http://www.worldsocialism.org.

NOTES

All italics in quotes are preserved from the originals.

1. Milovan Djilas, *The New Class*, London: Thames and Hudson, 1957.
2. Aneurin Bevan, *In Place of Fear*, London: Quartet Books, 1978 [1952].
3. Ludwig von Mises, *Economic Calculation in the Socialist Commonwealth*, Auburn, AL: Ludwig von Mises Institute, 1990 [1920].
4. See, for instance, Adam Buick, 'Why the market is not inevitable', *Free Life: the Journal of the Libertarian Alliance*, Vol. 6, No. 4, 1991, pp. 17–21.
5. Pieter Lawrence drafted the pamphlet *Socialism As A Practical Alternative*, London: Socialist Party of Great Britain, 1994.
6. Robin Cox, 'The "economic calculation" controversy: unravelling of a myth', *Common Voice* [online journal], 1, February–April 2004, accessed 30 June 2011, at http://www.cvoice.org/cv3cox.htm.
7. John Crump and Adam Buick, *State Capitalism: The Wages System under New Management*, London: Macmillan, 1986.
8. This section draws on Adam Buick's 'Marx: money must go', *Socialist Standard*, September 1985.
9. Karl Marx, 'On the Jewish question' in Karl Marx and Frederick Engels, *Collected Works* Vol. 3, London: Lawrence and Wishart, 1975, p. 168.
10. Ibid., p. 170.
11. Ibid., pp. 172, 174.
12. Karl Marx, 'Comments on James Mill, Elémens d'Economie Politique', in Marx and Engels, *Collected Works* Vol. 3, pp. 211–28, esp. p. 221.
13. Ibid., p. 212.
14. Karl Marx, *Economic and Philosophical Manuscripts of 1844*, in Marx & Engels *Collected Works* Vol. 3, p. 307.
15. This section draws on Adam Buick 'Bordigism' in Maximilien Rubel and John Crump (eds), *Non-Market Socialism in the Nineteenth and Twentieth Centuries*, Houndmills: Macmillan, 1987.
16. Amadeo Bordiga, 'Le programme revolutionaire' [1958] in J. Camatte, *Bordiga et la Passion du Communisme: Textes Essentiels de Bordiga et Reperes Biographiques*, Paris: Spartacus, 1974.

17. Amadeo Bordiga, *Structure Economique et Social de la Russie d'Aujourdhui*, Paris: Editions de l'Oubli, 1975, p. 310.
18. Amadeo Bordiga, *Russie et Revolution Dans la Theorie Marxiste*, Paris: Spartacus, 1972 [1952], p. 172.
19. This section draws on Adam Buick, 'Where LETS schemes fail', *Socialist Standard* (1994).
20. Harry Wears cited in G. Morgan, 'Bartering – an alternative economy or just returning the compliment?', *Woman & Home*, October 1993, pp. 32–4.
21. Donnachadh McCarthy cited in W. Bennett, 'Payment in kind is replacing the pound', *Independent*, 13 December 1993, p. 6.
22. Ed May, cited in John Vidal, 'Take a few pigs along to the Pie in the Sky Café and watch payment go bob-bob-bobbin' along', *Guardian*, 12 March 1994, p. 12.
23. Vidal, 'Take a few pigs along to the Pie in the Sky Café and watch payment go bob-bob-bobbin' along'.
24. Ibid.

8
Self-Management and Efficiency

Mihailo Marković

EDITORS' NOTE

Mihailo Marković was a prominent member of the humanist Marxist Praxis Group, constructively criticising developments in the Socialist Federal Republic of Yugoslavia (1963–1992). *Praxis* was an intellectual journal that drew on Marx's early humanist writings and advocated a creative use of Marxism within the Yugoslav model of self-management. Marković's analysis draws on his experiences, is engaged and practical, and, for non-market socialists, addresses some key questions associated with organisation and the satisfaction of human needs. Except for the two boxes with excerpts from other works by Marković, this chapter is a reprint of the final chapter of his *The Contemporary Marx: Essays on Humanist Communism* (Nottingham: Spokesman Books, 1974).

The following two questions seem to sum up most controversies about the idea and existing practical experience of self-management:

1. What is self-management?
2. How is the principle of self-management to be reconciled with the principle of efficiency in a modern economy?

That the former is a real problem follows from the fact that the term 'self-management' (see Box 8.1) is being used in a very indiscriminate way covering a number of different social forms which in fact lack some necessary conditions for correct classification as self-management.

Thus: *workers' control* is by all means an important, progressive objective in a class society. And yet it may only contribute to preventing undesirable decisions; it is still far from determining a positive policy in enterprises and local communities.

Workers' participation is also a progressive demand that has been gaining more and more ground in the international labour movement. And yet this is a broad, vague demand and in various forms could be accepted by the bourgeois ruling-class without really affecting the general social framework of a capitalist society. This is because: workers might be given rights to participate only in decision-making on some matters of secondary importance; they might be in the minority in a given body of management; they might be allowed only advisory or consultative functions and not the right to take decisions; finally, they might be denied access to information and left in the position only to endorse decisions that have been prepared by others and presented without any real alternatives.

Dictatorship of the proletariat, which in Marx's theory referred to a transition period of increasing democratisation, is nowadays associated with the experience of a strong, centralised authoritarian state which is actually in the hands of a political bureaucracy, and which uses the phrases 'the power of the Soviets' or 'workers state' in order to conceal and mystify the real oppressive nature of social relationships.

However, the idea of self-management should also not be mixed up with the idea of a mere *decentralisation*: an atomised, disintegrated society, lacking necessary coordination and conscious regulation would be at the mercy of blind, alienated social forces. Self-management is surely not the absence of any management and conscious direction within the society as a whole.

Here we come to the second question mentioned above. The most customary objection to self-management (as some form of social system in which people themselves somehow take care of matters of common interest) is that such a system is incompatible with the demands of technological efficiency and rationality in a complex modern industrial society. The argument is: self-management is a noble humanitarian idea but it cannot be brought to life because workers and ordinary citizens are not educated enough to run a modern state and a modern economy. Professional experts are needed to do the job. Therefore self-management is either a utopia or must be reduced to a rather limited participation in decision-making.

This kind of criticism surely overestimates the usefulness of the techno-structure and expertise in decision-making on crucial social problems. But it points to a real problem which can be resolved only by developing a rather sophisticated model of self-management – which leads us back to our first problem.

The idea of self-management rests on a more general philosophical principle – that of *self-determination.*

Self-determination is a process in which conscious practical activity of human individuals becomes one of the necessary and sufficient conditions of individual and group life. This is a process contrary to *external* determination, i.e. a process in which necessary and sufficient conditions of the life of some human individuals are exclusively factors outside their control and independent of their consciousness and will. To be sure self-determination is always conditioned by a given social situation, by the level of technology, the given structure of production, the nature of political institutions, the level of culture, the existing tradition and habits of human behaviour. However, it is essential for determination: (1) that all these external objective conditions constitute only the framework of possibilities of a certain course of events, whereas upon the subjective choice and conscious human activity will depend which of these possibilities will be realised; (2) that the subjective choice is autonomous, genuinely free and not heteronomous and compulsory. This means that the subject by his own activity creates a new condition of the process instead of merely repeating time and again an act to which he was compelled or for which he was programmed. This act need not be arbitrary and groundless; it should be an act of self-realisation, of the actualisation of basic human capacities, of the satisfaction of genuine human needs.

This active role in the course of events, this creation of new conditions instead of mechanical reproduction according to the laws of the system and inherited instincts, this extension of the framework of possibilities instead of permanently remaining within that framework, is a specific power of men, characteristic of every human individual, present at least in the form of a latent disposition.

Under certain social conditions this power can be *alienated*. It will be concentrated in the hands of a privileged social group and becomes its monopoly. Alienation is a consequence of: (1) the division of labour, (2) the accumulation of the surplus product, (3) the creation of institutions the function of which is to take care of common social interests, (4) increasing mediation between the individual needs and the needs of the whole society.

Political and economic alienation involves a process of social polarisation which at one extreme transforms a conscious, potentially creative subject into an object, into a reified, oppressed and exploited mass, whereas at the other extreme it transforms a normal, limited and fragile human subject into an authority, into a mystified entity that has supernatural power and control over human lives.

Such a critical analysis leads to the question: under what social conditions would the life of individuals and communities be less and less reified, less and less contingent upon external authority, and more and more self-determined? There are four such basic conditions.

The first such condition is negative: the coordination and direction of social processes must no longer be in the hands of any institution that enjoys a monopoly of economic and political power (such as capital, the state with its coercive apparatus, and the party with its bureaucracy and hierarchy of power). People themselves must decide about all matters of common interest. And this is possible only if the society is organised as a federation of councils composed of non-professional, non-alienated representatives of the people at all levels of social structure: in the enterprises and local communities, in the regions and whole branches of activity and, finally, for the society as a whole.

The second condition of self-determination is reliable knowledge of the situation, of its scarcities and limitations, of the existing trends, of the conflicts to be resolved, of the alternative possibilities of further development. Freedom is incompatible with ignorance or with a biased perception of reality. The right to take decisions without previous access to information is a mere formality: self-determination becomes a façade behind which a real manipulation by others, by political bureaucracy and technocracy, takes place. Therefore, a genuine self-determination presupposes the formation of critical study groups at all levels of social decision-making, from the local community and enterprise to the federation as a whole.

The third condition of self-determination is the existence of a powerful, democratic public opinion. The genuine general will of the people can be formed only through open communication, free expression of critical opinions, and dialogue. It is clear, then, that any monopoly of the mass media (by either big business, the church, the state, or the Party) must be dismantled. Such a monopoly enables a ruling elite to manipulate the rest of the population, to create artificial needs, to impose its ideology and to rule by consent of a 'silent majority'. Therefore *mass media* must be free and genuinely socialised.

The fourth condition of self-determination is the discovery of the true *self* of the community, of the real general needs of the people (see Box 8.2). This condition is basic and most difficult to achieve. Therefore, most of what passes under the name of freedom in contemporary society is only an illusory freedom: mere opportunity of choice among two or more alternatives. But alternatives are often imposed, choice is arbitrary and even when it has been guided by a consistent criterion of evaluation, this criterion is hardly ever authentic, based on a critical, enlightened examination of one's real needs and one's long-range interests. This condition clearly assumes a universal humanist point of view and practically implies creation of a new socialist culture and a humanist revolution of all education. Discovery of one's self, of one's specific individual powers and potential capacities, learning how to develop them and use them as a socialised human being that cares about the needs of other individuals – would have to become the primary task of a new humanist education.

The preceding analysis clearly indicates that the transition from reification and external determination to freedom and self-determination is a matter of a whole epoch.

Existing forms of self-management, seen in this broad historical perspective, are surely of great revolutionary importance but they should be regarded as only the initial steps. With general material and cultural development many other steps would have to be made, many present limitations would have to be overcome. Thus, organs of the class state (in the sense of an instrument of class rule) would have to be replaced by the organs of self-management composed of the workers' delegates who are democratically elected, replaceable, rotatable, and by no means corrupted by material privileges and the alluring career of a professional politician. Planning would have to be a synthesis of decentralised and democratic-centralist decision-making. The market economy, with its production for profit, would have to be gradually replaced by production for genuine human needs. With further technological advance, productivity of work will quickly increase while, at the same time, present-day hunger for consumer goods will be replaced by entirely different aspirations. Present-day overstressed concern about production and management will naturally tend to diminish. Self-determination in various other aspects of free and creative *praxis* will naturally gain in importance.

There are two possible ways in which a humanist philosopher might challenge the very idea of efficiency.

First, he might argue that beyond a certain high level of technological, economic and cultural development efficiency will begin to lose its importance. After all, efficiency in its present-day meaning is ability to produce a desired result, to perform well a certain defined role in the social division of labour. In a highly developed future society automata will increasingly replace man in routine physical and intellectual operations. As 'production of *specified, desired* results' and 'performance of well-*defined* roles' are typical routine activities, it would follow that man will let computers be efficient instead of him, and he will engage more and more in the production of *unique, beautiful* objects, and in playing *new, surprising, not-defined-in-advance* roles. In other words he will engage in *praxis* and in *praxis* the question of efficiency either does not arise at all or is of secondary importance.

Second, it might be argued that the concept of efficiency is devoid of any humanist meaning. It is apparently value-free and ideologically neutral. On closer scrutiny, however, it turns out to be ideologically loaded, and encouraging certain harmful and dangerous attitudes towards nature and existing society. Maximum efficiency in conquering and controlling natural surroundings means a dangerously growing rate of waste of scarce material resources and available forms of energy. Maximum efficiency in running present-day social organisations and institutions means full-scale endorsement of their inhuman, degrading practices. For unjust systems efficiency really is their best chance of survival.

Under given assumptions this critique is perfectly sound. In a highly developed future society both material production and the maximisation of efficiency will become social goals of secondary importance. But they are still a primary concern of every present-day society. Man will liberate himself from too-well-defined and ordered roles in material production and will afford to relax about efficiency only when he masters it, when he catches hold of it to such an extent that he will be able to relegate it to machines.

And even then there is a sense of the term 'efficiency' which will always be associated with achievement of goals of human activity, whatever these goals might be.

Which leads us to the second argument. From the fact that 'efficiency' is a neutral concept it follows that it could be – and as a matter of fact is – associated with all kinds of wasteful irrational and inhuman practices. But it also follows that its meaning would be entirely different with respect to progressive and rational human goals. After all, no theory and no program of social change is possible without some neutral concepts. There is an element of neutrality in most concepts, including self-management. There is no guarantee that self-management will always, in itself, make people happier, more rational, less alienated. It is only part of a complex project – not the absolute.

With these qualifications in mind one has to take the problem of compatibility of self-management with efficiency quite seriously. While dozens of countries average one hundred dollars of national income *per capita* or even less, there is still poverty of large segments of population even in Europe and North America, while human beings still spend the best part of their life in boring, technical work, further increases in efficiency are a necessary condition of human liberation and possible self-realisation.

Human liberation is certainly inconceivable without the right of every individual to participate in social decision-making. But is it really the case that full, meaningful participation of each citizen destroys efficiency?

This does not happen if the following three groups of conditions are satisfied:

(1) The first group follows analytically from the very concept of *integral self-management*. Workers' councils in the enterprises and the councils of local communities are not isolated atoms but elements of a whole network at different levels (from the *territorial* point of view: local–regional–national–federative; from the *professional* point of view: basic unit – the whole enterprise – the branch – the community of all producers).

Any individual has direct decision-making power in the basic units where he works and where he lives, and in addition he has an indirect decision-making power at higher levels through his delegates (freely elected, rotatable, always replaceable, responsible to him.) Any unit has all necessary autonomy and responsibility for decision-making on matters of its specific concern. But there must also be a readiness to cooperate and harmonise interests with other units of the system. On the other hand, higher-level organs of self-management must have the maximum possible understanding of the particular interests of each sub-system. They are vastly different from the organs of the state in so far as they are not instruments of any ruling elite, they don't oppress, and tend to reduce interference to the minimum. But in matters of common interest, after a certain policy has been widely discussed and accepted, its decisions must be binding. Otherwise, social life would lack a minimum of necessary organisation and coordination, and would tend to disintegrate.

(2) Another group of conditions follows from the general characteristics of self-determination discussed above. Organs of self-management operate in a field characterised by the following features: mass media of communication are free, they contribute to the creation of a genuinely democratic public opinion; political parties in the classical sense are absent but there is a plurality of various other forms of non-authoritarian and non-manipulative organisations, and there is an ongoing process of education and raising of socialist consciousness of all individuals.

(3) The third group of conditions under which the principles of participatory democracy and efficiency would be reconciled derives from analysis of the basic stages of the process of decision-making and of different kinds of knowledge and competence needed. Each rational technical decision presupposes (a) a critical analysis of the situation (including scrutinising the effectiveness of policies adopted in the past), (b) a *long-range program of development*, a set of basic *goals* of the organisation, with respect to which all concrete technical decisions would constitute the *means*. In other words, there are three distinct necessary functions in the process of rational decision-making: One is *fact-finding, analytic, informative*. Another one is *governing, political*. The third one is *technical, managerial*. Accordingly there are three distinct kinds of knowledge relative to these functions: factual knowledge (*know that*); theoretical knowledge of the basic needs of the people in a certain situation (*know what* is good and just to do); technical knowledge of the ways in which basic decisions can most effectively be realised (*know how*). Thus, in addition to the organ of self-management composed of wise, experienced persons who understand the basic needs at a given moment (who know what could and should be done), there must be, on the one hand, a group of analysts who critically study the implementation of adopted programs and the

changes in external and internal factors, and, on the other hand, the technical management, composed of people who 'know how', who elaborate concrete alternative policy proposals, and who try to bring to life the decisions of the organ of self-management in the most efficient possible way.

In this complex structure the technocratic tendencies are the main threat to self-management. (To be sure, while there is still a state and a ruling party, much greater danger comes from political bureaucracy. However, we are discussing here a model of a highly developed, integrated self-management in which the functions of the traditional state and authoritarian party have been taken over by the central organs of self-management.) A permanent source of technocratic tendencies is the fact that it is the managers who hold the executive power, who usually have better access to data and who, therefore, might try to manipulate the self-managing council. Excessive power of the managers, the executives, is dangerous because their understanding of social needs might be very limited and their scale of value very biased, giving priority to typically instrumental values of growth, expansion and order. Contrary to a common prejudice that modern society requires the rule of experts, the truth seems to be that experts are the least qualified candidates for good, wise, rational rulers, precisely because they are only experts, and their rationality is only technical.

Self-management has at least three powerful possible devices to resist manipulation by the techno-structure: (1) independent access to data, (2) the iron rule that the management always prepares its proposals for the organ of self-management in the form of alternatives among which to choose, (3) the right to elect, re-elect or replace the manager.

The organ of self-management must have its own informative and analytic service, and not depend on the manager. Otherwise, it will be at the mercy of the half-truths produced by the management whenever it is interested in having its own particular point of view adopted.

The organ of self-management must, time and again, assert its right of freely taking a decision after carefully examining other possible alternatives. Once it is reduced to an institution that merely votes on proposals prepared by the management it clearly becomes a victim of manipulation.

In order to keep the balance and to be able to assert its rights, the organ of self-management must have the power of rotating the manager. There is no real danger that a 'primitive', 'ignorant' workers' council will fire a good, efficient manager. The experience of Yugoslav self-management is that if the workers' council ever fires a manager this is either because he is utterly incompetent or because he is too authoritarian (or both). But the real danger is rather that the workers use this right too rarely or too late, after considerable damage has already been done, and the enterprise operates with heavy losses. This reluctance to react promptly indicates that what jeopardises the efficiency of production in socialism is rather too little than too much workers' participation.

A developed self-management has the historical opportunity to overcome both wasteful and irrational models of contemporary efficiency: one imposed by capital and the market, the other dictated by the authoritarian political machine.

Box 8.1   Mihailo Marković on Self-Management

In a restricted sense self-management refers to the direct involvement of workers in basic decision-making in individual enterprises. Means of production are socialized (owned by the workers' community or by the entire society)... In a more general sense self-management is a democratic form of organization of the whole economy constituted by several layers of councils and assemblies... At each level the self-management body is the highest authority responsible for the development and implementation of policy, and coordination among relatively autonomous enterprises.

In the most general sense self-management is the basic structure of socialist society, in economy, politics and culture. In all domains of public life – education, culture, scientific research, health services, etc. – basic decision-making is in the hands of self-management councils and assemblies organized on both productive and territorial principles. In this sense it transcends the limits of the state. Members of the self-management bodies are freely elected, responsible to their electorate, recallable, rotatable, without any material privileges... In contrast to parliamentary democracy it is not restricted to politics, but extends to the economy and culture; it emphasizes decentralization, direct participation and delegation of power for the purpose of a minimum of necessary coordination...

... As early as 'On the Jewish question' Marx expressed the view that 'human emancipation will only be complete when the

▶

individual... has recognized and organized his own powers as *social* powers so that he no longer separates this social power from himself as a *political* power'... In *Capital III* (Ch. 48) Marx explains the idea of freedom in the sphere of material production: 'the associated producers regulate their exchange with nature rationally' and 'under conditions most favourable to, and worthy of, their human nature'...

... All socialist revolutionary upheavals, whether successful or not, from the Paris Commune to Polish *Solidarity*, more or less spontaneously created organs of self-management.

Source: Mihailo Marković, 'Self-management', in Bottomore, Tom (ed.) *A Dictionary of Marxist Thought*, Cambridge: Harvard University Press, 1983, pp. 437–8.

Box 8.2   Mihailo Marković on Needs

Up to this point, science has not been highly engaged in the problem of human needs. With respect to a typology of needs, much less has been achieved than in the typology of minerals, insects, or nuclear particles. Still worse, as long as science is predominately descriptive and value-laden, it lacks the criteria for making an indispensible distinction between authentic and artificial needs...

The prevailing theory in all capitalist societies begins with the principle that the market is the basic regulator of production and that the market should indicate the type and quality of goods desired by the consumers. Therefore, the market is supposed to bring a knowledge of the structure of human needs, which individual companies can take account of in their production plans.

... However, the proposed [socialist] solution proved to be entirely unsatisfactory: if planning committees and political forums are to decide which human needs should be satisfied and developed, and which should not, then they obtain a tremendous power which exceeds every other in history...

Complete identification and fulfilment of authentic human needs are possible only under the condition of transcending manipulation by both the modern market economy and by bureaucratic authority.

▶

Only under conditions of free experimentation, self-government, and training for self-knowledge and self-improvement is it possible to develop a critical consciousness of artificial needs and to have an orientation which leads to the satisfaction of true needs – those which lead to the realisation of specific, fundamental human abilities.

Source: Mihailo Marković, 'Man and his Natural Surroundings', in his *The Contemporary Marx: Essays on Humanist Communism*, Nottingham: Spokesman Books, 1974, pp. 140–52, esp. pp. 150–1.

9
Labour Credit – Twin Oaks Community

Kat Kinkade with the Twin Oaks Community

How can anybody explain the purpose of Utopia? It's like explaining the purpose of Heaven. It's just the place you want to be, that's all.

Kat Kinkade[1]

EDITORS' NOTE

This chapter is compiled from edited extracts from two books by Kat Kinkade about the Twin Oaks Community, which is located in Virginia (USA). She helped to found this Community, which was established in 1967 on 123 acres of farm and forest lands. She died in 2008, so her material, which appears as the chapter proper, has been expanded and updated with edited extracts – in shaded boxes – from the Twin Oaks 'Labor Policy' written by Community members in 2009, to show how the system has worked recently.[2]

Basically labour credits are Twin Oaks' internal economic currency. One credit equals one hour of work. Other than the obvious exceptions for the sick and the aging, every member is required to work an equal number of hours for the Community each week. We call this 'doing quota'.

QUOTA

Quota is set by the planners according to the needs of the Community. [In 2009 it was 42 hours a week.] This may sound high at first, but it turns out to be a leisurely pace when one considers how much it covers, including: house cleaning, shopping, childcare, laundry, cooking, mowing, household repairs, volunteering, going to the doctor, voting, writing letters to Congress, going to relatives' funerals, and repainting our own rooms, in addition to virtually unlimited sick time. Every year we add some new projects to that list. Dozens of administrative and planning meetings are creditable, too.

Anyone may take credit for teaching anything to anyone, as long as the learner wants to learn it. Normal uses for teaching credits include teaching a language, a musical instrument, a recreational skill or academic subject. The situation becomes borderline when one person teaches their favourite friend to recognise forest flora, and they end up making love among the wild violets. Use your judgement and your conscience about how much of that to take credit for.

Counting your work in hourly units gives us a great deal of flexibility. Members may and usually do choose to vary their days and weeks by doing several different jobs. To as great an extent as possible, members choose their own work. People may well want to do more work than the minimum requirement, 'over quota' labour credits accumulated for future leisure/vacation time.

It takes two people about two days to do the labour assigning each week, juggling the personal requests with the Community's varying needs for different kinds of labour. Out of this investment in clerical labour we get:

1. individual labour schedules
2. general schedules posted where everyone can find out who is scheduled for what
3. bookkeeping in which members' surplus credits or deficits are recorded and data on all work areas is summarised and tallied.

The computer does what it is good for after the human has completed the part requiring judgement. All jobs are covered with assigned workers; all members have a fair share of the work. There are simpler ways of distributing work but none that grants a comparable degree of flexibility and personal choice. This is the main reason the basic system has survived.

The Labour Credit is the Basic Economic Unit of Twin Oaks

1. In general, the Community does not permit people to get more than one credit per hour, even for two jobs done simultaneously.

For example, chaining braid while attending a creditable meeting gives a person credit for either the braid or the meeting, or half each.

2. Work is creditable if it is part of the regular system or otherwise approved by a manager or the planners.
3. No one may claim credit for work done by another person. No one may pass credits to another person without the receiver doing work to earn them.
4. Credits have no cash value and cannot be converted to money. There is no good way for a member who is leaving the Community to do anything with their positive labour balance except take vacation.
5. Members do not earn any equity that they can take with them if they leave. Their work goes toward maintaining and improving the Community, as well as being a source of personal satisfaction.
6. Labour records for all members are the property of the whole Community. The information is not confidential.

The labour manager has various reports, which may be of interest to members, all available to be looked at any time.

1. Labour credit sheets for past weeks.
2. Quarterly reports of work in each area, summarised by person and by area.
3. Quarterly and yearly summary reports on all areas, not by person.
4. Weekly labour budget reports.
5. Monthly vacation balance report.
6. Products For Friends (PFFs) hours report.
7. Personal Service Credits (PSCs) claimed. The record of donations to various credit funds.
8. Weekly masters. Every week assigned work is put into the computer from the labour sheets. It prints out a report we can refer to during the week to see who is supposed to be doing what.

VARIABLE CREDIT EXPERIMENT

The idea of the labour credit was originally inspired by Skinner's *Walden Two*, but the way we use the system now is different in one fundamental way from the system suggested.[3] Skinner, having read Edward Bellamy's *Looking Backward*, was impressed with the idea that different kinds of work should be rewarded differently. That is, the more onerous a task, the more credit it should earn. Part of the charm of this idea, which we dubbed the 'variable credit', is that it reverses the traditional remunerative formula – that reward for work is determined by supply and demand, and therefore skilled work, however pleasant, pays better than unskilled, however wearing or demeaning. We agreed with Bellamy and Skinner that the traditional scheme is unfair and unnecessary, and we embraced the variable credit with a fervour almost ideological.

Ultimately we rejected the variable credit, both in theory and in practice, but in the five years during which we honoured and experimented with it, we assumed the principle was basic and important, and therefore gave it a very serious try. Our first problem was to find a fair and objective method to determine which jobs were in fact less desirable than others, so they could be given a higher credit value.

It didn't work just to ask people what they thought. The lure of higher credit tended to set people into competition with each other, sometimes squabbling with each other in their rival claims to personal suffering and sacrifice. A system in which each person rated all the jobs according to *personal* preference – the value of the credit varying accordingly – held certain logic, and we used it for over a year. This sometimes resulted in having two people on a shift, doing identical work, but one getting more credit than the other. Intuitively this felt bad to people, no matter how logically it had been arrived at. We kept trying to foolproof the system, but there were always people who figured out how to manipulate it for their own benefit.

We experimented with at least four variations on the variable credit system, and meanwhile vocal discontent with it grew louder and more convincing. What Skinner didn't have any way of knowing is that a group of forty members or more will have a broad enough range of taste and preference so that it becomes pointless to define 'more (or less) desirable work'. There is almost no type of work that does not attract someone. When we do run across jobs that nobody wants to do, manipulating the credit does not help.

The variable credit idea failed to make sense as soon as we were faced with any very large or endless task. Though it is pleasant to make hammocks in our sociable, relaxed workshop, making 12,000 of them every year gets tiresome, and toward the end of a high-production season, members complain. The same thing happens when we process hundreds of jars of tomatoes and peppers. No matter what the work, it will attract workers unless and until there is too much of it. Then it suddenly becomes 'undesirable'.

Recording Work

We keep records to only one decimal place. Thus, an hour and a quarter is either 1.3 or 1.2 but not 1.25. The accuracy to which labour records are kept varies. Some carry their sheets with them and write things down when they do them. Others estimate at the end of the day. Still others try to remember after several days have passed – definitely not recommended!

If you do work and don't know what to call it, ask almost anybody. Most members have a very clear knowledge of the basics. However, if you want to know something complex, you'll get the most accurate information from the labour manager or their assistants.

At the end of the week add up your sheet. If your sheet is late, you may lose the 2.5 credit bonus, but we need the sheet anyway.

Failure to turn the sheet in means no credits for the week.

A corollary is that work seems very desirable when there is not enough of it to go around. I remember a time when the Community had not done any construction for a couple of years and then decided to build a new residence. Under the bidding system, members were competing to be construction workers. Some said they would build for 0.8 credit per hour; then others offered bids of 0.7 and 0.6. In desperation someone said that if he was appointed to the crew, he would do it for no credit. Then someone else claimed to be willing to do it for negative credits – paying for the privilege from his labour balance.

We eventually made up the crew by drawing lots and assigning an arbitrary 0.8 per hour for the work. Within two weeks of the start of the building, the workers realised what they had done to themselves by competitive bidding. They could not meet quota. In order to get forty-six credits, they would have to work a steady fifty-eight hours a week throughout the construction season. Besides, after the first few days, construction work did not turn out to be as much fun as it had seemed.

During the same period, people forced the value of managerial work down to 0.9 per hour, on the theory that planning and management are more fun jobs than other jobs. Some managers responded by quitting their jobs. The people who replaced them soon discovered they didn't want the responsibilities after all, especially not at reduced 'pay'. We pronounced the variable credit system a failure in 1974, and since then almost all work earns one credit per hour.

Slack Labour

In the early years of labour budgeting we did the obvious thing – predicted the labour needs of each area, based on the previous years' records, added a small fudge factor, and set the resulting amounts as budgets. This is easy to understand, but it didn't work very well. There were always areas that needed more labour than budgeted, several others that didn't need as much as predicted, and plenty of spare people-power that couldn't be assigned within budgets. This is because predicting isn't accurate. The first solution was simply to ignore overspent budgets as long as the labour supply held up. But this method favoured managers who were careless and punished those who paid attention to their budgets. So we sought something fairer.

What we do now is give most areas a budget slightly bigger than we think they are going to need. This results in our apportioning more labour than we predict having. We calculate the amount of labour we believe we will have, and then add an amount between 5 and 20 per cent.

As a result, few areas run out of credits, and most areas use less than they have. The unused labour is called 'slack'. Very occasionally there is a crunch – insufficient slack is produced in a given week and managers collectively requisition more labour than is available. When this happens, it is up to the planners to decide which areas get the available labour and which have to wait. This happens rarely enough that in general we say that the slack system works. We have been doing it since 1985.

GETTING WORK DONE

We have to take turns washing the dishes. For years we attempted to assign that task only to those who minded it least, but they tired of it.

> Almost everyone is required to take a turn at kitchen shifts. Exceptions are for health-related reasons or substituting with specific other work, such as bathroom cleans or farming – if you can get assigned to them.

The move to a mandatory kitchen shift did not take place without a struggle. Two members adamantly refused to go along with it. After a good bit of indignant grumbling, the Community decided to put the new rotation into effect over the objections of the two holdouts. Everybody else would wash dishes. Those two men would not be assigned. Eventually one of them offered to clean bathrooms as a substitute. The other held out to the end, but when he left after many years as a member, there were those who still remembered his rebellion and who said, 'Well, at least now there are no exceptions.'

> **Twin Oaks' Labour System Requires Everybody to Plan and Record Personal Labour**
>
> The organisation, accounting, equality, liberty, and flexibility that Twin Oakers enjoy depend substantially upon this minor clerical chore.
>
> 1. The labour assigners have a file box of 3×5 cards (or file notebook of labour sheets), one for each member, with their preferences written on it.
>
> 2. Kitchen (K) shift preferences. If there is one particular K-shift that you very much don't want to do, let the assigners know, so they can put it on their chart. A request will generally be honoured.
>
> 3. Planning the week – turning in a sheet on Monday (by Tuesday morning 9 am). Take a blank labour sheet. Fill in your name, the dates of the week starting next Friday and ending the following
>
> ▶

Thursday, and the number of days you want to be assigned. If you intend to be gone on certain days, draw a line through that day or days.

Fill in your chosen K-shift, but also mark this choice on the culinary master sheet posted nearby. If somebody has already chosen the slot you wanted, pick a different one. Or let the assigners pick one for you. If you are a milker, fill in your milking shifts. To schedule time for some non-work activity, such as getting together with a friend, mark out this time in order not to get a work shift scheduled on top of it.

If you are willing to help with cooking, write that down in the 'notes' space. We frequently need cooking helpers. If you don't mind an extra K-shift, note that also. If you want to do some cleaning or housework (not usually popular), say so.

If you forget to turn in a sheet, the assigners will make one for you. This is when a well-filled-out personal preference card (sheet) is quite helpful, both to you and to the assigners.

Openings are not guaranteed in any area in any given time period, but certainly there will be many opportunities caused by people's changing jobs or leaving the Community. Watch the 3×5 board for work that interests you.

4. Turn your sheet in to the appropriate box. The labour assigners will finish it and have it ready for you to look at by Wednesday evening – sometimes earlier. The period between Wednesday-when-the-sheets-come-out and Thursday noon is called revision time. This means you look at your sheet and see if there is anything wrong with it. The assigner needs to make sure all changes get made correctly.

Frequently one person's revision causes changes on somebody else's sheet, so don't be surprised if your final sheet has changed a bit. On Thursday evening, the sheets are taken by the labour coder and the data entered into the computer. Late Thursday they are put in the box available for you to take.

There is a Friday work sheet posted in various public places, which tells who is scheduled for what work on Friday. Check it out to see if you by any chance are supposed to milk the cows or make lunch on Friday morning!

The concept of unemployment doesn't have any meaning in our environment. If we run out of valuable things to do, the labour quota goes down for everybody, and we all get more vacation. If sales and income go down, we all take the 'cut in pay' in the form of the Community's buying fewer or cheaper amenities or postponing them for a more prosperous year.

Vacation

Every member can be given or earn labour credits to take vacations, either on or off the farm. The Community gives 2.5 credits ('bonus' credits) per week to each member who turns in their completed sheet on time. Credits accumulated by this means add up to 130 credits per year (52 weeks times 2.5 credits), between two and three weeks, depending on quota. Vacation balances are cumulative and remain in the member's balance till used, carrying over year to year.

Vacation time may be taken either on or off the farm. It may be used in any increment, down to the tenth of an hour. A member may be gone for a month or a weekend or a single day or part of a day. They may stay right here on the farm and not do any work, lie in a hammock, walk in the woods, compose poetry, or spend the entire time in bed. That's also vacation.

Or, they may intend to work but dawdle at the dinner table, chat with friends, and unintentionally waste time, finding at the end of the week that they have done only 40 hours when they meant to do 47. The difference here is also called vacation. It is not intention that makes a vacation; it is the not-doing of Community creditable work.

The Community sometimes has members who never seem to have any off-the-farm vacation because they spend it all right here, doing less than quota frequently enough to use up what they accumulate. This is their choice.

Sometimes members can do Community work while on vacation off the farm. For instance, an indexer may take along an index to work on, or a manager might do some writing or phone calls.

Twin Oaks is just comfortable enough that it can support a few dependants. When an adult member slides into dependency – does less than quota for several weeks and accumulates a deficit, which we call 'being in the labour hole' – we don't always rise up in indignation against him or her, not right away at least. There are a lot of things we can try before resorting to extremes; only very occasionally has a member been expelled.

We try to make it obvious that leaving one's work undone is equivalent to asking other members to do it for you. A lot of people envy unearned vacation time. The first step would be for the labour manager to talk to the member who is getting behind. Together the two will look at the kinds of work that the member has been signing up for but not doing and talk about specific behaviour problems that get in the way. The Community can, on request, have someone wake you. Changing to scheduled work – like cooking, milking or dishwashing – might solve the problem. An arrangement will be made to make up the deficit a little every following week.

We patched this hole in 1987 with the 'labour hole policy' – any member remaining in the hole for seven months out of the last twelve automatically reverts to provisional membership. The member starts over with no deficit. But, in exchange, their membership may become subject to a poll taken by secret ballot. The Community offers several good ways to remain in good standing: vacations, occasional leaves of absence, time extensions, second chances, counselling, and a wide choice of work, all before encountering the teeth of the labour hole policy.

Visitors work too. Visitors' work assignments are fairly predictable – washing dishes and gardening – since there are many jobs they cannot do without training.

Credits for the Sick and Over 49-year-olds

1. In general, one hour of work equals one credit.
2. Sick time is creditable except that on a day in which sick leave is taken, total credit for the day may not exceed a day's quota.
3. Pension hours depend on the biological age of the person taking them. Every person over the age of 49 may take one pension credit (credit without doing any work for it) per week for every year of age past 49. (Example, a person 56 years old gets 7 pension credits per week.)
4. Doctor and dentist visits are fully creditable for the time one is with the doctor or dentist or waiting for the doctor or dentist to be available, plus the actual transportation time to the city where the appointment is. No credit for waiting due to car-pooling is given by health team.

CHALLENGES

There are problems with the labour credit system. It does nothing to control those few people who lie on their labour sheets. Some people can't handle freedom. Without any habits of self-discipline, they find themselves postponing work until late in the week, at which time they can't possibly make quota. The system's most serious flaw is one it shares with the wage system. There are sometimes people who set about earning labour credits as if they were dollars. This distracts them from the intrinsic worth and enjoyment of the work they are doing. The labour credit is so central to some people's thinking that they want labour credits for everything they do. Twin Oaks' labour system is controversial in the communal movement. People are put off by what they call the 'labour credit mentality'.

Dubious and Questionable Practices

Our labour system, like any economic system, is full of loopholes. It is easy to manipulate for various personal motives, some of which are perfectly legitimate.

1. *Claiming work that wasn't done.* We are vulnerable to this, because the whole system works on trust, and nobody is keeping close track of anybody else's work. Violating the Community's trust in this way is legal cause for expulsion, though that probably wouldn't be the first thing we'd do.
2. *Double-crediting.* Very sloppy record-keeping can result in remembering what one did, and taking credit, but forgetting that one did two of these things at the same time – such as doing data-entry on an office shift, or laundry during a primary shift. Remember that one hour's work gets one hour's credit, even if two things get accomplished.
3. *Estimating to the nearest hour.* It is reasonable for people to estimate the amount of time they spend working at various things, but you need to get closer than the hour. Rounding up to 6 hours when clocked time would have shown 5.2 is definitely not okay. Remember that some people are timing themselves to the minute, and this practice is unfair to them. Please keep better track. Rounding both up and down to the nearest half-hour is okay.

▶

4. *Claiming work on the wrong day.* It is possible, but not legal, to claim work on a day different from the day it was done. Nobody can spot this. If people do it, they get away with it, but it isn't right.
5. *Claiming sick hours during the week.* Sick hours are legitimate only to the extent that the day in which they were claimed does not total more than 1/7 of quota, including any work done that day.

There is no truth in the classic assertion that there is no incentive to work without personal financial gain. We have members who have the same intense dedication to their work that characterises happy professionals in the competitive outside world. Their involvement is with the work itself and with building the Community.

The point is, the labour credit system works. It is our security that everybody is doing a fair share. It is a way of earning free time. It allows us to work in a variety of areas. It gives us immense flexibility in scheduling. There is plenty of room to suit one's work preferences.

It helps minimise resentment and guilt. We do not look askance at a person who is lying in a hammock at ten o'clock in the morning. We get up and go to bed when we please, work the hours that suit us, take on responsibility when we feel ready for it, work with other members whom we get along with, and participate in the Community decision-making that controls how we define creditable work. I don't think our system can be matched for that combination of freedom and responsibility.

A COMMUNAL ECONOMY

Equality in labour is a large step towards social justice, but it is not the only step Twin Oaks has taken toward equality. Our financial and property policies reflect our determination to avoid a privileged class. The general arrangement is very similar to what is done in the Israeli kibbutzim. It is classic utopian communism.

We generate income almost entirely from on-premises activities, and all of that money goes into a communal bank account. We are not employees and we get no wages. Instead, the Community takes care of all our needs: food, clothing, housing, medical and dental care, toiletries, furniture, automobiles and trucks and their maintenance, recreation, and a dozen other things. I do not mean 'all our wants', which is different. The Community reserves the right to determine what is and is not a need. I consider that we have complete social security. Sick leave is unrestricted. If a doctor sends you to hospital, you don't worry about the bill. Either we qualify for financial aid or we will pay the bill.

The legitimacy of any business or domestic expense is decided by the manager of that area. After seeking input from the group, the library manager decides which magazines to subscribe to. There are no privately owned vehicles. Any member who wants to drive somewhere checks out an available car at the office. The cost is charged to the managerial area or personal allowance of the member who signed it out.

Members' contact with money is simply to check out some from the office for either personal spending (charged to their monthly account) or their managerial area, if they are in charge. The pocket-money allowance is spent entirely at the member's discretion. Children get an allowance too, about half the amount given adults. Some members have outside bank accounts, which remain frozen for the duration of a person's membership, and others get gifts from prosperous parents.

Personal Service Credits (PSCs)

Any member may 'pay' another member to work for them by having credits transferred. More than three credits claimed in a week should be accompanied by a brief explanation.

Pooled PSCs: If members wish to, they may donate labour credits from their labour balances to a pool of credits to be used by worthy projects, such as political action, or theatrical productions. Again, these credits may be claimed by the people doing the work.

PSCs are an exception to our overall labour economy. Since we have many years' experience with them, at this point we do not consider them likely to have a negative effect. However, it is the labour manager's responsibility to watch how large this segment of the economy becomes, and to curtail it if it should ever become a major, rather than occasional, way of allocating labour.

Some of our members do not automatically adjust their financial 'needs' realistically to the Community's per capita income. My guess is that it is because they are accustomed to thinking in terms of the income of their parents and peers outside. They plead they are not asking the Community to pay for these things. All they are asking is to be allowed to earn the money themselves in their free time. Thus members may, while on vacation away from the Community, earn money for personal purposes. We have several times tried to do away with vacation earnings in order to stop the angry (and perhaps justified) cynicism of those who cannot profit from it, but we've never even come close to a decision to abandon it.

We took a bold step the year we introduced 'Weeds and Knots' (spoonerism for Needs and Wants), a committee that distributes small amounts of money upon request to individuals who apply for it. People who envy those who easily earn vacation earnings are free to apply to Weeds and Knots for travel money or any other expense. Those grants are usually small.

Products For Friends

The Community allows members to earn hammocks or other products to give away or trade by doing products work without taking labour credit for it. There is a list of products and the number of hours it takes to earn each one kept in the products office. That person also handles the transaction when the actual product leaves our inventory.

Members may turn their positive labour balance into Products For Friends retroactively, but this creates extra clerical work. The usual reason for doing this is that the member is leaving and wants to take products with them. The labour manager and products general manager reserve the right to limit the number of products purchased in this way.

Overquota Products for Projects

This system allows members and others to make hammocks and other products without credit, a certain percentage of the profit from the product going to favourite, member-chosen purchases or expenses for the Community or donations to various causes. It is a piecework system. The accounting is done by means of tickets filled out upon work being completed. Overquota Products for Projects hours are not recorded on the labour credit sheet.

What many people want us to do is to provide a way to earn personal money within the Community, without having to go away. Unfortunately, we absolutely cannot pay our members any wages if we are to retain our valuable tax status. There is nothing, however, to prohibit our having an incentive program that benefits the Community, rather than individuals. People will work without labour credits for goals of their own choosing, even though they do not end up owning the purchased items. For example, people have used the Overquota Products for Projects program to earn CDs for the hammock shop music library, donations to causes they care about and for Community travel, such as a group going to visit another community or a vital conference.

In order to make even an adequate supply of anything go around, it is necessary for everyone to have simple and modest tastes and desires. That means the creation of an entirely new culture – non-competitive, non-consumerist. Twin Oaks is tackling both problems at once.

Labour Exchange

The idea of Labour Exchange is to give members of two communities the opportunity to experience the other community, without using up their vacation balances. Labour for these exchanges is not part of the yearly economic plan. No labour is set aside for it because we assume we will get the labour back during the same planning period. There is enough slack in our system so this condition need not be absolute.

The labour manager will approve members' doing Labour Exchange at another community if Twin Oaks owes labour to that community or if that community does not have a large debt to Twin Oaks and seems likely to pay back the credits within a year or so.

PLANNERS AND MANAGERS

Consensus government was sorely tested in the early years of the Community. Our by-laws leave us free to change our form of government any time two-thirds of the group wants it different. I personally think Twin Oaks would survive under a variety of government systems, including consensus or even democracy, as long as the managerial system was left intact.

The overall direction of the Community is in the hands of a three-person board of planners (a name derived from *Walden Two*). Their job is to appoint and replace managers, settle conflicts between managers, decide touchy questions having to do with ideology, and replace themselves when their eighteen-month terms expire.

Economic Planning

Once a year, in November, each manager needs to make up a plan for the upcoming year, as well as a quarterly breakdown of predicted labour use. The planners always help with this, since there are always new managers. If, between economic plans, a manager finds that the work that they are responsible for cannot reasonably be done within the budget allotted, and there are not people interested in doing it over quota, they can ask the planners for additional credits. These are not given lightly but, if reasons are sufficient, budgets are sometimes raised (or overspent). It is up to the planners to decide whether any changes will be made in budgets due to population changes.

Most of the authority of the Community, most of the important decision-making that affects the daily lives of the members, belongs to the group of managers, members in charge of various areas of work. Managerial positions are continually being created, and are awarded on the basis of interest and work.

Approving Labour – An Example

It is every manager's responsibility to decide what labour should be approved in their area. If someone wants to get credit for taking a class at a local university in a subject related to your area, and you suspect is not going to be a member long enough for the Community to benefit, you should deny the credit. But if you predict a long and fruitful Community career to which this class looks relevant, you would probably want to approve it. If this kind of decision-making makes you nervous, consult with your council, any experienced member or the labour manager.

▶

We have been told from time to time that the word 'manager' really turns people off. There is something about it that reminds one of 'authority' or 'boss'. After you have lived a while at Twin Oaks it loses those connotations. The actual job comes closer to 'servant', 'person responsible'. Managers use their best judgement in making decisions that benefit the group as a whole. They have nothing to gain by doing otherwise.

Choosing Crew Members

Twin Oaks allows managers to pick their own crews, because experience has shown that members in general are happier working in compatible crews. However, this privilege should be used carefully, always keeping in mind the basic egalitarian aims of the community.

We do not discriminate on the basis of sex, race, age, sexual preference, etc. Keep in mind that this rule works both ways. We don't discriminate against minorities or majorities. It is not okay to overlook a male candidate because one would rather work with a woman, for example. Affirmative action, for purposes of righting old wrongs, such as the formation of an all-female construction crew in order to encourage self-confidence, may be done occasionally if there really seems to be good reason for it, but this should be checked out with the council, planners, labour manager, or the Community, and not done casually. Attempts at keeping a sexual balance on a crew are legitimate if gender seems to be relevant to the job.

Temporary jobs: One-time or short-term jobs can be given to people who happen to be handy, without going through the formality of job posting. Otherwise:

1. Post the job opening on the 3×5 board. Leave it up about a week to collect signatures.
2. Interview all signers, either formally or informally. At a minimum, tell all signers who got the job. Preferably, talk to each of them and honestly consider them before making a decision.
3. Make your choice and post your decision on the 3×5 board. All of the above apply both to individual managers and to group managerships.

▶

Selecting Planners

New and stand-in planners are nominated by planners, then go through a group veto process and are appointed if the candidate is not vetoed (by more than 20 per cent). A planner can be recalled by a two-thirds vote of the full members. With a few exceptions, managers are appointed by a council of which the manager is a member and may be removed by the same council. Any time any job is open, it is posted on the 3×5 board in the ordinary way.

'Firing' Crew Members and Workers

On those rare occasions when it is obvious that a worker does not get along with the rest of the crew, or the work done is unacceptable and the worker unwilling or unable to improve, it is the manager's unpleasant duty to remove the worker from the crew or position. The member being removed from their work needs to be, at a minimum, notified of the decision. They can protest or appeal the decision to the council, which has the power to support or overturn the manager's decision. There are ways short of these formal channels to handle such a situation. Consult with people skilled in dealing with emotion-loaded processes about such methods as feedbacks, reviews and the like. The best course of action will vary with the individual and the situation.

What keeps our system from turning into a tiresome bureaucracy is its simplicity – that decisions can be made swiftly by at most three people, and usually by a single manager, using his or her judgement. What keeps it from being a dictatorship is that there is nothing to gain from being dictatorial. There is no police force here to carry out anybody's will. Our only technique is persuasion.

In spite of our hierarchical sounding government set-up, we are anti-authoritarian in both principle and practice. Planners are, in every sense, regular members of the Community, subject to their own regulations and serving without compensation. Nobody is on top of anybody. The plannership is not a position to be awarded to the manager who rates promotion any more than a managership is a promotion for a regular member with good behaviour. Managerships are positions of responsibility and trust. Bossy people are simply avoided. Managers point out things, make suggestions, define the job, and occasionally disqualify a sloppy worker.

NOTES

All italics in quotes are preserved from the originals.

1. Kat Kinkade, *Is It Utopia Yet? An Insider's View of Twin Oaks Community in its Twenty-Sixth Year*, Louisa: Twin Oaks Publishing, 1994, p. 257.
2. Kinkade, *Is It Utopia Yet?*; Kathleen Kinkade, *A Waldon Two Experiment; The First Five Years of Twin Oaks Community*, Louisa: Twin Oaks Publishing, 1972; 'Labor Policy', The Twin Oaks Labor System Principles, Policies, and Instructions 6/2001, compiled and updated by Jake, Labor Manager, accessed 21 February 2009, at http://www.twinoaks.org.
3. B. F. Skinner, *Waldon Two*, New York: Macmillan Publishing, 1976 (revised edition) [1948].

10
The Money-Free Autonomy of Spanish Squatters

Claudio Cattaneo

My doctoral research was part of my life: self-organised and without sponsorship with money or a grant of any kind. This helped me keep its content, ideals and message genuine and free, a part of the reality I live and believe in. This chapter is drawn and adapted from that thesis, which focused on the autonomy and ecological economics of living as a squatter in Spain.[1] My study of autonomy analysed the ability of a community to self-organise and achieve material sustenance directly, independent of the capitalist market. Squatters are characterised by avoiding paid work and the use of money, the market, in favour of autonomous self-organisation and collective sufficiency, but my thesis concluded that only neorural squatters have the material basis to achieve success.

Since I was a child, I have asked myself why we need to work eight hours a day if, in principle, we only need food to keep us alive. I also thought that all living comforts seemed to have been invented already, so there was no need for new inventions. At university I was told that marketing exists to satisfy needs, but I was convinced that marketing creates needs, which is a fundamental way that the market economy dominates alternative systems. My ideals prevented me from selling my time for a salary: for me, ecological economics is not a subject to study or an excuse to earn money in a 'politically correct' way: it is a way of life.

Nature taught me that we need no money to live. Fertile land is the source of life, and my life found fertile land in which to flourish in the urban and rural squatting communities of Barcelona and Catalonia where I arrived to begin my doctoral studies. I became close to the Can Masdeu project and people interested in alternative lifestyles living in urban squats, rural–urban ('rurban') ones in Collserola

Park, and fascinating villages in the Pyrenees, once abandoned and recently rehabilitated as 'neorural' squats. Connecting with these autonomous spaces provided opportunities to experiment for some years with an ecological lifestyle, to face the environmental crisis and the social one by beginning from the micro-individual rather than macro level. The Can Masdeu assembly allowed me to study and live within their project.

SQUATS

A squat is an illegally occupied private or public space – previously unused or abandoned – that functions as a home or social centre, free of capitalist or government control. Squats are for experimenting with new forms of social relations and democracy: collective, direct and deliberative decision-making. Self-organisation, using non-hierarchical structures, or real democracy ('people power') is the common managing philosophy.

In the Barcelona metropolitan area there is, on average, a stock of 200 squats and a flow of 50 evictions and squats each year. Most squats are homes for fewer than eight to ten people who have an active political neighbourhood agenda and a home assembly. Also, there are around 50 self-organised neighbourhood social centres providing public activities and services. The assembly of a social centre normally comprises people living in local home-squats. An info-list of their activities is released weekly.

The economy of the squatting community is rooted in radical political ideals: autonomy, freedom and respect for diverse people and living beings, a morality non-aligned with lawful practices. Since the new Spanish penal code was introduced in 1995, squatting has been a crime, the mass media criminalising the movement and justifying police repression. However, there is a moral code in squatting. Someone's home, even a second residence, would not be squatted in; the principle of right of use requires a place to be abandoned (those owned by real estate companies are preferred). It is highly immoral to rent a room in a squat. It is less acceptable to shop in big commercial centres rather than local shops or markets, and it is more acceptable to expropriate products from the former rather than the latter.

In general, it is moral to fight capitalism where possible. If a real estate property is a target for squatting, bank windows and automated cash-tellers are a target for street protests, as protesters have shown when supporting evicted squatters in street actions.

There has been no decision or any explicit collective process aimed at defining the political agenda of squatters. It is just what it is. To this extent, a squatter's resistance is not an ethical principle but a practice of freedom.

Squatters' Embedded Bioeconomies

The ecological economics of squatting communities is a bioeconomy beyond the market, based on self-organisation, mutual aid, reciprocity, urban gathering, material recycling, renewable materials, permaculture and agro-ecology. To satisfy their needs, squatters use their time to develop social and personal skills outside conventional labour and consumer markets. Permaculture, material recycling and the use of renewable materials are efficient ways to produce social benefit, the purpose of economic processes.

Squatters tend to avoid paid work and prefer to dedicate time to the direct satisfaction of material and other needs. 'Work' is not a category they use. Squatters free their time – the only scarce resource for need satisfaction – away from labour and capital markets to provide alternative satisfiers. Conviviality, non-monetary entertainment and *la joie de vivre* are important but all squatters are free to determine how they allocate time to create, mutually cooperate or earn money.

Urban squatters who live in Barcelona have a smaller environmental impact than the average urbanite because they shun the market. They are ethically opposed to consumerism; they 'recycle' abandoned houses to live in. In contrast to modern goals – 'become independent', 'live by yourself', 'be free' – squatters live in communities independent from banks, real estate business and paid work. Many squatters are vegetarians and some are vegans, which has environmental benefits. They do not charge, or charge little, for workshops they offer; some benefits of not paying rent and being free from paid work do 'trickle down' to society. They develop skills and promote cooperation within the squat and the local community, as much as possible growing their own food and collecting rainwater.

Squatters tend not to save and, even if they do, refuse to profit by lending money. Squatters' morality with respect to speculation has solid roots. Today, charging an extortionist interest rate is immoral and punished by legislation in most countries but, historically, *any* rate of interest was condemned as usury. Aristotle, early Christian thinkers, St Thomas Aquinas and the Muslim religion have condemned usury. The Old Testament defined certain limits:

'Thou shalt not lend money to thy brother on usury, nor corn nor any other thing, but to the stranger.'[2]

Rural squatters achieve higher degrees of autonomy than urban ones. Urban squatters achieve a certain degree of monetary, temporal and political autonomy, while rural squatters can achieve ecological (material) autonomy as well, being satisfied directly from their surrounding natural environments. Neorural settlements – such as those in Alta Garrotxa, described below – have lower population densities, rely on photosynthesis and constitute a system with greater autonomy than urban squats, which depend on the energy inputs and material recycling of an urban system. Therefore the urban squatter movement has a particularly ambivalent relationship to the dominant market economy.

In city squats some food – especially vegetables, fruit and out-of-date packaged food – is garnered from local shops. Major food (such as for social events) can be found in the Mercabarna port area, where hundreds of kilograms can be 'recycled' in one go, and plenty of edible tonnes are destroyed. Dry foods and grains are bought from supermarkets or local shops. Expensive food might be expropriated from supermarkets. There is marginal participation in cooperatives, buying organic fruits and vegetables directly. Finally, the production of organic vegetables is marginal, being more of symbolic and educational value than materially significant.

More opportunities for gardening exist in rurban squats. However, the composition of their diet is similar to urban ones. They have the same practices: collecting food from local markets, distributors of organic food and weekly street stalls. Organic gardens supply fresh vegetables and fruit. Some food is bought from cheap supermarkets. Gathering of mushrooms, olives, wild herbs, chestnuts and carob is common, but of marginal significance. Exchange with major agricultural producers, for example of fruits, olives and olive oil, is common. Eggs and chickens provide minor amounts of animal protein.

Squatters' internal networks are not mediated by traditional rules or the market, and links with wider social and ecological environments are mediated by the market only to a small extent. Between themselves, they adopt tornallom, which is the Valencian farmers' expression for mutual aid and cooperation: one day you help me, another day I help you, without the need of money. They provide a micro model for local solutions to the ecological crisis: social self-organisation and decision-making that is neither top-down nor bottom-up, but rather 'bottom–bottom' decision-making.

Production, consumption, supply, demand and other elements of an exogenous market tend to dissolve into a micro 'embedded economy'.[3] In a way, this self-organised bioeconomy is a return to pre-market origins, to household modes of production and communal land management. Squatters live next to and within the market yet try to revive alternatives, which had existed when competitive markets were only marginal aspects of life. Neorural and squat economies bear similarities with the gift economy of Malinowski, the domestic mode of production of Marshall Sahlins, and incorporate the theory of time allocation of Becker and Kropotkin's analysis of mutual aid in the evolution of social life.[4]

A squat is self-organised at several levels: through spontaneous order, where 'everything just happens', as in the anarchic natural state of 'order out of chaos'; through the formal act of plenary government that stems out of the assembly of its people, acts of will where consensus is moulded on a plurality of values; but also through informal communication of values, wishes and conflicts in the day-to-day life of a squat – an imperfect form of direct deliberative democracy (as discussed in Chapter 4).

Squatters make minimal and efficient use of the market, buying only what cannot be easily home-made, recycled or expropriated – see Box 11.1 on 'freeganism' and Box 11.2 on the United Kingdom freegans' views on 'fair trade'. Social self-organisation manages a common resource providing a use value, such as water or the squat. Management of a non-market service is likely to cause less environmental harm because it is not mediated by money and profits. Co-managers offer collective intelligence through multiple expertise, knowledge and values.

In rural and rurban squats that practise permaculture, self-organising biological systems contribute to personal and social needs-satisfaction through material and non-material services. Urban squatters' philosophy of material recycling marginally contributes to the preservation of the integrity of natural systems that otherwise would be affected by market consumption, representing a practical and participatory ecological economy.

However, squatters cannot transcend the system; they need a little money to live on. They dedicate time to search for minimal 'quality' self-employment or one-off jobs. Their resistance places them at the periphery of the market system. Squatters' ideals have resulted in creating a network of antagonist micro-realities within the political and economic arrangements of modern capitalism. Their independent ethical base is the necessary condition to commit the crime of squatting. The sufficient condition to put ethics into practice is to be collectively organised towards mutual political support and to resist repression.

Squatting is political. Evictions are an opportunity to show the conflict between housing speculation and legitimate housing crimes; between representative democracy and self-empowered deliberative democracy. Need for money is an indicator of dependence, insufficiency as opposed to self-sufficiency. Money does not originate from nature; it is an abstraction formed by the human mind. Capitalist processes imply artificiality and social inequalities.[5] In contrast, self-organisation represents a direct form of democracy, ethical independence and autonomy, a type of social ecology.[6] Nature is the central element and people are part of living nature.

In reality 'a squatter' is a fuzzy continuum of different people: one lives in a squat and has a paid job; another pays rent but participates in a social centre; yet another is evicted and obtains an agreement to stay in a rural house; one stays with a friend living in a squat. No matter where they live, some support squatters with donations, participate in squatter activities and sympathise. Who is a squatter and who is not? In this sense, 'squatting' is a social phenomenon rather than anti-system. Squatters can be seen as either anti-system or an appendix of established political-economic systems. Many of their practices contain contradictions and are not yet ideal.

TWO SOCIAL CENTRES IN BARCELONA

The oldest squat in Barcelona, the Kasa de la Muntanya, was in a building abandoned by the Guardia Civil in 1982. In 1989, a group of 20 people seeking self-organisation occupied it. Soon after it began, the Association of the Friends of Recycling was born along with many workshops: screen printing, mechanics, tailoring, electrical, small publishing and a library of recycled books. Kasa de la Muntanya has been a political laboratory for radical autonomy. For almost two decades it organised events for the Gracia neighbourhood, keeping the memory of Barcelona's anarchist history alive. The weekly *cenador* – a popular restaurant meal for less than €5 – helped to finance household needs and other social causes or squats. For several years, a modest orchard and garden has provided vegetables. Children born in Kasa de la Muntanya are already teenagers. The occupants were illegally evicted in the summer of 2001, but, after a street fight between squatters and the national police, the building was reoccupied. In the autumn of

2003, they were nearly evicted, but a widespread protest from all over Europe showed that the project deserved to continue.

Kan Pasqual, inspired by permaculture and energy autonomy, was the first squat devoted to ecological living. The squatters refused to use electricity from nuclear power even if it was a free service. First they installed a 12-volt system made up of a few recycled solar panels and car batteries. In 2006, a 500-watt windmill was constructed in a two-week workshop and lifted on a homemade steel tower in a couple of afternoons. Vertical integration reduced the need for the market: the 'aerogenerator' is made mainly from locally produced materials and about 30 people raised the 18-metre-high post. When the electrical system was upgraded, the old one was moved down to La Santa, a nearby building that has a famous bread oven and has been a home for squatters since 1998. The following testimony, which I translated from Catalan, appeared as an Internet post from an anonymous Kan Pasqual resident:

> I live in a rural squat with 15 adults and three kids. We have a relatively low level of carbon dioxide emissions – about two tonnes per person per year, compared with the Spanish level of nine and a half – like that of a poor country, but poor we are not. We have a very rich and diverse lifestyle...
>
> We recycle a lot from the recycling point... Garbage containers are full of surprises. Our furniture and house appliances come from the street. Our friends give us things that do not fit in their flats... Recycling extends the life cycle of products and no carbon dioxide is wasted in its production and neither is money. Even our house is recycled! If it wasn't for us, it would already be a ruin and to build a home for 15 people would release hundreds of tons of carbon dioxide.
>
> Solar panels are expensive and release a lot of carbon dioxide when they are made, but the windmill works very well and so do the hot water panels for the shower.
>
> We use the car and van only a minimum, the bicycle dominates ...
>
> We heat the house up with wooden stoves and, in part, we cook with wood. We collect only fallen wood, leaving something to regenerate the forest. Not everybody can use wood but a lot is not collected and makes the forest very flammable. We bake ecological bread in a wooden oven once a week and, on another day, so do our neighbours. We distribute it to friends and through ecological cooperatives. Flour is made without the use of nitrogen dioxide-

producing fertilisers, pesticides or herbicides. We tend to eleven orchards, some of them very big, and we use the manure of two retired horses that shit a lot. We do some permaculture, mulching to hold moisture, encouraging biodiversity with mini-habitats and a pool. We do two jobs in one.

We do not get water from the mains. We collect it from roofs and paths into reservoirs and pump it (with diesel, it's true) from a well. It is easy and cheap to collect water from the roofs when you have a place to store it.

We have chickens and ducks eating the rest of our food, dry bread and some grains. The city used to be full of chickens and orchards and, in time, could again. We have some beehives that give us honey and wax. We make beer, conserves, jam, crafts, medicinal creams, spirits, wine, magazines; we have a massive library, workshops for wood, mechanics, mycology, natural health, astronomy, etc.

We recycle from the kitchen and what the chickens do not eat is used to produce compost for the gardens. We have a super compost toilet built by German carpenters.

We hope that what we do in Kan Pasqual will continue to inspire practical change, whether a mini-orchard on the terrace or to foment social revolution![7]

A RURBAN SQUAT: CAN MASDEU

The rurban squat of Can Masdeu lies next to the city bypass and, in less than five years, suffered one eviction attempt, one criminal trial and one civil trial. The attempted eviction of Can Masdeu in 2002 illustrates the creativity of the squatters and their popularity in their neighbourhood. The squatters in Can Masdeu knew an eviction order could be made any day in the fortnight beginning 29 April 2002, so they experimented with positions to hang from and trained people in the darkness of night: to be secretive was fundamental to taking the police by surprise on the day of eviction and delay the eviction order. On 30 April, police arrived in the morning and set up barricades. There was just enough time for a backdoor escape for one group, who went to call supporters and media, while another group activated the plan.

Ready for active resistance, police found the squatters adopting passive resistance. They called the fire brigade, who refused to pull down those hanging because they were not in danger. The judge simply ordered the police to wait for the squatters to give up out of tiredness. Police blocked the entrance to the passage of food, water and blankets from supporters in the gardens below. This created a climate of social alarm: the next day, 1 May, there was talk throughout Barcelona about how these people were resisting without food and water while 300 supporters encamped in the valley were planning to enter to make the riot police retreat. The police were acting on behalf of San Pau Hospital, which had abandoned this public heritage building 50 years ago and now planned to destroy it to build an urban residence for retired doctors. The squatters won popular support and several months later the prosecutor did not appear in the court trial.

I have observed the importance of human-powered work among squatters, their ingenuity in reusing and recycling waste or employing renewable materials – a path that slows down material degradation. For instance, Can Masdeu's community gardeners use renewable or reused materials for infrastructure. When an old man picks out a bed frame from garbage and uses it as a gate, his human energy represents a means of production, producing a gate and disposing of waste. Production, maintenance and use of a rubbish truck are associated with entropy increases and material degradation, but our farmer, being alive, does not wear out and is self-organised as a dissipative structure, through rejuvenation and reproduction. Social self-organisation in the monthly assembly is replicated at a biological level, representing an economic alternative to market self-organisation.

Rather than using electrical heating during cold winter days, residents prefer to wear more clothes or use blankets and wood fuel. Using firewood requires labour time and effort, but is a simple technique for sourcing energy and is ecologically more efficient. Its high-entropy waste has functions. Recycled by human activity or bioprocesses, high-entropy ash becomes low-entropy fertiliser for gardens. High-entropy carbon dioxide is low-entropy input for photosynthetic growth; charcoal encourages the growth of, for example, trees and garlic. The tree is a cooling system in summer, producing lime blossom for tea (to reduce stress), and garlic serves as a tasty nutrient and medicine.

DECISION-MAKING

An assembly is an ideal democratic tool for making decisions. It is relevant to the small scale of the squat it manages and all people with a stake in it are represented. A well-structured assembly has different roles, with a facilitator or moderator, a note-taker, a timekeeper, a translator and an observer; there is an agenda with specific, short and informative discussion points. In some cases, speakers' interventions follow an order and have a time limit. However, sometimes conflicts on contrasting values generate tensions and conflicts. There is a trade-off between keeping a meeting short and effective and dealing only with practical points or having strong political debate on basic values, which risks inconclusive results.

A preference for practical over political debates is likely to depend on the size of the assembly and the challenge of organising 25 people. For 25 people there can be 325 different one-to-one relationships, while for 13 there are only 91. In contrast, from my experience in the small Alta Garrotxa case, discussed further below, practical decisions can be made informally at the dinner table, freeing assembly time for political debates or more work. In Can Masdeu, assembly decisions regularly involve commissioning those interested to investigate and report back or place a note on a notice board where comments are welcomed. Sometimes people simply do a job that they consider is necessary and obviously good. If they haven't even discussed their intensions informally, this can create resistance or malcontent.

However, tensions arise between making decisions and taking action so flexibility is a prerequisite. Take, for example, making a decision on our willingness to keep donkeys in Can Masdeu. A high-level debate included animal liberation and personal conflicts. The issue became too complex and was postponed to another meeting, then to another and, finally, was classified as a long-term discussion point. More than 20 people spent 40 minutes talking about how to talk about the donkeys. By then, the debate turned to methods for making decisions: should we have a monolithic meeting on donkeys, talk informally in the corridors, dedicate a wall for written proposals, decide now, have a trial and then an evaluation? No decision was made. A year later, a woman came by without asking the assembly and dropped off a couple of donkeys, who lived happily in the valley for two months. A man was keen to look after them. An ideal place was found. Water, care and companionship from others all just happened. This case shows that adaptability and resilience are essential.

Under other circumstances, decisions have to be made in advance: driven by scope or by purpose, people desire things that are not spontaneously supplied by the external environment, be it nature or a city. Participatory assemblies still might not be the best option:

even if they contribute better to direct democracy, deliberation processes are often limited by participants' rhetorical skills. Some people provide better arguments more quickly than others, finding it easier to clearly express values, be critical, and assess the pros and cons of a proposal. Sometimes, speakers compete or arguments are monopolised; some people get too tired to keep contributing to discussions, or think of good arguments too late.

There are processes to deal with this, such as 'rounds', where each person has the right to talk only once. Rounds are used to communicate personal feelings or high-stake values, or as a stage of an important decision-making process, such as a defence strategy or regarding the entrance of a new house member. Rounds are useful for enhancing direct communication and showing different visions.

Most decisions tend not to be as strict as a law; rather they are behavioural norms applied as much as possible without force. Social control is often more powerful than physical strength. In most cases, control and punishment mechanisms are lacking and self-responsibility, combined with common sense and enhanced communication, improves implementation.

STATUS AND CONSUMPTION

Squatters consume less energy and save time otherwise spent working for money. With their critical mass, they can redefine non-competitive social rules and feel socially included. Maximisation of spare time can reduce material consumption, money flows and central control. Social positioning is one of the most important non-material needs driving material consumption. The satisfaction of non-material needs with material satisfiers can be a psychological mirage – short-lived false satisfiers contributing to environmental crisis. Squatters care very little for social positioning. They have clear ideas and are quite smart: if everybody is racing and only one can win, then it is better to not race. They might be worse off than the winner but better off than many losers.

Karl Polanyi questioned the philosophical and moral fundamentals of the development of the market. He argued that it was not 'natural' for human beings to make a profit or expect a wage. Instead, incentives to work can be based on reciprocity, competition, happiness from work and social approval. Reciprocity and redistribution are principles of economic behaviour in small primitive communities, and in large and rich civilisations. Division of labour does not depend on trade or exchange, but on geographical, biological and other non-economic factors, whereas the 'natural law' of the market imposes a specific world-view to which humans must adapt.[8]

Similarly, Kropotkin argued that cooperative behaviour ('mutual aid') exists even alongside competition.[9] Among squatters there are many occasions for mutual aid, economic reciprocity and redistribution, which are typical characteristics of non-market economies. Solidarity against evictions is the best example. In a newly squatted property, cleaning, restructuring and securing the building are important and often difficult tasks, so help from others is always welcome and often organised. Building materials are often given away in expectation of future generosity in return, or freely given if a squat does not need them or has been evicted. Special tools are often shared without many problems.

Competition creates hierarchies while squatters' ideals tend towards egalitarianism. To be 'number one' is meaningless. Not to participate is a sovereign decision in a pluralistic society. Time (what I do now) has a practical use-value rather than an exchange value set by competitive rules, as in how much can I sell my labour for? Marshall Sahlins has observed that a group of a few people is enough to solve most of life's problems: use of time focuses on diversity rather than specialisation, and is limited mainly by biological, rather than social, constraints.[10]

NEORURAL SETTLEMENTS IN ALTA GARROTXA

If urban squatters are characterised by what they do not consume, the 'neorural' economy is characterised by patterns of ecological production and consumption, and the management of the pristine rural landscapes in which they live. Common to both are non-material satisfiers for most of their needs. While urban squatters are ecological because they consume economic waste, neorurals are ecological because they produce in an ecological way. The neorural Alta Garrotxa project offers a good example.

In the early 1970s, a new ecological movement of urban youth returned to country life. In the 1980s, neorurals, mainly from Barcelona and other Catalan towns, arrived at Alta Garrotxa. The radicals chose the austerity, isolation and savage beauty of this territory. The Alta Garrotxa project was established in the late 1980s and had a high turnover of squatters. Rather than infrastructure rehabilitation, the main activity has been childcare.

One nucleus of public property in Alta Garrotxa is a popular place; many people have lived, passed by or gathered there. The car park for the four-wheel-drive track is a 40 minute walk uphill, the nearest village is half an hour's drive away and the capital is one hour's drive away.

The main house serves as the social centre for local celebrations and other activities, and a lot of people use it. The main living area can fit more than 40 people into it. It is built on a hillside with two floors on one side. The goats are kept underneath the bedrooms, which are warmed by the animals' heat. One of the four bedrooms is at the same level as the goat shed. The fireplace is on bedrock, around which the house was built. The storage room is for food and garden tools, while the water well is on the outside terrace. Irrigation and animal water come from a recently dug pond uphill, combined with another farther up, near the four-wheel-drive track. Close to the small house is a hayloft, used to keep dry fruits, hay for winter or people sleeping during a gathering.

Fire is the most important source of energy for heating and cooking with a wood-fired kitchen-stove. A small solar panel provides light and energy for a radio. Animal traction – and their heat – is another source of energy, for work in the fields and for milk, cheese and meat. A lot of materials come from wood, while many tools are homemade and others exchanged with the wood carver. A donkey is a better tractor than an engine here because, if something fails, the engine cannot be easily repaired.

Staying in Alta Garrotxa

I visited the Alta Garrotxa project at Easter in 2003. As gifts, we brought food that was difficult to find there: sugar, coffee, tobacco, food for kids, wine and olive oil. At the first house, the five people living there were hand-clearing land for a common garden, for foods for subsistence and possibly to market. When the light faded, we all went to the kitchen. The solar panel had not worked that day, so we lit a candle and talked for a few hours, celebrating the reunion. Anti-war demonstrations were the main topic. There was an informal meeting to organise the next day's activities.

The next day I interviewed a person while he was cutting firewood with a chainsaw, to stock under a roof in the chicken yard because they expected heavy rains. He told me that when they first arrived, half of the roof was missing and other beams had to be replaced. First they rehabilitated the kitchen and sleeping areas to avoid living in a caravan like other neorurals. It was complicated by police intervention because they did not have permits. They argued that people traditionally built and maintained their homes without permission, and that they were mainly using traditional manual techniques. Now that the roof was finished, they planned to restore the traditional kitchen with a fireplace and wood-burning stove, and to build a dry-food storage room, an extra bedroom, a sitting room and a library. They planned to extend the orchard for commercialisation and keep more animals (pigs, goats or just more chickens).

Drinking water came from half a kilometre away. Irrigation water was stored in a couple of ponds onsite. We searched for stones in a nearby mound for reuse with sand, to fill in the basement. During lunch time, decisions were made about the next day's tasks: one person would go to the county capital to buy vegetables to plant, exchange food and meet people; others would continue with local work; and three more would go to a neorural meeting.

In the afternoon, three people chose to work in the garden while six more continued to prepare the stone and cement basement for the hut. The total cost of the hut (€6,000) was mainly due to purchasing Finnish wood planks. Most of the work was arranged by reciprocity and mutual aid. This non-monetary work is typically organised informally, using popular know-how, personal techniques and complex ecological approaches rather than advanced technology. It was regarded a worthwhile experience – as personal growth. By evening, we were all very tired.

With plenty of agricultural land, food comes mainly from the gardens: many vegetables and fruits, and some corn or wheat. Recycling is a minor, not marginal, food source. Dry food is bought, especially for winter. Animals provide eggs and milk and, marginally, meat and honey. Food and gift exchange is more common than in cities or rurban squats.

On the morning of Good Friday, we divided into four working groups: collecting stones, collecting wood, planting onions and cutting long grass with a scythe. I cut grass, quickly learning the motion and improving the precision of the cut. However, hitting just one rock could damage the blade so I did not cut very close to the ground. Over lunch, we talked about two formal repopulation projects refused by the authorities. The conversation on rural abandonment and government responsibilities continued in the afternoon as we went on collecting stones. In the late afternoon, some people came from Barcelona for the Easter weekend, making a total of 15 people.

On the Sunday, working activities were replaced by a more relaxed and mixed use of time. People slept a bit longer and took time for breakfast, then some went for a walk on the hills while some prepared lunch. The rhythm was, as usual, very calm. Since some people did not know each other, we spent most of the time talking – all the Barcelonians in this isolated house of Alta Garrotxa. In the late afternoon, the group that had arrived last went back to Barcelona. The remaining seven of us continued with the slow comfortable rhythm of the day.

Our last day began very early: a long walk was ahead. We were told to take a new route down to the valley and, although the walk was not difficult, we still relied on natural signs and common sense rather than maps and signposts. Luckily, we were given very clear directions from local experts. We walked for four hours back to the same river where we had stopped at the beginning of the trail. We ate sandwiches and then continued to walk down along a track by the river.

When we came across a few cars, rock climbers, a ranger patrolling in his four-wheel drive and foreign tourists driving to an old church, we immediately felt that we were back in civilisation. Even if we were still in Alta Garrotxa, we met more people in that hour than we had seen in the previous week. As the track turned into an asphalt road, we began hitchhiking and quickly got a ride from the neighbour of our first hosts, who dropped us off at the bus stop to Girona. Before dark, we had made it for a train to Barcelona.

MARKET FORCES VERSUS SQUATTERS' BIOECONOMICS

A recent political-cum-ecological conflict involving Garrotxa neorurals, traditional locals, landowners and excursionists illustrates tensions between the market and the squatters' bioeconomics.[11] In the Hortmoier Valley (near Oix), on the path to some neorural settlements, a non-local owner had fenced his property to open a reserve for hunting. No enclosure had ever happened in the valley and the news shocked the commoners: locals always used the forest freely, neorurals used the pastures and excursionists enjoyed its natural beauty. While goats mainly bred on the land, so reducing its market value, an enclosure for wild-pig hunting would be a major business opportunity.

The conflict peaked when the landowner killed some goats that had 'trespassed' onto his property. The landowner, interested in encouraging wild pigs, opened cornfields. Because the government of Catalonia supports transgenic fodder, the corn was thought likely to be genetically modified. Corn pollen can spread extremely easily, which might result in transgenic contamination of traditional and ecological varieties in the valley. In contrast, on the mountainsides, neorurals cultivate cereals and manage a branch of a seed bank to preserve a diversity of traditional seeds, maintaining specific varieties that best adapt locally. Preservation of seed diversity in transgenic-free zones is preferable to avoid a transgenic invasion, so the project was organised by a network of rural houses.

On the one hand there is a huge, possibly transgenic, monoculture grown for sale to the market and involving wage labour. Here, ecological and social biological processes are suffocated by market rules. On the other hand, the seed bank of locally adapted plant life represents biodiversity and future growing potential; fertile soils, networks of self-organised social movements, squatters and cultural diversity reproduce squatters' values and common sense. As such, dissidence, antagonistic positions, resistance to adverse external conditions, visible diversity and direct action represent the movement's political role, which differs little from a battlefield.

Autonomy in Stages: From Barcelona to Alta Garrotxa

Barcelona's squats are characterised by a political economy centred on autonomy from both money and time. Social autonomy only indirectly implies ecological autonomy: reducing expenditure on material consumption, recycling or reusing the waste of speculative capitalism to satisfy basic material needs. Barcelona squats have a social autonomy that can be understood as a form of social ecology: both social and natural self-organisation are fundamental prerequisites for a bioeconomic system. Even though they marginally benefit from the quality of homegrown food, their social relationships and individual freedoms improve their physical, mental and spiritual health. These are the characteristics of a better human ecology, adapted to the natural environment. But where would their food and housing come from without the present economic system and its waste?

In rurban squats the picture is slightly different. Beyond some autonomy from money, Can Masdeu and Kan Pasqual show a degree of economic autonomy: use of renewable materials, producing and consuming renewable and endosomatic energies. Rurban life is not so rural because of the proximity to Barcelona, where they spend a lot of time (but little money) having an active socio-political life. Land and water allow for organic agriculture but caloric and protein autonomy is still quite marginal. Rurban squatters could hardly survive without external sources of food. Available land is insufficient for pastoral activities and cereal cultivation. Ecological autonomy is foregone for social participation and political activism.

Different degrees of autonomy exist along an outward-moving path from mental to monetary and, finally, whole-of-system autonomy. Freedom of thought is the core element of the first stage of autonomy: more sustainable and less consumerist practices free people to pursue more autonomous social relations, for example balancing work with family and leisure, and supporting fair trade or ethical banking.

The second stage is more radical. Not paying rent is illegal. If the first step modifies consumption, the second modifies production through paid-work time. For every euro that an employee earns, there are overheads and financial and material costs of a superior order of magnitude. Autonomy from money reduces the multiplier effect as squatters earn only to survive. Social ecology produces social technology, allowing for household production, economies of scale, skill and know-how growth and alternatives to employment.

The third stage towards ecological autonomy is material, not just metaphorical. It is impossible in urban squats because of the lack of both land and preserved nature. Neorurals in the Iberian Pyrenees have a higher degree of material autonomy: rebuilding a house from a ruin surpasses the rehabilitations of urban squatters; animal care is more complex than growing vegetables, and provides more protein, calories and autonomy. In the Pyrenees, the distance from the city and the richness of local nature enables a lifestyle that is relatively materially independent. For all squatters, autonomy from the market system develops in co-evolutionary ways from endogenous preferences and exogenous social and natural opportunities. However, the stronger material autonomy of neorurals implies greater resilience to shocks in the economic system.

Urban squatters' energy-use in households does not appear to be particularly environmentally friendly: no gardening, animals or renewable energies. However, the human ecological values of non-sedentary life are significant. This is the starting point for an ecological economy. Can Masdeu has become more materially autonomous in infrastructure (but not food security) by constructing a small beer distillery, thermal solar panels, two wooden ovens and a bakery, and by digging a new large pond in the community gardens. Kan Pasqual has constructed a wind turbine, a water pool, a terrace for agriculture, a tree house and a bioclimatic house, and reconstructed a guest room and a wall in La Santa, near the bakery. Urban examples of material autonomy include constructing a public park in El Forat de la Vergonya and the transformation of a military garrison into four fully furnished flats in Kasa de la Muntanya.

Neorural settlers provide better examples of material autonomy than urban squatters who, at first glance, live as parasites on – or possibly even in symbiosis with – the established system. From the practice of their reality and beyond abstract ideals, neorurals provide a distinctive way of life, a real material alternative. This is necessary because establishing and maintaining links with market systems in the valley are more costly than developing ecological opportunities in the mountain. In the unlikely event the market system fails, a high value lies in neorural systems.

Urban squatters seem the most controversial: do they bridge two realities, or are they stuck midway between them? What do they produce? What is the value of their contribution? Their achievement is remarkable in effort, originality and hope, but they do not provide a material alternative: they depend on abandoned buildings and tend to survive from the waste of the economic system. Their contribution to reducing the costs of waste management is insignificant in the macro-economy. Their contribution to environmental preservation through non-consumption, though positive, is still ambivalent: squatters are parasites, even an overall brake to social progress.

Urban squatters' ecological impact is as unviable as the mainstream economic system is unsustainable. If urbanites were more efficient materially and produced less waste, squatters could barely exist. Is the planet improving through squatters' reduced material consumption? To what extent will their contribution retard environmental collapse? Not much. Nevertheless, the urban squatters, who form less than 0.03 per cent of Catalonia's population and are widely regarded as living in the most densely squatted region in the Western world, have other impacts. Their main value is non-material: increasing awareness at a macro-political level.

SELF-ORGANISATION AND BOYCOTTING THE MARKET

Market capitalism is harming people and nature. As long as we all spend money, we are all saying that capitalism is necessary. You either choose to use the market or choose to get self-organised. I advocate effective self-organisation and a market boycott.

Rural squatters achieve the most ecological (material) autonomy: neorural settlements constitute a system with greater autonomy than urban squats dependent on the energy inputs and material recycling available in cities. Both in the Collserola Park squats and in the neorural settlements of Alta Garrotxa, ecological impacts are reduced by use of organic agriculture, renewable energy and greater self-determination in the allocation of time and production of need-satisfiers. Beyond a dematerialised ecological economic system, all squatters create a demonetised polity and economy and, in avoiding spending money, avoid harming the environment. While urban squats are ecologically not as autonomous as neorural communities they do create social and political values.

To create a self-organised lifestyle, squatters reject the external controls of the state and capitalism. Squatters create spare time and participate in social networks. Social self-organisation is similar to, and in symbiosis with, self-organising dissipative structures, order out of chaos and diversity – possibly their most meaningful contribution to social learning. Urban squatters are more autonomous than the average urbanite in terms of economic (money) and political (self-organisation) autonomy. Political activism, direct action, resistance and disobedience are local examples of a global frontier line resisting the competitive pressure of capitalistic markets, and where the limits of competition are set by cooperation and mutual aid. New forms of making decisions are visualised along this global frontier and a new process beyond top-down and bottom-up is identified: social self-organisation is characterised by a new process of 'bottom–bottom' operating at a local level, not only tolerating diversity but requiring, and even highlighting, diversity.

In the twentieth century, reformism and uprising revolutions were regarded as vectors of social innovation, and the state was the agency of change. This millennium conditions are very different. Parliamentary democracy has shown limited potential. Bottom–bottom will always exist somewhere at the micro-scale – already a victory, a sign of resistance, producing real results. Bottom–bottom developments include direct deliberative democracy through assemblies, socially and virtually connected networks, the physical hubs of social centres in squats, neighbourhood associations or consumer cooperatives that split to grow on, ever bigger. Bottom–bottom is a never-ending revolution.

Box 10.1   Freegans on Freeganism

- Freegans are people who want to reduce waste, limit their consumption, save money, strengthen their communities, and opt out of the cycle of working for socially irresponsible corporations to buy the goods of other socially irresponsible corporations.

- Through dumpster diving, squatting, guerrilla gardening and other strategies, freegans transform waste into resources to meet real needs, allowing us to live our values of ecological sustainability, cooperation, and sharing while reducing our contribution to capitalism's abuse of humans, animals and the earth.

- As an alternative, freegans believe we can create a society based on local self-sufficiency, cooperation on a community level, respect for the earth and other living beings, limited consumption, and wise conservation and voluntary sharing of the resources available to us.

- Many freegans seek alternatives to the tired debates between left wing advocates of 'big government' and right wing 'big business' enthusiasts, believing instead that we need to renew traditions of local communities where people support each other and wisely use and conserve finite resources.

- Freeganism is about believing that we can create a better world and live better lives than the ones that this 'free society' tells us are our only option. In our society we are told that happiness is found in acquiring wealth and using it to buy material commodities. We cede the hours of our lives often to jobs that we hate as the price of survival so that we can pay the bills, and never have enough time to do the things that really matter to us. Freegans believe that life can be an adventure, that we can be the masters of our own time, that we can find joy and fulfilment volunteering in our communities, spending time with our families, working with groups working to fight social and environmental injustices, and in appreciating nature rather than in shopping.

Source: 'Essential points on freeganism', FREEGAN.INFO [website] accessed 29 October 2010, at http://freegan.info.

Box 10.2   United Kingdom Freegans on Fairtrade

Such schemes are often run with the best of intentions, however there are always flaws. Sometimes guidelines are cynically disregarded, and the scheme is nothing more than a marketing ploy for the retailer. At other times the markup on the selling price of the product is grossly out of proportion to the extra wage given to the producer. In cases such as these, a better way to help the poor is to buy the cheapest product and to donate the saved money directly to them. And the same problems with huge environmental and human costs of transport and waste exist when purchasing goods from remote locations... What people in developing countries need rather than our money is the food and resources that are being exported from their own countries. The bottom line is that even the fairest system that involves people being motivated by profit, is still a system built on greed and distrust. Such a system will fail to deliver what is necessary regardless of any good intentions.

Source: United Kingdom Freegans, Frequently Asked Questions [webpage], accessed 29 October 2010, at http://freegan.org.uk/.

NOTES

1. Claudio Cattaneo, 'The Ecological Economics of Urban Squatters in Barcelona', unpublished doctoral thesis (supervised by Professors Lupicinio Iñiguez and Joan Martinez-Alier), Institut de Ciència di Tecnologia Ambientals, Universitat Autònoma de Barcelona, 2009.
2. Deuteronomy 23:19.
3. Karl Polanyi, *The Great Transformation: the Political and Social Origins of our Time*, Boston: Beacon Press, 1944.
4. B. Malinowski, *Argonauts of the Western Pacific* [*Argonauti del Pacifico Occidentale*], Rome: Newton Compton, 1978 [1922]; Marshall Sahlins, *Stone Age Economics*, London: Tavistock, 1977; G. S. Becker, *The Economic Approach to Human Behavior*, Chicago: University of Chicago Press, 1976; Peter Kropotkin, *Mutual Aid: A Factor of* Evolution, London: Kessinger Publishing, 2004 [1915].
5. N. Georgescu-Roegen, *The Entropy Law and the Economic Process*, Cambridge, MA: Harvard University Press, 1971.
6. Murray Bookchin, *The Politics of Social Ecology: Libertarian Municipalism*, Montreal: Black Rose Books, 1977.
7. Cattaneo, 'The Ecological Economics of Urban Squatters in Barcelona', pp. 45–6.

8. Polanyi, *The Great Transformation*.
9. Kropotkin, *Mutual Aid*.
10. Sahlins, *Stone Age Economics*.
11. J. R. Tornès, *Si Vas a Hortmoier*, Olot: Grup de Defensa de la Vall d'Hortmoier, 1991.

11
Contract and Converge

Anitra Nelson and Frans Timmerman

All of the contributors to this book bring diverse understandings from different political and philosophy currents to support the major principles of non-market socialists, who advocate a money-free, market-free, wage-free, class-free and state-free global society. This chapter offers a vision for a non-monetary society based on collective sufficiency within bioregions and 'contract and converge' strategies for achieving it. It is not proposed as a one-and-only solution to current socio-political and environmental problems. Rather, it simply illustrates what other contributors to this collection have argued, that non-market socialism can be realised here and now. Although they might disagree with details of the vision and strategies advocated – in certain ways made clear in each of their chapters – we all agree that capitalism prevents us from addressing social injustice and achieving substantive democracy, and works against the establishment of sustainable living practices.

Clearly a non-monetary system *per se* cannot ensure that we achieve self-organisation, substantive democracy, communality, relative autonomy and sustainable practices in terms of the planet's natural limits. However, we argue that a money-free world is a *necessary*, even if not *sufficient*, condition. People would share power and exercise it in transparent ways, basing their decisions on the real, natural and human qualities that constitute our existence, so shaking free from the domination and contortion of exchange values. This would enable us to appreciate and better use our skills and knowledge, better assess our basic wants, and work with nature's complex needs and bounty.

Using Australia as an example, this chapter begins with a brief discussion of environmental challenges to demonstrate the imperative for non-market socialism, specifically from a state-of-the-environment perspective. The following discussion suggests that a 'contract and converge' strategy, which has been proposed to cut greenhouse gas emissions, can be expanded into a framework for addressing global social injustices and environmental crises. Finally we propose some building blocks for a global–local non-monetary system to achieve bioregional, community-oriented production with decision-making and activities determined by use values and wants using the principles of ecologically sound and humane values.

The strategies and structures proposed generalise many of the themes and practices already discussed. They draw on our personal experiences of political campaigning in the trade union, peace, environmental and women's liberation movements. Furthermore, during the 1990s, Anitra Nelson lived at Commonground, an intentional community strongly influenced by feminist, anarchist and socialist values, which had been established in Seymour (Victoria) in 1984. Later, she bought a share and lived in Round the Bend Conservation Cooperative in Christmas Hills (Victoria), which began in 1971 with environmental missions to preserve the local box-ironbark forest while living in harmony with it. Soon afterwards, the cooperative's objectives were taken up within a more expansive Environmental Living Zone, later classified in Victoria's planning legislation, and managed at a local level by the Bend of Islands Conservation Association.[1] These experiences of the challenges and benefits of community-based decision-making and the potential of achieving sustainability in local ways inform the vision and strategies proposed.

CLIMATE CHANGE

Throughout the second half of the twentieth century in particular, scientists have increasingly warned about widespread environmental damage and degradation using analyses based on use values (rather than exchange values). As such, the international Union of Concerned Scientists issued the 'World Scientists' Warning to Humanity' on 18 November 1992 (see Box 11.1). This statement, with 1500 signatories (including 101 Nobel Prize winners) was issued before the specific impacts of global warming were well known and pointed to the broader environmental damage of capitalist practices. In its constant references to 'collision', 'irreversible damage/loss' and the need for social change, the warning was a call to action for fellow human beings to reverse current practices and instil a 'new ethic... for caring for ourselves and for the earth'.

Since this scientists' plea, environmental problems have increased in extent and severity. Global warming driven by human-induced carbon and other greenhouse gas emissions has become the most discussed issue this century, even though it is just the most obvious symptom of environmental challenges facing human beings today. Global carbon emissions reached 387 parts per million by November 2010.[2] Among many international experts Dr Megan Clark, head of Australia's Commonwealth Scientific and Industrial Research Organisation, confirms: 'We are now starting to see CO_2 [carbon dioxide] and methane in the atmosphere at levels that we just haven't seen for the past 800,000 years, possibly even 20 million years.'[3]

Slightly leading the global average, Australia's mean temperature rose by about 0.7 degrees Celsius from 1960 to 2009, with some regions warming by 1.5 to 2.0 degrees. In the 1960s, the average number of record hot day maximums was ten, with 22 cold day maximums; four decades later this had reversed to over 22 hot day maximums and 10 cold day maximums. In many areas heatwaves are increasing in severity and in number, while frosts and cold periods are diminishing. But the impacts are not uniform. Rainfall is increasing in some regions, such as the north-west and north-east, contributing to damaging floods, while other areas such as the south-west and south-east mainland are becoming drier.[4]

Off the Queensland coast the most extensive coral reef system in the world is disintegrating as the oceans surrounding Australia become warmer. Australians face massive challenges from land salinity and in creating systems for sharing scarce water resources with one another, especially in our ever-growing state capitals, and with nature for the maintenance of crucial ecosystem services. Irrigation for agriculture has proved environmentally harmful in many areas, disrupting natural water flows and cycles, but farmers and regional businesses strongly oppose the efforts to redress this imbalance.[5] Meanwhile, government agencies project that average temperatures in Australia will rise 0.6 to 1.5 degrees Celsius over the next 20 years and, under stable levels of global greenhouse gas emissions, warming would reach 2.2 to 5.0 degrees Celsius by 2070.[6]

Biodiversity loss has waxed and waned in severity since the European invasion of Australia in the late eighteenth century. Another 'wave of extinctions' of species has begun, this time associated with global warming, and will probably be worse than ever before. Causes include land clearing and climate changes, specifically heatwaves. What has surprised scientists is that many indigenous species, such as the prolific possum, cannot endure temperature rises outside their tolerance level even for very short periods of time, such as occur in acute weather events that are becoming more frequent.[7] Such developments are not isolated to

Australia. From 1970 to 2007, populations of vertebrate species across the world were reduced 'by almost 30 per cent'.[8]

Both 2009 and 2010 opened with record-breaking rainfalls and floods in the north, which cut off vast areas of Australia, damaging agriculture and infrastructure, and isolating residents. Simultaneously, in early 2009, heatwaves occurred in the south-east, leading to massive bushfires in Victoria, where strong winds, scarcely any rain for the preceding month and low humidity encouraged conflagrations that razed entire towns and killed 173 people. These extraordinarily high temperatures were one of the world's most extreme weather events in 2009, which was one of the hottest years on record for Australia.[9] The forest fires in Victoria in 2009 not only released hundreds of millions of tonnes of carbon dioxide but also reversed the more normal cycle of forests as carbon sinks into sources of carbon emissions.[10] Although not included in the accounting of the United Nations Framework Convention on Climate Change, carbon emissions from those forest fires in Victoria were equivalent to around one-third of Australia's total national greenhouse gas emissions for 2003.[11]

Per capita, Australians in 2011 were the world's second-greatest producers of carbon emissions. However, despite the damaging impacts of climate change already being experienced and forecast, successive governments have failed to establish an effective policy – based on targets and a means of achieving them – to arrest and reverse the growth of carbon emissions into the atmosphere. Meanwhile, all of the evidence suggests that a cut of over 95 per cent in emissions by 2050 is needed and, even then, Australia would be on trend towards 2 degrees Celsius warming above pre-industrial levels, which is likely to mean plant and animal species extinctions at a level of 15 to 40 per cent worldwide and widespread drought, including in Australia.[12] As international expert James Hansen has said, 'the oft-stated goal to keep global warming less than +2 degrees Celsius is a recipe for global disaster, not salvation'.[13]

In his introduction to the Worldwatch Institute *State of the World 2010* report, Erik Assadourian wrote:

> Preventing the collapse of human civilization requires nothing less than a wholesale transformation of dominant cultural patterns. This transformation would reject consumerism – the cultural orientation that leads people to find meaning, contentment, and acceptance through what they consume – as taboo and establish in its place a new cultural framework centred on sustainability.[14]

Referring to overuse of the Earth's resources today – 'people are using about a third more of Earth's capacity than is available' – Assadourian compared the sixfold increase in consumption between 1960 and 2006 (measured in 2008 in US dollars) with the population increase over the same period of just 2.2.[15] He continued:

> According to a study by Princeton ecologist Stephan Pacala, the world's richest 500 million people (roughly 7 per cent of the world's population) are currently responsible for 50 per cent of the world's carbon dioxide emissions, while the poorest 3 billion are responsible for just 6 per cent.

> Indeed if everyone lived like Americans, Earth could sustain only 1.4 billion people... But even at middle-income levels – the equivalent of what people in Jordan and Thailand earn on average today – Earth can sustain fewer people than are alive today.[16]

Clearly, failure to make decisions and address the multiple environmental crises, such as global warming resulting from human activities, threatens our survival as a species. The illogicality of trying to use the market to confront the ecological challenges facing the human community – spelled out in certain chapters in Part I of this book – reinforces all the contributors' arguments that people must take direct control of their lives and the natural environment by abandoning market mechanisms and exchange values.

Non-market socialism offers the quickest, most effective and efficient way of curbing the kinds of human practices that cause environmental damage. Other contributors to this book have offered ways to establish more sustainable as well as fairer relations. The holistic vision and strategies that follow are indicative, not prescriptive, suggestions.

GENERALISING A CONTRACT-AND-CONVERGE STRATEGY

Although we know how to satisfy our needs more sustainably, the ways and principles of more sustainable living clash irreconcilably with capitalism. For instance, the speed, scale and variety of changes required to bring human activities into balance with the natural capacity of our planet means that we cannot pursue an economic system that depends on growth and ever-increasing world trade. We need to reorient our economic, social and political relationships around local collective sustainability. Such reorganisation must focus wholly and solely on use values, the qualities and quantities of natural matter and forces and human capacities and potential as they exist and might become through human energy and skills. To move from 'here' to 'there' will require strategies that achieve a general and shared modest standard of living in communities across the planet.

'Contraction and convergence' has been proposed as a global strategy to reduce emissions of greenhouse gases (carbon compounds) and, thereby, ultimately reduce global warming. This strategy was developed by the Global Commons Institute in the 1990s as its research revealed divergences between different countries' per capita emissions and the global expansion of greenhouse gases.[17] The principles and vision of contraction and convergence are simple: to reduce overall emissions – at a safe level agreed on by all countries – by evening out all countries' emissions based on an equal quota of emissions per capita.

However, implementing a contract-and-converge strategy proves complex under existing economic and political structures. Negotiations would require participants to agree on a maximum 'safe' emissions level, a time line of targets for the entire process and each country, global and national 'safe' population levels and controls, diverse models for how countries pursue their targets, how and who monitors the process, and what punishment would be appropriate for non-compliance. Based on the limited achievements of the United Nations Framework Convention on Climate Change, and even assuming a modified (say, more 'ethical') form of capitalism, such agreement might take so long that the limited opportunity will be missed for taking the immediate action needed to diminish the threat to our existence as a species.

At the same time, a contract-and-converge strategy seems appropriate. So, is it possible for individuals and groups to implement such principles, altering many of their activities accordingly, and lobbying for local policies that support renewable energy infrastructure and use? Transition Towns and carbon rationing schemes are examples of attempts to go in this direction.[18] In other words, instead of a top-down approach, people can and do act at a grassroots level pursuing the bottom–bottom connections that Claudio Cattaneo discusses in Chapter 10. Still, the extent of this response is limited by current structures in as much as people have little influence on what is produced and how and where it is produced. The most significant barrier to broad change towards meeting environmental needs within capitalism is resistance from the drivers of society, namely business people and politicians.

Furthermore, as discussed, climate change resulting from human activity is associated with deeper environmental crises that complicate such change. These other environmental crises – water shortages and contaminated water that reduce productivity and habitats, wholesale clearance and damaging incursions into forests that contribute to loss of biodiversity, ocean acidity related to pollution from agricultural and industrial contaminants – all relate to destructive capitalist activity, including the concentration of overproduction and overconsumption in certain regions, typically countries of the so-called 'North', to which Australia belongs. All of this suggests that human practices must change at the grassroots, with individuals and groups exercising the kinds of freedoms and responsibilities discussed by all the contributors to this book.

We have known for decades that human activities are using many natural resources at unsustainable levels, especially through production and consumption in advanced capitalist countries, while others, most victims of capitalist underdevelopment, fail to have their basic needs met. Thus the 'contraction' we propose would be an uneven process guided by the social justice concept of convergence in terms of material equality – to each according to their needs, from each according to their talents – between all people over the world. Therefore, people who today do not get enough would have their basic needs met under this new strategy.

The contract-and-converge strategy has strong parallels with 'degrowth' strategies (see Box 11.2). Contraction is not simply a matter of reducing the sheer amount of things processed and consumed but of improving the principles and techniques of production and consumption so less is used and wasted. For instance, we need local production from regional resources so that there is a minimum of travel and transport involved in making and getting food and other daily requirements.

Contraction implies environmentally friendly lifestyles, ecologically sensitive techniques for satisfying our needs and appropriate technologies for producing things. Following principles of contraction and convergence in community-based collective sufficiency implies resettling populations so some areas would contract and others expand. Because all areas of the earth have different environmental conditions, potential and limitations, local answers would be distinctive. However, generally applicable forms would match generally applicable principles: compacts and spheres of exchange intertwining local collectively sufficient 'bioregional' units.[19] (See Box 11.3 on bioregionalism.)

LOCAL AND COLLECTIVE SUFFICIENCY

To achieve local collective sufficiency, people would need to take over the use rights and responsibilities for the catchment landscapes that substantially support them. Local, community-based forms of living, producing and exchanging that emphasise communal sufficiency are the most environmentally friendly because they minimise energy and resources otherwise wasted on transport and economise through providing directly for most daily needs. Claudio Cattaneo's practical Chapter 10 on the money-free autonomy of Spanish squatters featured these kinds of developments.

In as much as local regions develop in communally sufficient ways they are socially and environmentally semi-autonomous, robust and resilient. Communal sufficiency overcomes limitations of self-sufficiency by economising on effort and by making use of economies of scale through the use of resources, including energy. Subsistence activities include growing, harvesting, collecting, storing and preserving foods in ways as environmentally friendly as possible, exercising principles such as those developed by the permaculture movement.

A 'whole' person exercises skills and develops knowledge in a range of activities. Similarly, what we call a 'compact' society – where significant relations are based on compacts, rather than contracts as in market-based societies – would nurture people and be nurtured by people who have a range of skills and apply them regularly in various ways, namely subsistence, sharing, caring, learning and teaching. Work time would be divided between these activities so that, ideally, every person would participate, say one day a week, in production and exchange of the provision of subsistence goods and services, including food, clothing, houses, furniture, equipment and buildings for households and neighbourhoods, and all the goods and services involved with electronic communications. Another day would be spent in caring activities: caring for children, sick and aged people, in a range of duties, including exercising the skills of 'barefoot doctors', complemented by highly skilled practitioners. Yet another day would be spent on making decisions and communicating with compact partners and in the activities of networks.

All of these activities would involve training on the job, and learning in specific places would be restricted to intensive skills and knowledge acquisition such as those involved with learning to read, write and exercise basic arithmetical skills. Thus, ongoing training for all members would characterise compact communities. Another day would be spent on cultural and recreational activities in which people would participate as both creators and enjoyers. We estimate that, once established, living in a compact society would require not more than three days (say 20 hours) of work per week from each able person over and above certain household and self-maintenance tasks. People would be free to offer more time in such activities and to spend time travelling by foot, or helping transport goods, for a range of purposes.

Spheres of production and exchange would be local, regional and global. These spheres would follow ecological as well as social rationales, with local economies based on the scale of catchments, along bioregional lines. Households would develop, say every six months, lists of basic needs and work out to what extent they could fulfil these needs through self-sufficiency, such as through their household and neighbourhood gardens, kitchen baking, preserving and storing, and milk, meat and other products from domesticated animals, including fowls and goats. Households would grow and create according to appropriate principles and technology, such as prioritising indigenous vegetation and animals, and sustainable practices infused with permaculture approaches.

Neighbourhood farming and industrial facilities would complement the needs of households and provide workspaces for householders to exercise a wider sphere of activities related to collective sufficiency. Each neighbourhood would identify its landscape's specific potential for easily producing surpluses that met deficiencies in other neighbourhoods. The neighbourhood might share or offer the right to use, say, pockets of forest or marine areas or bordering neighbourhoods to meet their subsistence needs. Neighbourhood audits would estimate production to account for accidental shortfalls and unpredictable losses and also coordinate with wider catchment-based networks so that such surpluses could act as a wider safety store to avoid waste.

Explicit and formal agreements, 'compacts', on production and the exchange of products as well as other social activities imply a network of agents who create, comply with and receive benefits from such compacts, which would be similar to contracts but would not involve money, as contracts often do in capitalism. Compacts would deal only in use values and the needs, capabilities and wants of the parties participating in the compact. Their formalisation would involve the engagement of an independent mediator responsible for ensuring proper conduct in making the compact and the negotiation of all details through the life of the compact, including compliance with and changes to the compact.

Short-term compacts between two parties might appear like formalised barter or promises in use values. Perhaps neighbourhoods or even more distantly placed communities would make a compact for an exchange that involved passing over surpluses to fulfil unexpectedly unmet needs in return for supplying crafted goods or art services now or at a specific time in the near or medium-term future. Long-term compacts between peoples to provide one another with wants that they could not produce themselves might well involve multilateral, not simply bilateral, exchange. Bioregions would negotiate with other bioregions (starting with neighbouring ones) to exchange, say, seafood for indigenous forest nuts, in particular seasons of the year or even all the year round. The compacts would involve deliberations over minimising the environmental and labour costs of transporting such goods.

Collective self-sufficiency implies personal and collective attachments to and deep respect for environmental birthplaces and migration places, and familial, household and neighbourhood bonds recognised and celebrated in various cultural ways. However, despite these characteristically place-centred polities and collective sufficiencies, compacts would allow people mobility for visiting and changing living spaces, acting, as such, as citizens of the world. Attachment to spaces and landscapes would involve livelihood responsibilities and rights, protected by global compacts outlining basic principles, rights and responsibilities for humankind the world over, yet flexibly managed to respond to changed natural and social circumstances. Thus living simply would not focus on simply living, but on establishing and maintaining a holistic sense of security and well-being for all.

A person would make their life journey as an individual who accumulated skills, capabilities, experience and knowledge. Singular self-sufficiency and independence would be impossible (just as these states are impossible to achieve even now in our 'individualistic' world). Developing social and physical powers would be aspects of personal journeys as people would grow in households, their natural parents and kin-parents charged with the responsibility to care for them. Households would comprise backgrounds and histories of all those people grouped under one roof, sharing their living space for shelter, eating and socialising. Personal space, a room of one's own, and personal belongings would be universally established and protected rights.

Groups of households would make up larger neighbourhood precinct units, the size of which would be determined by environmental as well as social rationales, the particular sufficiency enabled by areas of landscape within which they lived and were sustained. The collectively sufficient-as-possible neighbourhood community would exist in balance and in regular contact with similar neighbouring groups in order to exchange and share cultural and material surpluses and challenges with them as well as with more distant communities, all participating in numerous webs of compacts or 'networks'.

While compacts would involve specific aims and outcomes and might often be temporary, networks would exist as continuous relational channels of communication and interaction, fulfilling purposes of sharing information, mutual support, and guiding and protecting universal rights of individuals, communities and environmental landscapes. These networks would involve very broad political compacts, including co-production of those limited numbers of goods and services that are most easily and efficiently created for multiple communities, such as research and learning on macro-scales related to both environmental and social phenomena and developments, transfers of technical skills and knowledge, and managing the electronic communications systems to support networks and compacts.

The transition to a world without money – which is only to say that the conditions are laid for humans to establish communities based on social justice and environmental sustainability – would be created by, on the one hand, diminishing production and exchange based on a monetary, capitalist rationale and, on the other hand, progressively taking over production and exchange using compacts. Already many communities, such as Indigenous and peasant communities existing at the margins of capitalism, would have rights and responsibilities acknowledged for traditionally occupied country. At the same time they would be required to recognise sharing of country and resources through non-monetary compacts where appropriate.

Non-monetary production and exchange already exists within, despite, and at the margins of, monetary exchanges that dominate capitalism today, as well as having proliferated in non-capitalist societies, where non-monetary exchanges have enabled the sharing of responsibilities for production, distribution and redistribution of goods. The transition would focus on cutting and more evenly distributing work for wages, depriving the market of labour, to rely more and more on non-monetary production and exchange, while developing general political support and structures based on collective management of localities and bioregions. Our point is that non-monetary exchange can complement social and political practices in communities where sharing power in making decisions over production and distribution is transparent and, as such, has the potential to be more reliable than in capitalism.

COMPACTS AND NETWORKS, NOT CONTRACTS AND TRADE

Formal spheres of non-monetary exchange have always relied on customary rights and responsibilities with local and personal variations associated with social and environmental circumstances and developments. Non-monetary exchange will involve compacts and networks that allow groups access to basic needs and wants from outside the local area. Studies of non-capitalist societies reveal spheres of exchange involving specific goods and exchange protocols. For example, in areas without a natural source, salt or a useful metal might be provided in a continuous and reliable way in exchange for another natural product or craftwork, all by way of an established customary arrangement.

Complicated mixtures of environmental and social rationalities have driven the principles, protocols and rules developed for such exchange. Rules about what and how much is given or bartered is logically linked with reproducing certain social relations and with environmental balances deemed necessary by those creating the rules. Emerging market-based societies not only dissolved customs associated with non-monetary exchange but sometimes also incorporated or adopted practices from them (for example slavery, especially common in early stages of capitalism). We will not go back to old ways, but we do know that we can develop new ways that have antecedents and that, from historical viewpoints, capitalism has been the exception rather than the rule in human– human and human–nature relationships.

The values in the compact model are non-monetary: community-oriented production must be determined by decision-making and activities based on use values (that is, qualities and quantities [potential uses], and human abilities and capacities, in terms of ecologically sound and humane values). The political model is of subsidiarity, that is, control that is as local as practicable and appropriate: the household, neighbourhood and bioregion. The rights model is universal: equal rights for people and nature across the globe, such rights embracing diversity in the expression of set principles – such as the right to shelter – rather than expressed in uniform standards. The economic model is 'collective sufficiency', a version of relative self-sufficiency achieved by neighbourhood groups.

Like the other contributors to this collection, we argue that a world without private property would allow for genuinely democratic forms of management and evenly distributed and locally focused power to all people. This would enable greater effective freedom and, through diversity, more choice. As outlined, non-monetary material reproduction can be achieved through community-based ownership and responsibility for collective self-sufficiency facilitated by 'compacts', meaning formal agreements between individuals and groups to support all kinds of essential and continuous activities, including collective production and exchange within spheres, organised in local and local-to-local networks. Compacts together with 'networks' offer viable structures for people to take and share direct power. Once appropriate principles and values have the force of common rights and normal responsibilities, compacts and networks have the potential to institute societies alternative to capitalist ones.

Currently capitalist practices do not directly fulfil, but rather, in many ways, contradict universal human rights to basic needs such as food, clothing, shelter, safety and care. Every activity involves monetary considerations at some level, shackling direct and sensible responses to human and environmental needs. Compacts and networks would work directly with available human skills and effort, and energy and materials would be assessed in terms of their use values. Every person would have the right to basic needs and would be a member of compacts designed to fulfil those needs while belonging to networks that would make them responsible for fulfilling other people's basic needs and caring for the local environment.

Within existing capitalism people have experiences of using techniques for sharing power to create products and services within families, collectives, cooperatives, and state and community-based voluntary organisations. Certain public media bodies, emergency organisations based on volunteers and private charitable organisations demonstrate that people are very capable of developing and delivering high-quality and diverse products and services to cater for special interests as well as general consumption.

Currently such practices are limited and frustrated by market-based and market-oriented activities, money-raising being a common concern and distraction from, as well as obstacle to, good works. Volunteers often feel 'used' and tensions arise with salaried members of such organisations. In the transition to a compact society these organisations would benefit from interlocking support networks with similar organisations, developing compacts that involve the production of goods and services directly for one another in fair exchanges, sharing skills and knowledge, and passing on surpluses, unused resources, 'waste' for re-use and so on.

In compact societies, networks of exchange involving goods and services could be established and dissolved according to compacts involving wants and abilities. These networks would involve formal compacts dealing with use values and negotiated in terms deemed fair by diverse models developed through local experiment and evolving into universal customs. Agreements (compacts) would be formalised and dissolved by official independent mediating parties. Most importantly these exchange networks would complement communities living simply on production for direct use values, exercising independence as well as benefiting from efficiencies evolving from collective sufficiency, by offering complementary and supplementary goods and services in exchange for the same.

Compacts and networks would be diverse, fulfilling various purposes for numerous members. As basic ways of organising, formal compacts would offer robust and stable forms for local-to-global organisation of all kinds of activities, from those directed at fulfilling basic needs and wants to cultural and recreational ones. The principles of simple, local and small can guide efficient and effective techniques for fulfilling basic needs to ensure more socially and environmentally friendly developments all over our planet. Permaculture and alternative appropriate technologies for generating energy and extracting and processing resources offer ready-made and tested ways to proceed.

WORK AND FREEDOM

Even though we suggested that such a future might involve people in just around 20 hours' work per week, perhaps you think our proposal would mean working more and harder? If you had lived in the Twin Oaks community (discussed in Chapter 9) in 2009, as long as you were not sick, you would have been responsible for fulfilling 42 hours of effort towards collective tasks per week in exchange for the group's meeting your basic needs: from food and shelter through to training, care during illnesses, and holidays. If 42 hours sounds a lot, because you are thinking in terms of paid work outside the domestic sphere, compare it with more analogous data, such as Australian Bureau of Statistics figures for paid work (outside the home) and household work (which includes child-rearing activities).[20]

Australian trends in the period 1992–2006 show an increase of around two hours per week (or four days per annum) in the average combined work tally for both of these spheres per adult. In 2006 adults spent, on average, just over 50 hours per week on paid and household work combined. However, some Australians were working much longer than others, and a gender imbalance also persists. The average mother in a couple family with children under 15 years of age spent 53 hours a week just doing chores around the house and associated with child rearing, compared with an average 22 hours for the domestic input of fathers in the same situation.

If we look closely at paid work by couple families with children under 15 years of age, in more than 40 per cent of cases the mother works part time, on average 19.5 hours per week compared with the father's average of 51.5 hours per week of paid work outside the domestic sphere. (The general definition of part-time work used by the Australian Bureau of Statistics is working between one and 34 hours in paid jobs.) The average working week combining work inside and outside the home for such couples was around 69 to 74 hours for females, either part time or full time in the paid workforce, and around 72 to 73 hours for employed males. A national Go Home on Time Day survey conducted by the Australia Institute found that most workers wanted to work fewer paid hours per week (except those being paid for just two days or less who, understandably, wanted to work more).[21] In this comparison, the simple 42 hours' work at Twin Oaks seems most attractive.

Now, compared with the resident member of Twin Oaks, the average Australian family might consume more goods and services for all of their work, but they are facing having to reduce consumption for environmental reasons. It is significant that at Twin Oaks the expectation in terms of working hours is standard and therefore fairer than in free-market economies, such as Australia, where the 'average' statistic levels out great disparities in working hours between those on higher salaries and in receipt of income derived from profits and those on very low wages or running struggling businesses. In terms of the environmental challenges we face, today Australians have the largest homes in the world, which often means more onerous mortgage responsibilities, maintenance and consumption to fill the house. One has to take into account that consumption itself consumes time. So, arguments that advanced capitalist lifestyles are characterised by less work and more leisure than non-capitalist ones are fallacious. The option of working less and using alternative technologies is not only achievable but also more efficient and more environmentally beneficial.

We also estimate that direct control and collective decision-making over basic needs and fulfilling them locally would need less time than all of the financial and management activities needed by capitalist production and markets, which would become obsolete in the process. Simply consider all the workers and managers employed in financial positions from banking through to accountants, advertising and gambling: as an exercise, estimate how many work hours in your local, regional and national communities focus on the requirements of a monetary economy. Also think about working in more meaningful ways than under capitalist monetary discipline.

CONCLUSION

This spare vision of a global compact society comprising local compact communities indicates basic processes, namely compacts and networks, sufficient to establish political structures to organise the planet, from local to global spheres, on the basis of the principles of social justice and environmental sustainability. At the same time we have indicated strategies necessary to achieve this vision: the conscientious avoidance of any monetary rationale in restructuring socialist organisations and activities, and a focus on restructuring production and exchange to fulfil needs and wants related to social justice and in accordance with environmental sustainability. This common vision clarifies both the necessary and the sufficient principles and strategies for coordinating, expanding and amplifying efforts towards instituting local compact communities and a worldwide compact society. Our defence is entirely ethical: the institution of substantive democracy for human well-being and the protection of a living planet.

Where we live, in the Blue Mountains (Australia), we have a very active food cooperative open every day of the week. It is said to have the largest membership of any food cooperative in the southern hemisphere. Similarly, the largest LETS in Australia operated in the Blue Mountains until 2001, when it broke down.[22] In Chapter 7,

Buick suggested why LETS are inadequate in terms of our utopian goals. Other people throughout the world are experimenting with hybrid and genuinely non-monetary forms of production and exchange, as discussed by Terry Leahy (in Chapter 6), Kat Kinkade and Twin Oaks (in Chapter 9) and Claudio Cattaneo (in Chapter 10). Common examples of alternative lifestyles include growing and processing vegetables and fruit in gardens and neighbourhoods for direct use, to share within collective structures, or in less formal and more *ad hoc* ways. Today these kinds of informal food security networks are proliferating the world over. This book was written because we believe that these efforts to confront the key challenges of our day are most usefully discussed using theoretical frameworks associated with non-monetary socialism, as the contributors to this collection have explained.

Revolutionary periods are marked by instability, challenges, soul-searching and creativity. The global financial crisis has already made people question our systems of want-satisfaction and governance. With the environmental crises, especially global warming, there is a growing sense that we must shake ourselves free from unsustainable practices because the future of our species depends on it. The vision is not complex and only needs combined willpower. Ultimately and globally, we need to establish systems within which local human and ecological requirements determine what we produce, and how and why we produce it.

Box 11.1   World Scientists' Warning to Humanity, 18 November 1992

Human beings and the world are on a collision course. Human activities inflict harsh and often irreversible damage on the environment and on critical resources. If not checked, many of our current practices put at serious risk the future that we wish for human society and the plant and animal kingdoms, and may so alter the living world that it will be unable to sustain life in the manner that we know. Fundamental changes are urgent if we are to avoid the collision our present course will bring about...

The irreversible loss of species, which by 2100 may reach one-third of all species now living, is especially serious...

Much of this damage is irreversible on a scale of centuries, or permanent...

▶

The earth is finite...

Pressures resulting from unrestrained population growth put demands on the natural world that can overwhelm any efforts to achieve a sustainable future...

No more than one or two decades remain before the chance to avert the threats we now confront will be lost and the prospects for humanity immeasurably diminished.

Warning!

We the undersigned senior members of the world's scientific community, hereby warn all humanity of what lies ahead. A great change in our stewardship of the earth and the life on it is required, if vast human misery is to be avoided and our global home on this planet is not to be irretrievably mutilated.

What We Must Do

Five inextricably linked areas must be addressed simultaneously.

1. We must bring environmentally damaging activities under control to restore and protect the earth's systems we depend on...
2. We must manage resources crucial to human welfare more effectively. We must give high priority to efficient use of energy, water, and other materials, including expansion of conservation and recycling.
3. We must stabilize population...
4. We must reduce and eventually eliminate poverty.
5. We must ensure sexual equality, and guarantee women control over their own reproductive decisions.

The developed countries are the largest polluters in the world today. They must greatly reduce their over-consumption...

A new ethic is required – a new attitude towards discharging our responsibility for caring for ourselves and for the earth.

Source: Union of Concerned Scientists, '1992 World Scientists' Warning to Humanity: Scientist Statement' issued 18 November 1992, Cambridge, MA. Available at: www.ucsusa.org/about/1992-world-scientists.html (accessed 10 March 2010).

Box 11.2   From the Declaration of the Paris DeGrowth Conference, 2008

We... call for a paradigm shift from the general and unlimited pursuit of economic growth to a concept of 'right-sizing' the global and national economies.

1. At the global level, 'right-sizing' means reducing the global ecological footprint (including the carbon footprint) to a sustainable level.
2. In countries where the per capita footprint is greater than the sustainable global level, right-sizing implies a reduction to this level within a reasonable timeframe.
3. In countries where severe poverty remains, right-sizing implies increasing consumption by those in poverty as quickly as possible, in a sustainable way, to a level adequate for a decent life, following locally determined poverty-reduction paths rather than externally imposed development policies.
4. This will require increasing economic activity in some cases: but redistribution of income and wealth both within and between countries is a more essential part of this process.

The paradigm shift involves degrowth in wealthy parts of the world...

Source: Participants in Economic DeGrowth For Ecological Sustainability And Social Equity Conference, 'Declaration of the Paris 2008 Conference', held in Paris, 18–19 April 2008, accessed 10 March 2010, at http://www.degrowth.eu/v1/index.php?id=56.

Box 11.3   Graham Purchase on Bioregional Interfederations

Bioregionalism begins by emphasizing and observing that the accumulated accidents of geology, compounded by the vagaries of spontaneous biological evolution, have created a living planet containing a plethora of unique ecological regions and subregions... the existence of regional biotic diversity is a vital component of world ecological stability. Inhabitants of distinct biotic regions

▶

must engage in modes of socio-ecological behaviour and interaction consistent with the preservation of such regions as life sustaining and self-renewing macrobiological entities.

The prime geographical unit according to the bioregional perspective, the natural or 'ecocommunity,' represents a matrix that, although astoundingly diverse, cannot be regarded as a closed integer. It is dependent on wider external determinants for its survival. The need for clean air and the intercontinental migration of bird and marine life, etc., not only show us that bioregional boundaries are extremely permeable but also illustrates their extreme interdependence on a global scale. Bioregions must be capable of existing in a dynamic ecological and federative harmony with other bioregions, both neighbouring and remote. Each bioregion must not only strive to ensure its own continuous happiness but must strive to take a responsible place in a delicately complex interregional, continental, intercontinental and global federation of environmental forces.

Source: Graham Purchase, *Anarchism and Ecology*, Montreal/New York/ London: Black Rose Books, 1997, pp. 100–1.

NOTES

All italics in quotes are preserved from the originals.
All URL addresses were accessed on 20 October 2010.

1.   Glen Ochre, 'From a Circle of Stones to Commonground Dreaming', in Bill Metcalf (ed.), *From Utopian Dreaming to Communal Reality: Cooperative Lifestyles in Australia*, Sydney: University of New South Wales Press, 1995; Anitra Nelson, 'Two models of residential conservation; communal life in an Australian box ironbark forest.' *International Journal of Heritage Studies*, Vol. 7, No. 3, 2001, pp. 249–72.
2.   The Earth System Research Laboratory global carbon emission updates are available at the National Oceanic and Atmospheric Association [website], at http://www.esrl.noaa.gov/.
3.   Dr Megan Clark cited in S. Clarke, 'CSIRO chief defends climate science', ABC News, 15 March 2010, at http://www.abc.net.au/.
4.   All data in this paragraph are sourced from the Australian Bureau of Meteorology and Commonwealth Scientific and Industrial Research Organization (CSIRO), *State of the Climate* [Brief], Canberra: Australian Government, 2010, at http://www.bom.gov.au.
5.   For instance, see report – and links to further reports – on regional conflicts over the Murray-Darling Basin Authority plan and irrigators: Bronwyn Herbert and

staff, 'Murray-Darling cuts "could spark riots"', ABC News, at http://www.abc.net.au/.

6. Australian Government Bureau of Meteorology and CSIRO, *State of the Climate*.

7. All data in this paragraph to this point are sourced from Tim Flannery, 'The third wave', *The Monthly*, April 2009, pp. 14–17.

8. Duncan Pollard (ed.), *Living Planet Report 2010: Biodiversity, Biocapacity and Development*, Gland: WWF International, 2010, p. 7.

9. D. S. Arndt, M. O. Baringer and M. R. Johnson (eds), *State of the Climate in 2009*, Bulletin of the American Meteorological Association, Vol. 91, No. 7, pp. S180–3.

10. Expert Mark Adams cited in D. Fogarty, 'Australia fires release huge amount of CO_2', *Reuters* (26 February 2009).

11. Reuters, 'Victorian fires release huge amount of CO_2', *ABC News*, 27 February 2009, at http://www.abc.net.au/.

12. David Spratt, 'Climate countdown', transcript of talk given at Moreland Climate Group meeting, 20 April 2009, posted on the Climate Code Red blog, 21 April 2009, at http://climatecodered.blogspot.com/. David Spratt co-authored, with Philip Sutton, *Climate Code Red: the Case for Emergency Action*, Melbourne: Scribe Publications, 2008.

13. James Hansen, 'Guest Opinion: Global warming twenty years later: tipping points near', Worldwatch Institute website, 23 June 2008, at http://www.worldwatch.org/.

14. Erik Assadourian, 'The rise and fall of consumer cultures', in *State of the World 2010*, Washington: Worldwatch Institute, 2010, p. 3.

15. Ibid., p. 4.

16. Ibid., 'The rise and fall of consumer cultures', p. 6.

17. Global Commons Institute [website] at http://www.gci.org.uk/.

18. For 'Transition Towns', see the Transition Network [website] at http://www.transitionnetwork.org/; for 'carbon rationing schemes', see Carbon Equity: Ration the Future [website] at http://www.carbonequity.info/.

19. For more detail on this vision and strategies see Anitra Nelson, Compact [website] at http://www.moneyfreezone.info.

20. Australian Bureau of Statistics, 'Trends in household work', *Australian Social Trends* Cat. No. 4102.0 (March 2009), Canberra: ABS, at http://www.abs.gov.au.

21. Josh Fear, Serena Rogers and Richard Denniss, *Long time, no see: the impact of time poverty on Australian workers*, Policy Brief No. 20, Manuka: The Australia Institute, 2010.

22. 'Blue Mountains Community Exchange', *The Echo*, Issue 22, October 2010, p. 4, at http://issuu.com/districtgazette/docs/october_2010_.

Notes on Contributors

Adam Buick has been a member of the Socialist Party of Great Britain since the early 1960s, speaking and writing on socialism as a moneyless and wageless society. He regularly contributes to the party's *Socialist Standard* and contributed a chapter to Maximilien Rubel and John Crump, *Non-Market Socialism in the Nineteenth and Twentieth Centuries* (1987).

Claudio Cattaneo did his PhD at the Institute for Environmental Science and Technology (Universitat Autònoma de Barcelona), where he remains a Research Associate. Practising degrowth by living on fewer than €250 per month, he teaches ecological economics at Carlo Cattaneo University (Italy) and is a squatter, bicycle mechanic and olive farmer.

Harry Cleaver is Associate Professor of Economics at the University of Texas (Austin). An autonomist Marxist, his many publications include the classic *Reading* Capital *Politically* (1979). His activism has centred on university campaigns and struggles of Mexican immigrants and Zapatistas, and he maintains the Texas Archives of Autonomist Marxism.

Kat Kinkade (1930–2008) was a founding member of Twin Oaks Community, established in Virginia (USA) in 1967. She helped found the East Wind and Acorn communities, and the Federation of Egalitarian Communities, which still exist today. She wrote two books on her experiences at Twin Oaks: *A Waldon Two Experiment* (1972) and *Is It Utopia Yet?* (1994).

Terry Leahy is a Senior Lecturer in Sociology and Anthropology at the University of Newcastle (Australia). He teaches and publishes work on food, agriculture, permaculture, a gift economy and anarchism. Recent publications focus on the global environmental crisis and strategies for sustainable agriculture and food security in developing countries.

Mihailo Marković (1923–2010), a widely published Serbian philosopher and scholar, worked for many years in the University of Belgrade Faculty of Philosophy. He became a leading proponent of the Marxist humanist Praxis School, which emphasised the dialectics and humanism of Marx's earlier writings and produced the international *Praxis* journal.

Anitra Nelson, Associate Professor of RMIT University (Australia), is an expert on Marx's theory of money (*Marx's Concept of Money: the God of Commodities*, 1999) and community-based sustainability (editor of *Steering Sustainability in an Urbanizing World: Policy, Practice and Performance*, 2007). She lives in the Blue Mountains, Australia.

John O'Neill is Professor of Political Economy at Manchester University. He has written widely on philosophy, political economy, political theory and environmental policy. His books include *Markets, Deliberation and Environment* (2007), *The Market: Ethics, Knowledge and Politics* (1998) and, as co-author with Alan Holland and Andrew Light, *Environmental Values* (2008).

Ariel Salleh, a researcher in Political Economy at the University of Sydney (Australia), was Associate Professor in Social Ecology at the University of Western Sydney and is on the editorial boards of several international journals. Widely published on eco-political thought, including *Ecofeminism as Politics* (1997), she edited *Eco-Sufficiency & Global Justice* (2009).

Frans Timmerman has been a prominent socialist faction leader in the Australian Labor Party for decades and a political adviser to several members of parliament. Associated with publishing since 1970 – as a journalist, academic editor and bookseller – he co-edited *Free Palestine* published by the General Palestinian Delegation in Australia (1979–90).

Index

Compiled by Sue Carlton